presents...

The (nearly) Complete Guide to Airstream Maintenance

© 2015-2019 Church Street Publishing, Inc. All rights reserved. This publication may not be reproduced in whole or in part by any means whatsoever without written permission from Church Street Publishing, Inc., 411 Walnut St #4468, Green Cove Springs FL 32043.

Airstream® is a registered trademark of AIRSTREAM Inc., and is used under license.

The information contained in this book is derived from a variety of sources, including Airstream Inc., product manufacturers, and other third-party sources. Although every effort has been made to verify the information in this book, the author and publisher assume no responsibility for inconsistencies or inaccuracies, or liability for any damages of any type arising from errors, omissions or advice given herein.

Neither the author nor the publisher assume responsibility for the services of any business mentioned in this guide, damage to your Airstream or its contents, or for any loss, injury, damage or disruption in your travel for any reason.

ISBN: 978-0-9833458-3-1

Illustrations by Brad Cornelius. Interior page design by Lisa Coe. 1st printing August 2015. 2nd printing May 2016. Updated 2nd edition printed August 2019.

Thanks to the contributing writers of Airstream Life, including Terry Halstead, John Irwin, David Tidmore and Roger Siminoff, as well as Dave Schumann, Colin Hyde, Alex Kensington, and Brett Greiveldinger, who all provided expertise for this book.

How To Make Your Airstream Last Forever	**9**
Your Tool Kit	**11**
Your First Aid kit	15
Vintage Airstream needs	15
Learning to Inspect	**17**
When and why to perform inspections	17
The "Storage inspection"	18
Tools and procedure	*18*
Exterior	*19*
Interior	*23*
Pre-departure check	25
On The Road inspection	27
Learn the song your rig sings	*28*
Other inspection opportunities	28
Budgeting for maintenance	29
Interior Cleaning and Appearance	**30**
Curtains	30
Windows	31
Window blinds	31
"Day/night" pleated fabric shades	*31*
Aluminum mini blinds	*32*
Wood blinds	*32*
Formica laminate countertops	32
Corian® solid surface countertops	33
Stove and oven	34
Ozite interior ceiling/wall covering	35
Vinyl flooring	36
Shower maintenance	36
Minor furniture repairs	37
Adjusting cabinet door hinges	*37*
Adjusting or replacing cabinet and drawer latches	*39*
Adjusting overhead cabinet spring hinges	*40*
Tambour doors	*40*
Loose screws	*41*
Repairing edge banding on countertops	*41*
Flooring replacement	42
Flooring options	*43*
Trimming out floor edges	*45*

Exterior Cleaning and Appearance — 46
- The aluminum clear coat finish — 46
- Washing the Airstream — 46
  - *Cleaning hard-to-remove contaminants* — *48*
  - *Removing hard water deposits* — *48*
  - *Cleaning the front wrap protectors and front window stoneguards* — *49*
  - *Cleaning after salt exposure* — *49*
- Getting on the roof — 49
  - *Cleaning the roof and solar panels* — *50*
  - *Washing trailer wheels* — *51*
- Zip-Dee awning — 51
  - *Awning hardware maintenance* — *52*
  - *Awning fabric maintenance* — *53*
  - *Awning tips* — *54*
- Belt line trim replacement and front wrap protectors — 54

Aluminum Body Repair — 56
- POP® rivets — 57
  - *Replacing a POP rivet* — *57*
  - *Rivet stuck in tool* — *58*
- Solid rivets — 59
- "Olympic" or shave-head rivets — 60
- Fixing minor aluminum blemishes — 61
  - *Removing decals* — *61*
  - *Filiform corrosion* — *62*
- Polishing — 63
- Belly pan repairs — 65

Leak Prevention, Detection, and Repair — 68
- Leak detection techniques — 69
  - *Plumbing leaks* — *70*
  - *Rainwater leaks* — *71*
- Roof inspection — 72
- Sealants — 74
  - *Sealant replacement technique and tools* — *77*
- Identifying floor rot — 78

Windows, Doors, Locks, and Vents — 81
- Lubricants — 82
  - *Cleaning and lubricating gaskets* — *83*
  - *Stabilizers (squeaking)* — *83*

Door hinge maintenance	*84*
Entry step maintenance	*84*
Locks and latches	*85*
Entry door and screen door adjustment	85
Fan-Tastic Vents	87
Replacing window and door screens	89
Replace Hehr window crank	90

Plumbing 93

Plumbing tools	94
Sanitizing the fresh water system	94
Common water supply problems and solutions	95
Water filtration	*95*
Hard water problems	*96*
Freezing weather	*97*
Overflowing fresh water tank	*98*
Other water tank issues	*99*
Draining the water tank	*99*
Water pump	100
Types of plumbing	101
Basic leak repair	103
Threaded fittings	*103*
Dripping hose connection	*103*
Leaking sink	*104*
Leaking faucet	*105*
Drain system maintenance and cleaning	105
Toilet maintenance	106
Toilet seal maintenance	*107*
Sewer hoses	*108*
Black tank maintenance	108
Leaking dump valves	*109*
Gray tank maintenance	109
Calibrating the tank monitor (Catcon Micropulse System Monitor)	110
Getting out of calibration mode	*113*

Running Gear and A-frame 114

Hitch coupler and ball maintenance	114
Hitch receiver inspection	115
Breakaway switch	117
Power hitch jack	119

Tire maintenance	119
Inflation	*119*
Using a Tire Pressure Monitoring System (TPMS)	*120*
Rotating the tires	*121*
When to replace the tires	*122*
Preventing tire damage	*124*
Accessing and maintaining the spare tire	124
Spare tire maintenance	*124*
Changing a tire	125
Jacking up the trailer	*126*
Using a torque wrench	*126*
Three wheel towing	*128*
Patch, plug, or replace?	*128*
Replacement tires	*129*
Wheel balancing	*129*
Brakes	130
Drum brake adjustment	130
Drum brake inspection	*131*
Disc brake maintenance and inspection	*132*
Wheel bearing and brake service	133
Nev-R-Lube bearings	*134*
Standard bearings	*135*
Troubleshooting electrical problems with brakes	137
Axles	139
Shock absorbers	140
Loading	**143**
Weighing before your next trip	144
Carrying bicycles	148
Storage and Seasonal	**150**
Choosing a place to store	150
Short-term storage	152
Rodent and insect problems	152
Winterizing	153
Winterizing procedure	*154*
Winterizing the Dometic macerating toilet	*157*
Over-winter battery storage	*157*
Final winterizing steps	*157*
Routine checks while in storage	158
Springtime de-winterizing	160
Expiration dates	161

Electrical	**164**
Electrical overview	164
Solar panels	*165*
Preventative maintenance	*165*
Fuses, circuit breakers, and Ground Fault Interrupters (GFI)	166
Troubleshooting power problems	169
No AC power	*169*
No DC power	*170*
Replacing light bulbs	171
Exterior lights	*172*
LED versus incandescent	*173*
Maintaining the 7-way trailer plug	174
Battery basics	175
Battery maintenance	176
Routine battery inspection	*177*
Topping up battery water	*178*
Understanding battery capacity	178
Monitoring your battery capacity	*179*
Extending battery capacity with equalization cycles	*180*
Charging batteries	181
Generator or solar for recharging?	*182*
TV antenna	183
Propane System	**185**
Propane tank inspection	186
Checking for propane leaks	186
Replacing propane "pigtail" hoses	189
Filling the propane tanks	189
Propane regulator inspection and adjustment	190
Humming regulator	*192*
Adjusting the regulator	*192*
Propane leak detector	193
Resecuring gas lines	193
Climate Control	**194**
Air conditioner	195
Air conditioner filter cleaning and replacement	*196*
Top side inspection of the air conditioning	*196*
Air conditioner tips	*197*
Furnace	198
Catalytic heaters	200

Gas Appliances   **202**

  Refrigerator   203
    Adjusting the door gasket   *204*
    Defrosting   *204*
    Operating tips   *205*
    Troubleshooting   *206*
    Gas burner maintenance   *207*
  Stove/oven   208
  Water heater   208
    Routine maintenance   *209*
    Inspecting for leaks   *210*
    Removing and reinstalling the drain plug   *210*
    Flushing the water heater tank   *211*
    Inspecting the electrical connections   *211*
    Inspecting and adjusting the water heater burner   *211*
    Disassembling and cleaning the burner tube and flue   *212*
    Inspecting the gas orifice, ignitor, and gas valve   *213*
    No hot water or very little   *214*
    Rotten egg odor from hot water   *214*
    Dripping P/T valve   *215*
    Replacing the P/T valve   *216*

Keeping Your Perspective   **217**

Resources   **219**

How To Make Your Airstream Last Forever

As Editor of Airstream Life magazine, I've seen many Airstreams that have been lovingly maintained and passed on through families for fifty or sixty years. I've also seen far too many that have been run down in just a few years. The difference is usually just knowing what to do to maintain the Airstream.

This causes problems for some well-intentioned owners. It's sad when I meet them, only a few years into what should be happy ownership, and hear that they are facing expensive repairs because they didn't know how to prevent them. Often they are considering getting out of RVing entirely, out of frustration.

This book is intended to prevent that. You can keep your Airstream investment in excellent running condition for the rest of your life with just a little knowledge and a few tools. **Most Airstream maintenance is simply a matter of inspecting, cleaning, lubricating, and easy adjustments — and this book will teach you how to do all of those things.**

You don't need to have a giant chest of tools in your garage. (You can almost entirely disassemble an Airstream with a cordless drill and a screwdriver.) So don't be intimidated by the idea of doing your own winterization, replacing sealants, checking tires and wheels, or anything else you see in the Table of Contents.

It's important to recognize that this book is primarily about preventative maintenance. It's not a service manual or repair guide. Also, there are some maintenance items that require specialized tools or which should be done by a trained technician for safety reasons. For those things, you'll still want to bring your Airstream to the shop—and for that reason they're not covered in this book.

Still, many common minor problems and solutions are explained here, so that instead of dragging the trailer off to have every little thing checked out by the shop, you can make simple repairs yourself and avoid interrupting your trip.

If you are a new Airstream owner, you may want to get *"The Newbies Guide to Airstreaming,"* since it contains numerous tips on non-maintenance aspects of Airstream ownership, and is designed to be a companion to this book.

If you take care of your Airstream, it can take you on wonderful adventures for your entire life and still be in great shape to hand down to another generation. I wish you many happy years with your Airstream! See you on the road,

Rich Luhr

Editor & Publisher, Airstream Life magazine

PS: You might be wondering why the title of the book says "(Nearly) Complete." That's because you can help improve future editions. If you find a routine maintenance procedure that's not covered here, or have a great tip to share that makes a job easier, please write to me at rich@airstreamlife.com. I'd be happy to hear from you.

Your Tool Kit

Airstream maintenance isn't hard, especially if you have the right tools to get the job done.

Naturally, the tools you need depend on the jobs you are willing to take on. For most of the tasks in this book you can get by very comfortably with just a few things.

At home you may have a lot of tools, or none at all. But you should have a small collection of tools and parts that stay in the Airstream to deal with on-the-road problems. Consider carrying the parts and tools needed to:

- change a tire
- replace a fuse or light bulb
- disconnect / reconnect the battery
- clean up corrosion
- detect a gas leak and tighten a gas connection
- remove and replace a rivet
- tighten a loose screw
- test a power outlet
- fix a simple plumbing fixture leak
- stop a rainwater leak
- lubricate hinges, latches, and hitch

Most of the tools and supplies you will need are readily found in hardware stores, and the rest can be ordered from RV suppliers or found in RV stores.

Probably the most useful (and expensive) tool you might need is a cordless drill. Get a powerful one, 18 volts or better. Obviously it's great for drilling holes if you need to install a new hook somewhere, but you will end up using it the most to raise and lower the stabilizers on your trailer.

(You'll need a socket adapter and the correct size of socket.) This turns a tedious chore into a 30 second non-event. You will appreciate this the first time you set up or break camp in a heavy rain.

The cordless drill is essential for drilling out broken rivets so you can install replacements, so you'll want a set of drill bits as well. The usual size drill for an interior rivet in an Airstream is #30, or 1/8", but you should get a set that ranges from 1/16" to 1/4". With a small set of screw bits, your cordless drill can also be used as a high-speed, high-power cordless screwdriver. Owners who have equipped their Airstream with either a Hensley Arrow or Pro-Pride 3P hitch can also use a cordless drill with the 3/4" socket and socket adapter to run their weight distribution bars up and down.

The only other expensive tool you need for maintenance is a good torque wrench (and a 12" extension and socket), so you can be sure you've got the lug nuts tightened properly when you change a tire.

The rest of the tools most people need are pretty simple and not terribly expensive, even the rivet tool used to replace POP rivets. A list of suggested items is below.

If you travel for long periods, or if you've got an older Airstream, then you'll want more stuff. The trick is not knowing what to bring, it's knowing when to stop packing tools. I've seen guys traveling with pickup trucks that were basically big rolling tool boxes. Most of the time this is overkill, and can even be dangerous if you are overloading your tow vehicle with heavy tools you won't need.

On a long expedition, it might make sense to carry a hard-to-find tool or part, if it's light or small, but there's a point at which it makes more sense to find a service center—or just buy the part when you actually need it. This is a judgment call.

You should be prepared for anything small that might seriously disrupt a trip, which is why this book puts emphasis on tires, fuses, gas leaks, electrical problems, and water leaks. It's really frustrating to be somewhere wonderfully remote, like Big Bend National Park in Texas or the north rim of Grand Canyon, and find you have power problems because of a simple bad ground. Do you really want to hitch up and tow 70 miles to the local garage just to have a technician spend one minute cleaning a ground wire that you could have fixed yourself if you'd brought a simple piece of sandpaper and this book?

There are many things you might bring that are extremely handy or even essential. Here are the maintenance tools we carry in our Airstream, for your consideration:

ITEM	NOTES
leveling blocks and chocks	necessary for uneven campgrounds, but also useful for changing tires on double axle trailers
bottle jack	for changing a tire (single axle trailers only)
in-line water filter	keeps sand and debris out of fresh water tank, improves taste
tire pressure gauge	if no TPMS is installed (see "Tire maintenance"). Should read from 20 to 120 psi
socket wrench with 6" or longer extension and correct size socket for your lug nuts	for loosening lug nuts on wheels when changing a tire—lug nuts are typically 3/4" or 13/16"
torque wrench	for torquing lug nuts to proper spec
cordless drill	18 volt or better recommended
socket adapter	allows sockets to be used with cordless drill
drill bit set	1/16" through 11/32"
box of vinyl gloves	useful for dirty jobs
holding tank chemicals	septic safe, non-formaldehyde type
hitch ball lube/ hitch grease	as needed for your hitch type
junk beach towel	handy for many uses, see "Belly Pan Repairs"
silicone spray or BoeShield T9	for lubricating hinges, latches, locks, etc.
headlamps	very useful for hands-free nighttime work, setting up camp after dark, etc.
first aid kit	
high visibility shirt or vest	for emergency roadside repairs
voltage meter	for electrical diagnosis

Teflon (PTFE) plumber's tape, rated compatible with propane	for preventing leaks in threaded fittings
Parbond	see "Sealants" in the Leak Detection, Prevention and Repair section
rivet tool	for replacing broken or missing rivets
small hammer	useful for tapping stubborn parts
combination screwdriver or screwdriver set	slotted and Phillips type
kitchen/utility shears and/or retractable safety knife	will cut through almost anything
electrical tape	for minor 12-volt repairs
silicone tape	excellent for temporary repair of small leaks in plumbing
wood glue	for minor furniture repairs, reattaching edge banding, etc.
medium sized adjustable wrench	useful for tightening gas fittings
pliers	
wire cutter/stripper tool	for minor 12-volt repairs
zip ties or Velcro straps	for tying up loose wires or bundling cables, etc.
sandpaper or emery cloth	for removing corrosion on ground wires and various other uses
butt splices and crimper tool	for minor 12-volt repairs
spare bulbs for interior and clearance lights as needed	(if your Airstream is not equipped with LED lights)
assorted 12 volt automotive-style blade fuses	various amperages
single-sided razor blades	multiple uses
#8 and #10 wood screws	replacement and repair
rubber hose washers	for fresh water hose
1/8" aluminum POP® rivets (grip range 1/8-1/4")	for interior repairs
3/16" aluminum "large flange" POP® rivets (grip range 1/8-1/4")	for belly pan repairs
Aerospace 303 Protectant	good for preventing sticking windows and vents

It may seem like a lot, but most of this fits in a small fabric tool bag (except the hoses, tire changing tools, cordless drill, and blocks).

Don't take this list too seriously. Your Airstream probably has a few different components, and the jobs you care to tackle on the road may be different, which will change the things you need to bring along. You don't need to be able to repair anything that might happen, just the little things that are easily done along the way. Start with the basics and add to your traveling tool bag as you identify specific needs. Eventually you'll end up with a tool kit that fits your style, skills, and Airstream.

Your First Aid Kit

You probably don't have one, because it didn't come with your Airstream trailer (Interstate motorhomes do come with a First Aid kit). It is surprising to me that the RV industry safety code calls for installation of a fire extinguisher but not a First Aid kit. This suggests that they are more worried about saving the trailer than they are the people inside it. Seems ridiculous, doesn't it?

Be sure to correct that oversight as soon as possible. From personal experience I can assure you that minor domestic injuries seem to happen more often when you are miles away from health care, or on the Friday night of a long weekend in a small village like Jackson Center, Ohio. I don't know why.

You can buy First Aid kits pre-made or just build your own. We went to Wal-Mart the day after my wife sliced her finger open with a kitchen knife, bought a zippered case, and filled it with goodies like bandages, tape, gauze, anti-bacterial ointment, scissors, gloves, hydrogen peroxide, and Benadryl. We also got some advice from friends who are nurse practitioners, EMTs or MDs about treatment methods and tricks.

The next time we have a domestic injury while camped somewhere remote, or while doing some maintenance, we'll be much more able to take care of it ourselves. Make sure you are ready, too.

Vintage Airstream needs

Airstream has been making aluminum trailers for over 80 years (albeit with a shutdown during WW II). Not surprisingly they've changed substantially in all that time, so that it's virtually impossible for this book to cover all the differences in models, floorplans, options, and years of manufacture. Mostly we're focusing on the non-vintage years, and especially those trailers manufactured since 2000.

The other challenge relating to vintage Airstreams is that they have usually been heavily modified since new. So it's impossible to predict what model of water heater, vent, furnace, refrigerator, awning, power converter, and many other components your trailer has installed. Similarly, some parts and systems in older trailers will be in different places, or may not exist at all.

For owners of vintage trailers, it's still important to understand how the systems work in a general sense, and then learn for yourself the particulars of your trailer. The members of the Vintage Airstream intra-club of the Wally Byam Airstream Club (WBAC) are an excellent resource for new owners of vintage trailers. You can also find support from Vintage Trailer Supply (online) and learn quite a lot by attending vintage-oriented rallies, which are held all over the country.

Your tool kit for basic maintenance will probably be very similar to that of new trailer owners, but you may want to put more emphasis on certain specialty tools and parts. For example, the owner of a vintage trailer with no clear coat will have no concern about filiform corrosion, but may want to investigate aluminum polishes. Vintage owners might not be as concerned about electrical repairs if they have a gas-only refrigerator, a gas-only heater, a pilot-light water heater, and even a gas lamp—but those owners will probably want to learn more about propane gas systems and repair tools.

Assess your trailer as you read through this book, and decide for yourself which systems or components are most likely to need help as you travel, then outfit your tool kit accordingly.

Learning to Inspect

When and why to perform inspections

A big part of maintenance is simply paying attention to your Airstream. It's also the easiest part of maintenance, so it's something that anyone can do. All you need is a pair of eyes and a little bit of knowledge about what you're looking at.

These inspections will really pay off. Most on-the-road problems can be caught during routine inspections and fixed before they become big problems, saving you a trip delay or an embarrassing wait by the side of the road for help.

The following sections talk about the things you'll need to understand when you are inspecting your Airstream, but first let's just think about when to inspect. You've got many opportunities to catch maintenance problems when the inspection process is virtually painless.

The first opportunity is a week or two before you actually plan to leave for a trip. We'll call this the "Storage inspection." This inspection is designed to find any problems that might have developed while your Airstream was in storage. You may be surprised to learn that most serious problems happen (and fester) when you aren't using the trailer, like flat tires, water leaks, frozen plumbing, electrical corrosion, rodent intrusions, decaying sealant, and seized-up moving parts. Airstreams are happiest when they are frequently used. They don't like to be stored for long periods of time without attention.

If your trailer has been sitting for a while, doing an inspection two weeks before a trip will give you time to fix or maintain anything you might find that needs attention. It's an awful feeling to be ready to pull out and discover a trip-killing problem that you could have fixed earlier, had you only known about it.

The second great opportunity to inspect is during the packing process. This is the "Pre-departure inspection." You'll learn to check the appliances and systems while you load up for your travels. With practice, this inspection becomes second nature, and you won't even have to think about it.

A third and very important time to check is during your trip—what we're calling the "On The Road inspection." We'll describe some things you should check at every fuel stop or rest stop along the way to catch common problems that crop up during long road trips.

Finally, as part of the annual winterization process in the fall, and de-winterizing in the spring, you'll have the opportunity to inspect key plumbing and electrical systems that are usually overlooked otherwise. This is also a good opportunity to check for hidden problems in your tow vehicle's hitch receiver.

The "Storage inspection"

This inspection is primarily designed to uncover problems that might affect the safety and/or road-worthiness of your Airstream, as well as find major problems that would prevent use of the plumbing or electrical system.

A thorough Storage inspection includes everything that you'd check before leaving a campground (see Suggested Checklists in *The Newbies Guide to Airstreaming*") and also includes the tires, brakes, exterior trailer lights and signals, roof vents, smoke and carbon monoxide detectors, fire extinguisher, belly pan, plumbing system, electrical system, and the hitch.

Because this inspection is done after the trailer has been sitting unused for a while, it's a great opportunity to identify problems that might take some time to be obvious, like tires that lose air slowly, a battery charging problem, or a rodent infestation.

Tools and procedure

You don't need many tools for this inspection. You should have a tire gauge and a good flashlight so you can see inside cabinets and underneath the trailer. A notepad is useful to keep track of problems you want to correct. A few sheets of paper towel are helpful to locate moisture inside small spaces.

The Airstream does not need to be plugged into power for this inspection, but it should be de-winterized. If it hasn't been de-winterized, you will have to skip a few parts, or you can read about de-winterizing and complete that procedure before continuing. In particular you need the battery connected and fully charged, and for plumbing inspections you'll need to have some water in the fresh water tank.

The easiest way to start is to circle the Airstream slowly, touching or looking closely at every item that might need attention. Begin outside, at the front of the trailer, and after completing your exterior inspection, go inside and move from front to back to check all the interior items.

You're verifying that everything works as it is supposed to—with special emphasis on safety items—and looking for anything that might be amiss. Use all of your senses: look for items that are loose, broken, corroded, or wet; sniff for propane gas or mustiness; feel for moisture in places you can't see; listen for abnormal sounds from the gas appliances or plumbing.

If you've got a newer trailer, inspecting all these items might seem silly. After all, it's new, so nothing should need inspecting, right? Actually, learning how things are supposed to look and feel when new will help a lot later, because you'll notice readily when something doesn't seem right. And even new Airstreams can have problems with leaks, critters, or failed components. So regardless of the trailer's age, this is an important inspection to practice.

Exterior

At the front of the trailer, check these items:

- **Power hitch jack.** It should go up and down normally without any strange noises.

- **Breakaway switch.** When you pull the pin out, you should be able to hear a click and hum from the trailer's drum brakes. With disc brakes, you'll have to listen for the hydraulic actuator to make some noise. Don't leave the pin out for more than about 10 seconds.

For details, see the "Breakaway Switch" section of this book. If the pin seems to need lubrication, use a little silicone spray.

- **Hitch coupler.** This should move smoothly (not stuck with rust or from lack of lubrication). There should be some light lubrication inside the coupler. If not, apply a little silicone spray or BoeShield T9.

- **Weight-distributing hitch components.** The hitch should have tight bolts and be lubricated as recommended by the hitch manufacturer, with no broken, cracked, damaged, or missing parts. Look for rusty lines on all components that may indicate a crack forming in the metal. If the hitch is generally rusty, you should plan to remove the rust with a wire brush and repaint it soon (see "Receiver hitch inspection" in the Running Gear and A-frame section). There may be other things to check depending on the type of hitch you have, so check the manufacturer's documentation.

- **Batteries.** These should be clean, undamaged, and dry. Replace batteries that appear to be cracked, damaged, or leaking. If you have the type of batteries that take water (standard equipment on Airstreams unless replaced), pop off the caps and check the water level, and add distilled water as needed. See "Battery Maintenance" for details.

- **Propane hoses.** Check that they are not cracking or damaged. Open the gas valves to pressurize the system. There should be no sign of leaks (see "Checking for Propane Leaks"). Be sure to follow the propane lines downward from the propane regulator, under the frame and belly pan of the Airstream. The propane lines below the trailer are copper and thus easily damaged, so check that they are in good shape and that all the clamps holding the propane lines in place are still attached.

- **Propane tanks.** These should be securely tightened down, and of course they should have enough propane in them for your trip. If the tanks are damaged or rusty they should be replaced. Tanks over 12 years old need recertification. See "Propane Tank Inspection" for details. Once you've verified the gas system is OK, turn the gas on at least one tank so you can test the gas appliances inside the Airstream later.

- **Front window stoneguard(s) should be secured.** Note any problems with the latches or the window itself.
- **Front ground wire.** Beneath the A-frame, look for a thick copper wire that is bolted to the frame or to a propane gas line with a small clamp. The location may vary—on some trailers it is located near the front curbside stabilizer jack. There may also be more than one connection point. On vintage Airstreams the ground may be inside. If this wire looks corroded or exceptionally dirty, unscrew the clamp that holds it in place and clean up the clamp and wire with sandpaper or wire brush. The copper should be shiny where the wire makes contact with the clamp, for a good electrical connection.

If your Airstream has a front storage compartment, open it and inspect for signs of water intrusion (such as water stains, a moldy smell, soft wood in the floor, dampness, or condensation). Use your paper towel to be sure. It should be dry as a bone inside the compartment, otherwise there's cause for further inspection to find the source of the moisture.

Now move to the curb side of the Airstream (right side) and continue your inspection by checking for any sort of damage to the body. Are the windows closing fully? Is the awning secured? Are any rivets popped loose or missing? Any of these signs would be reason to investigate further.

- **Sealant.** Check around the windows, entry door, the mounting points of the awning, and any appliance openings on the body. The sealant should be complete and not cracked. Gaps and dried out sealant can be repaired easily (see "Sealants").
- **Tires.** Look at condition, wear, and inflation. Use a tire gauge to check that they are at the correct pressure. See the section entitled "Tire Maintenance" for details on the signs of a failing tire. Each tire stem should have a screw-on cap.
- **Wheels.** Problems with wheels are usually pretty obvious (e.g., noticeable damage). Any damage to a wheel should be checked by a professional. Also notice if there's a lot of grease streaking out from the center of the wheel hub. This is grease from the wheel bearings. A small amount isn't cause for alarm, but a lot of grease could indicate a bad grease seal, which could cause catastrophic failure of the wheel bearings.

- **Wheel lug nuts.** Check for correct torque with a torque wrench, especially if a wheel has been removed in the last 100 miles. See "Using a torque wrench" in the Running Gear and A-frame section.

Now bend down and take a look under the trailer. You're looking for anything dangling from the trailer, such as a loose propane gas line or pieces of the belly pan. Sometimes the rivets that hold those items to the frame will come loose from corrosion or from hitting road debris. Any loose metal items should be re-secured with new rivets. See "Belly Pan Repairs" in the Aluminum Body Repairs section, and "Re-securing Gas Lines" in the Propane System section for details on how to make these repairs.

If your Airstream has hydraulic disc brakes (most don't), take a moment to look at the black flexible rubber brake hoses that lead to the brake calipers behind the wheel. They should not have cracks, swelling, or other damage. If any hose has a problem, it's time to replace all of them and have the brake fluid replaced.

Continuing around the trailer around the back and street side (left side) of the trailer, continue looking for signs of damage or sealant failure as before. Also check these items:

- **Exterior compartment doors and appliance outlets.** As before, you're looking primarily for signs that water may be able to get inside, but of course any sort of damage is cause for further investigation and repair.
- **Rear ground wire.** There may be a second ground wire located inside the rear bumper compartment. Follow the instructions for the front ground wire, above.
- **Refrigerator and water heater compartments.** Open the water heater cover and the refrigerator cover on the outside of the trailer and clear out any spider webs, wasp nests or bee hives.

Interior

Now it's time to check a few things inside the trailer. Your interior inspection starts as you unfold the entry step and open the main entry door. Are either of them squeaking at the hinge? Does the door lock work correctly? A little lubrication may be called for on the hinges or in the lock. Silicone spray works very well in both places (not WD-40, please).

In the following steps you'll notice a number of different checks for leaks. You might regard this as paranoia, but one of the few things that can kill an Airstream is water damage, whether from a rainwater leak or a plumbing leak. So we'll be extra cautious about that after a period of storage.

As you go into the Airstream, notice the atmosphere. It shouldn't be any more humid inside than outside. Is condensation on the windows? Is there a moldy odor? All of these are hints of moisture intrusion and reason to check extra carefully in the following steps. If the Airstream has been stored with the city water disconnected and water pump off, it should be dry inside. (However, some condensation may occur normally on inside metal walls during temperature changes or if there's no ventilation.)

- **Put the battery disconnect switch into the "USE" position (or reconnect the battery if it was disconnected) and turn on the lights.** This is just so you can see well for the rest of the inspection, and incidentally note if any light bulbs or LEDs need replacement.

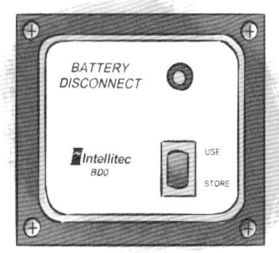

- **Turn on the water pump** and run water at each faucet, shower head, and toilet for a few seconds to verify the pump is working and there are no plumbing leaks. Run each of the faucets until all the air is out of the water lines and you're just getting water at each outlet. After you've shut off all the faucets, leave the water pump on. During the rest of your inspection, notice if the water pump runs again. It might run once for a couple of seconds because of air in the lines, but if it runs repeatedly when no faucets are on, that's a strong hint that water is leaking from the plumbing system somewhere.

- **Check inside cabinets under the kitchen and bathroom sinks for any hint of leaking plumbing.** Use your paper towel and flashlight. Water drops will show as shiny reflections in the light. You might find a little condensation on cold water lines, which is normal if the air is humid and the water in your fresh water tank is very cold, but it could also be a sign of a leaking plumbing fitting, so wipe the moisture off and double-check to see if the water reappears. A drip or a puddle is probably not condensation. Also if you hear hissing while the system is pressurized, you've got a big leak that needs immediate attention. Turn off the water pump and disconnect the city water hose before continuing. If you find a leak on a plumbing fitting, read "Quick Leak Fixes" in the Plumbing section. While you're doing this, notice whether there are any signs of rodents. Little black specks of droppings, chew marks, or fluffs of material that a rodent might use for bedding are dead giveaways. If you see these things, read the discussion on "Rodent and Insect Problems" in the Storage and Seasonal section.

Now we can check for rainwater leaks. Rainwater leaks are typically not detectable by actual moisture unless it is raining while you inspect. So instead we'll look for the secondary signs that a leak has occurred in the recent past. You're checking for funky smells, rusty screw heads, water stains, black streaks on the walls (this is aluminum oxide being pulled down by water, typically under a seam in the aluminum), splatter marks on a countertop, stains or rust on the ceiling vents, stains on the curtains, or even a soft spot in the floor (usually near the wall). If you suspect a rainwater leak, read the section on Leak Prevention, Detection and Repair to find out how to address it.

- **Check all of the gas appliances for proper function.** Start with the stove, because that's the easiest way to get air out of the propane lines. It might take a minute or more before all the air is purged and the burner lights, if the trailer has been stored for a while. Then check the other propane appliances (water heater, furnace, refrigerator) and verify they light on propane. The refrigerator will take several hours to get cold, but turn it on now just to make sure that it fires up on propane and make a note to check later to see if it got cold.

Open the windows you commonly use. If they are sticking, see "Windows" in the Interior Cleaning and Appearance section for tips on how to open them without damaging the seal. Then open the vent fans and turn them on to verify operation. If a vent is sticky and hard to open, make a note to lubricate the seal (see "Fan-Tastic Vent" in the Windows, Doors, Locks and Vents section of this book).

If the 9 volt batteries in the CO (carbon monoxide) and smoke detectors have not been replaced in the past year, put in fresh batteries now and press the "TEST" buttons on each detector to verify they are working. The propane detector mounted down low on a wall (often below the refrigerator) is wired into the 12 volt system and doesn't require a battery.

With those checks, you've checked the essentials: heat, light, air, and water. You can't test the air conditioner until the trailer has a 30-amp power connection (or 50-amp if your trailer has dual air conditioners), but air conditioners usually don't fail during storage. You'll check some other essentials in the Pre-departure check, described below.

Finally, even though it's not part of your Airstream, check the hitch receiver on your tow vehicle. Get down on your knees and take a good look, with your flashlight. The receiver should be free of cracks, heavy rust, or stretched metal. The bolts and the ball mount should be tight. For details, read "Hitch Receiver Inspection" in the Storage and Seasonal section of this book.

You've checked over thirty separate items in this inspection—congratulations! You'll find that after doing it a few times you can complete this inspection almost automatically, in just about 10-15 minutes. It's well worth the time to save your Airstream from long-term problems.

Pre-departure check

You've got a great chance to quickly check all the major systems of the Airstream while you are packing up to go. This is almost second nature, because as you pack you are likely to turn on the lights, fire up the refrigerator, run the faucet (maybe to clean up something with a damp sponge), hitch up, and perhaps run the air conditioning or furnace. It's a good idea to start your pre-departure cleanup and packing a few days early just in case you find a problem.

We already did a thorough check of the exterior in the Storage inspection, so the only outside thing to check now is the operation of the clearance lights and brake/turn signals. Of course, you can only check these if you have a tow vehicle plugged to the trailer, and you'll need a helper to check the lights while you press on the brake, turn on the lights, and flash the turn signals.

Before you connect the 7-way cable from the trailer to the tow vehicle, take a look inside the cable end (plug). Check for green or whitish corrosion inside the plug. If you find an exterior light that doesn't work, or the 7-way cable end has problems, go to the Electrical section for tips on troubleshooting and repair.

We also checked most of the appliances and plumbing during the Storage inspection, but it doesn't hurt to use everything again as you are packing. If you treat your Airstream more like a house and less like a cargo trailer when you getting ready to go, you'll find that you will "automatically" check most of the systems, and enjoy the packing process more.

Run an extension cord out and plug in. If you can, hook up the water line or fill the water tank. Use the Airstream's bathroom instead of going back to the house. Open a window and run a vent fan. Turn on the stereo for a little packing music, or maybe even throw on a DVD movie for the kids to watch while you're getting ready. This way you are testing everything without even having to think about it.

When you are accessing storage bins and closets, take a moment to shine your flashlight in and check for signs of rodents as you did in the Storage inspection.

It's a good idea to turn on the refrigerator at least a day before you depart, so it has time to cool down. (The freezer should be cold enough to make ice within 24 hours.) Run either the furnace or the air conditioner during your pre-trip prep, if you can plug the trailer in and expect to need heat or air conditioning during your trip.

You'll still need to run down your normal checklist for departure, which would include things like closing the windows and vents, hitching up, stowing cargo, etc. Sample checklists are in our companion book, *"The Newbies Guide to Airstreaming."*

On The Road inspection

Once you are on the road, you should do quick mini-checks of the Airstream and tow vehicle at every rest stop or fuel stop. This is the easiest inspection of all and it takes only a couple of minutes. Just walk slowly around the entire rig, looking up and down for anything unusual.

In particular, keep an eye on the tires. You don't need to crawl around under the trailer to do this. Just take a good look at the tread and sidewall. You're looking for suspicious bulges, uneven wear, nails or screws in the tire, cracks, and other physical damage. You won't be able to see the bottom of the tire of course, but if you make a habit of looking at every stop it will average out.

Touch the wheels to see if one of them is much hotter than the rest (this can indicate a dragging brake or bearings about to fail). Some people use an infrared thermometer for this check, but your hand will tell you as well. The wheel hub (center) should feel pretty warm but not hot enough to burn you immediately. A normal operating range for the wheel hub is about 130°- 175° F, and sometimes brake components will get hotter after a long downhill run. Wheels on the sunny side of the trailer will normally be hotter. As you are doing this, look at the lug nuts to see if any of them are missing or loose.

As you circle back to the front of the trailer, look at the hitch to see if any parts have come loose, are missing, or need lubrication. Notice if there are any rub marks in unexpected places.

Then, as you are walking to the rest area or to get lunch, stop about 50 feet away and give the Airstream final glance. At that distance you can admire the whole rig. While you are enjoying the view of your beautiful Airstream, make note: Is the belly pan up nice and flat, or is it sagging at some point? Is anything dragging on the ground?

After your stop and when everyone is back in the tow vehicle, double-check that all the windows, vents, hatches, and doors have been closed.

That's all you need to do for a quick on-the-road inspection, and if you make a habit of doing this quick walk-around at every stop, I guarantee that one day it will pay off when you catch a serious problem in the making.

Learn the song your rig sings

One advantage of using your Airstream frequently is that you will get to know it very well. When something is not right it's usually very apparent. For example, you will learn to anticipate the stance it takes when it sits in a campsite with all tires fully inflated.

You will also learn the "happy noises" that your tow vehicle, trailer hitch, and brakes make when they are operating normally. You'll recognize the "seat of the pants" sensations that come with accelerating, turning, braking, and bumps. With time, you'll find that everything flows along like a familiar song, which is what you want, because it sensitizes you to any off-key notes. A little squeak may be all the warning you get before a problem crops up, but it will be enough if you are in tune with your Airstream and tow vehicle.

Other inspection opportunities

There's a section in this book about seasonal storage, which details what you need to think about when you put your Airstream away for the winter, so it's not repeated here. But in general, just before you wrap up for the season is the best time to check for possible leaks that can cause big problems during storage, and get things fixed that might take some time at the shop (at off-season labor rates!).

Keep in mind that you can do the Storage inspection anytime. To avoid a potentially big job in the spring, try to visit the Airstream several times while it is in storage, and maybe tweak a few things while you're there. In this way you can give your Airstream a little winter love and enjoy it while it's waiting for the snow to melt. Unlike a boat or a summer cabin, the Airstream is perfectly usable (except for the winterized plumbing) during the winter with just an electric outlet to plug into—and it makes a great getaway if you've got too many relatives in the house around the holidays!

Budgeting for maintenance

Often people ask in public forums what they should budget for "unexpected repairs." The problem with this question is that by definition such expenses are unexpected. You can't accurately budget for them.

On the other hand, maintenance is predictable, and helps reduce your cost of ownership by catching problems before they get more expensive. Routine maintenance as described in this book should cost relatively little, because it's mostly a matter of inspection, cleaning, and lubrication. The supplies you need are inexpensive, like lubricants and cleaners, and you don't need a lot of tools.

If you really want to have a budget for emergency repairs, think about the worst repairs you might have, barring a collision or a fire. Most problems that are likely to crop up will cost a few hundred bucks to fix at most, like a blown tire or a failed appliance. A big repair would be a complete replacement refrigerator, out of warranty. Figure somewhere between $1000 and $2000 depending on the fridge size. Keep in mind that a complete replacement refrigerator is not a common repair.

With a new-trailer factory warranty, your annual repair cost will likely be very low as long as you keep an eye on everything and fix problems promptly (especially leaks or integrity issues). Without a warranty you can still have low annual repair cost if you do the small things yourself and stay ahead of the maintenance.

Most of the "unexpected" repairs on trailers are the result of lack of attention. Check your Airstream regularly as described in the Inspection procedures above, and you'll find problems before they get expensive.

Interior Cleaning and Appearance

Cleaning the Airstream is just like cleaning your house. The major difference is that it doesn't take nearly as long! You'll want to periodically mop the floor, vacuum the carpet, dust, and wipe down surfaces — the basics.

Household products for floors, countertops, etc., generally work just as well in an Airstream as they do in a house. But because the interior is much more confined, try to use cleaners that are unscented and don't contain volatile chemicals. The odor of some cleaning chemicals can be overwhelming in a small space. Also, you don't want to dispose of cleaners containing bleach or ammonia down the sink. They can combine in the holding tank and create toxic fumes, and bleach will kill the beneficial bacteria in the tank.

"Natural" products are a good choice. For example, orange cleaner is an excellent general purpose cleaner for surfaces. You may be able to find it in natural foods stores or at auto parts stores. Baking soda makes an excellent light abrasive that can be used for numerous cleaning tasks. It removes odor in carpets, fabrics, refrigerator or freezer, and drains.

Airstream recommends using Pledge® Multi-Surface Everyday Cleaner to clean interior surfaces including exposed aluminum interior panels. But don't feel obliged to stick with that just because the factory likes it. You're not likely to cause damage with any household product, so use what you like.

Curtains

Airstream uses two different curtains in travel trailers: a loose-weave type for Classics and a polyester type for all other travel trailers. Both types can be machine washed on gentle cycle (air dry only), but dry cleaning is recommended in Sport, Safari, Bambi, and International CCD models. Airstream provides more detailed cleaning instructions by fabric type in the owner's manual.

Remove the curtains by unsnapping them from the wall, removing a screw or POP® rivet from the end of the curtain track, and sliding them out. The POP rivets are removed by drilling through the head with a 1/8 in drill bit. If you have a rivet tool, this rivet is easily replaced after you've reinstalled the curtains. (See "Replacing a POP rivet" in the Aluminum Body Repair section.)

Windows

The windows have rubber seals around the edges, which sometimes get sticky after long periods of storage. A sticky window should be opened carefully, using a plastic scraper or credit card to gently pry the seal away from the glass. You can help prevent this problem by annually cleaning the window seal with soapy water and applying Aerospace Protectant 303 or silicone spray.

If the trailer is going to be stored for a while and has the "International" type windows that are hinged at the top and open fully, you can also leave strings of waxed dental floss between the glass and the rubber. When it's time to open the window after storage, you can gently pull the dental floss sideways to help release the glass from the rubber seal.

Window blinds

"Day/night" pleated fabric shades

The day/night shades can stain easily, so don't use any cleaning products on them. Instead, vacuum them periodically with a brush attachment to prevent dirt from getting embedded. Be sure to clean the vacuum attachment before you use it so you don't inadvertently add dirt.

Hardware stores carry a dry sponge used for fine sanding of wallboard. This sponge can be used dry to wipe over the surface to brush dirt out.

Microfiber towels will do the same job. These can be lightly dampened with water (wring out all the excess moisture) and quickly wiped over the blinds. Don't let the towel wet the blinds, or it may erase the pleats.

Storing the shades in the closed position will help keep the pleats well defined.

Aluminum mini blinds

These mini blinds are pretty durable, but they do get dusty, especially near the kitchen where small amounts of airborne oil from cooking tend to make them sticky. For a quick cleaning you can use a spray bottle of water with a little liquid soap. Spray this mixture on a lint-free towel and wipe the slats individually. You can turn the slats toward you to make cleaning easier, but don't bend them too much or you may put a crease in the metal.

If the blinds have gotten really dirty, it's easier to remove the blind assembly entirely. Pull up the tabs on each end where the blinds mount, and slide them out. Airstream suggests spraying them with foaming bathroom cleaner, and then—believe it or not—shaving cream. You can use other products that are good at removing grime, as long as they aren't harmful to plastic or fabric (because of the cords and other parts of the blind).

To dry, just wipe with a clean damp sponge and let them air dry on a towel before re-installing.

Wood blinds

Some older Airstreams came with real wood blinds. You don't want to wash these, because too much water can warp or discolor them. Instead, just dust them periodically or use a vacuum cleaner brush attachment.

Formica laminate countertops

The laminate countertops are almost maintenance free. Just clean them periodically with a mild general purpose cleaner. The main thing to avoid is anything that might scratch the surface, so never use steel wool, Scotch-Brite® pads, or abrasive cleaners—and always use a cutting board.

Stubborn stains can sometimes be removed using a paste of water and baking soda. Apply the mixture gently on the stain and blot it up, but don't rub since it is abrasive.

For really tough stains the manufacturer says you can try undiluted household bleach or nail polish remover (acetone), but since both of those items are dangerous, take care. The fumes can be nasty, and neither of those chemicals are things you want to touch. Wear gloves and clothes that you don't mind ruining, and open the vent fans and windows.

Saturate a cotton ball with the cleaning chemical of your choice and gently rub the stain for up to two minutes. Rinse thoroughly with water and wipe dry using a soft cloth. This procedure may be repeated if the stain appears to be fading and the color of the laminate has not been affected.

Corian® solid surface countertops

Solid surface countertops look great and are very durable, so as with the Formica laminate, cleaning is pretty easy most of the time. If the surface starts to look blotchy or uneven, it may be because water was left to dry on the countertop. This eventually allows a hard-water mark to build up which dulls the look of the countertop, so always wipe the countertop completely dry after spills and cleaning.

The manufacturer recommends cleaning with soapy water, ammonia based cleaner (not window cleaner), or products made specifically for solid surface cleaners. If your countertop has hard-water marks, you can use try something like Soft Scrub® on a damp sponge or cloth, or a cleaner made for removing minerals such as CLR® or Lime-A-Way®. A more environmentally friendly option is white vinegar.

Darker colors tend to require more attention than lighter colors. You can use a polish to enhance the shine on darker colors but always use a polish formulated for food contact areas, such as Countertop Magic®.

Unlike Formica, you can use abrasive cleaners to remove stains or marks caused by cigarettes, alcohol, food, lipstick, hair dye, shoe polish, iodine, marking pens, etc. A Scotch-Brite® pad is also fine. If your countertop has a matte finish, use a green pad. If it has a gloss finish, use a white pad.

Minor cuts and scratches can be removed or minimized with a very light sanding using pads recommended by DuPont (the manufacturer of Corian). You'll need to obtain those pads from DuPont.

The procedure starts with washing the area where the scratch is located. With the surface still wet, start rubbing lightly with the peach colored side of the DuPont abrasive pad. (Pressing too hard may actually leave deeper scratches). Rub over the scratch using a straight line motion. Periodically switch rubbing direction ninety degrees. Rinse the pad periodically to remove any built up residue. Be sure all of the scratch is removed.

Then, inspect. Clean the area with water and dry thoroughly. Check to see if the sanded area blends with the rest of the top. It may not match perfectly, but if you want to try again you can do a larger area so there's more surface area to blend the borders.

If needed to get the gloss right (particularly on semi-gloss surfaces), continue the sanding process using the DuPont aqua-colored pad and then the gray-colored pad.

DuPont also says a matte finish can be restored with 220 grit sandpaper followed by hard buffing with a green Scotch-Brite® pad in a circular motion. To restore a semi-gloss finish, use 220 grit sandpaper, followed by 320 grit, followed by 400 grit. Then blend the finish in by using abrasive cleanser and a sponge or rag. A high gloss finish is best restored by a professional.

If your countertop is looking particularly rough and you can't get the scratches out using the procedure above, get a quote for professional refinishing before you consider replacement.

Stove and oven

The oven of an Airstream is the most under-utilized appliance. It's not uncommon to find trailers from the 1960s with ovens that look like they've never been used. Most people use them for bread storage. Should you be one of the dedicated few who actually bakes or roasts in the oven, the good news is that cleaning it is pretty much the same as a household oven. You can use typical household oven cleansers, but beware of the fumes inside the Airstream—open up windows and ceiling vents.

However, the stove often does get used, so cleaning it is more commonly needed. Most newer Airstreams have stainless stovetops. For daily clean-ups, a mild general purpose cleaner is fine, or just a soapy sponge. Clean up food spills promptly, because even the "stainless" steel top can get stained or etched by acidic foods. Don't use anything abrasive or acidic. A plastic scrubbing pad is OK.

Of course, make sure that the stovetop and all burners are cool before you start cleaning.

When you are cleaning around the burners, watch out for the metal igniter electrodes. If your sponge catches and bends or damages this electrode, you might find that the burner will not light the next time you go to cook.

Ozite interior ceiling/wall covering

This fuzzy white fabric found on the walls of some older Airstreams is pretty tough stuff. It's polyester fiber made from recycled plastic bottles. It adds a little soundproofing and insulation value to the interior, you can hang pictures on it using Velcro tape, and it lasts forever.

However, if it gets stained it can be hard to get clean. It's difficult to give a universal solution since cleaning depends on what caused the stain. For example, sometimes it shows black streaks caused by aluminum dust from seams or rivets rubbing. Brownish stains are typical of water leakage. Or maybe a little spaghetti sauce splashed onto it near the dinette.

Airstreams recommends using compressed air first to remove as much loose dirt as possible so it doesn't get worked into the fabric. Most people don't have an air compressor handy, so a vacuum attachment with a brush is probably more practical. Be careful about this if the problem is aluminum dust coming through the fabric, since the vacuum can pull more dust through and make the problem appear worse.

You can start cleaning with a mild bleach solution (carefully, of course, and in a small area first). Soak lightly and blot more so than rub so you don't cause the woven fabric to pill. You can also try a mild solution of detergent, OxiClean, or carpet stain removers. Work this gently into the stain with a plastic scrub brush. Use microfiber towels to rinse the area with clean water.

If this covering needs to be replaced or repaired, check out Ozite "hull liner" fabric for replacement options. The Ozite in your Airstream is glued to the aluminum but can be peeled off (with some effort). You can make a patch as needed and glue it into place. Note that getting the old glue off the aluminum is next to impossible, so you'll probably prefer to choose some sort of replacement covering rather than trying to expose the bare aluminum.

Vinyl flooring

What's the hard-surfaced floor in your Airstream? Vinyl. People often call it "linoleum," but that's something entirely different and Airstream doesn't use it.

Sheet vinyl floors are easy to clean with a soft broom and/or non-abrasive cleaning pad. The Swiffer brand pads work well. The amount of traffic the floor gets will determine how often you will need to clean it. If it doesn't come clean after the Swiffer treatment, you can use a mild detergent or household floor cleaner. Don't use abrasives of any type, because they will damage the surface layer of the vinyl. Once the surface layer starts to erode, the floor will tend to look dirty all the time and be much harder to clean.

If the vinyl gets a tear, there is a repair procedure to replace a small section of vinyl, but it's tricky and requires you to have a piece of identical flooring to use as a patch. This is a job best done by a flooring specialist.

The vinyl floor will be good for years of use, but no floor lasts forever. If yours is getting sort of tired-looking, at some point it will be a better option to replace it. Read the discussion "Flooring replacement" later in this section for details.

Shower maintenance

The only routine maintenance jobs in the shower are to clean the surface, which you can do with any fiberglass-safe shower cleaner, and periodically replace the silicone sealant, especially around the flexible Shub shower door found in corner bath models.

Waxing the fiberglass walls (not the floor) once a month can reduce water spotting and deposit build-up.

If you notice water dripping outside the shower door, it's time to strip out <u>all</u> the old sealant with a dull blade, thoroughly dry the area, and replace with a quality silicone kitchen and bath sealant. Get a color that matches your shower (typically almond). Applying it is not difficult but it takes a little practice to make a nice clean bead. Use a wet finger to smooth it out. Have plenty of paper towel on hand to clean up, and if possible have someone show you the technique the first time.

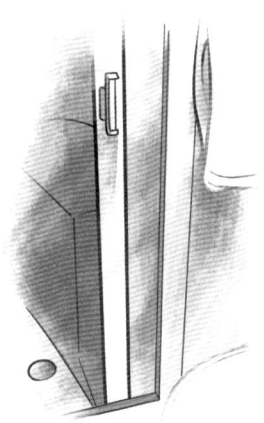

The Shub roll-up shower door is made of a very tough polyester material that the manufacturer says cannot be torn or ripped. It won't grow mold or mildew either, so there's no maintenance for it except wiping it down with cleaner periodically.If the Shub shower door won't retract fully, check for obstructions in the track and spray both the upper and lower tracks with silicone. If it still doesn't operate well, check that the bottom rail hasn't been pushed upwards in a curve from too much silicone sealant being forced under the rail. There's a 1/8" gap under this rail that should be filled by sealant, but not overfilled.If the screen spring is broken and the screen won't retract, you'll need to get a new "refill" screen. The manufacturer provides instructions on how to install it.

Minor furniture repairs

The furniture is generally pretty durable and needs only occasional cleaning. In this section we'll focus on a few issues that sometimes crop up.

Adjusting cabinet door hinges

Doors that don't close right can really be frustrating, and yet it's a relatively simple thing to adjust them. The trick is to be methodical and understand how each of the adjustment screws on the hinges affects the position of the door.

Late-model Airstream cabinet doors use a hinge that has five screws. Two screws hold the hinge in place, and the other three adjust the position of the door. If the door isn't adjusted correctly, the black snap latch won't engage smoothly, and the result will be a door that is hard to close.

Open the door and take a look at the part of the hinge that is attached to the inside of the cabinet (not the part on the door itself). There's a black plastic or stainless cover on the hinge, which just pops off with a fingernail or screwdriver.

With the cover removed, you'll see that the screws form a + shape on the hinge. The top and bottom screws hold the hinge to the wall, and don't offer any adjustment, so we can ignore those. They should be tight.

The center screw provides a little up-and-down adjustment, raising or lowering the door about 1/8". Start with this one to get the relationship of the door striker to the latch in alignment vertically. Loosen the screw at both hinges and then raise or lower the door. (It's much easier if you have a helper to reposition the door after you've loosened the screws, and hold it there while you tighten the screws again.)

Then work with the two screws at the left and right of the hinge. Loosening both screws will allow you to move the cabinet door closer or further from the cabinet, thus changing the gap between the door and the cabinet frame. You want the door to sit tight to the cabinet when it is closed, but not so tight that it binds at the hinge side of the door when it is closing. Get this adjustment right on both hinges before you move on to the next adjustment.

Now you can adjust the door left-to-right (as viewed when closed) as needed to get the latch to mate smoothly. Slightly tightening or loosening those two screws will change the door's position from left to right. For example, if you tighten the left screw, it will cause the door to move slightly left. Loosening the right screw will move it left a little more. Since there's a limited range of adjustment in each screw, you may have to use a combination of both screws to get the position the door needs.

Take your time. Make small adjustments to one screw at a time, and test the door after each adjustment. Watch the latch to see how it is engaging, and don't force it.If you prefer, you can remove the door and hinge entirely to make large adjustments, then hang it again. To do this, look for a small tab on the inside short edge of the hinge. Squeeze this tab and the hinge should pop free from the base that is screwed to the cabinet wall. To reattach, align the hinge to the base and snap it back in starting from the outer short edge (door end of the hinge).

Adjusting or replacing cabinet and drawer latches

One day you might go to close a drawer or a cabinet door, and find that you can't get the drawer or door to close fully. It will stop about an inch before full closure, and bang into the latch. This is because the black latch has snapped shut prematurely.

You can reset this latch with a screwdriver, by inserting it into the space behind the snap and carefully prying the snap to pop it back out. Try not to gouge or bend the soft plastic edges of the groove that the snap rests in, otherwise the latch may not align correctly and the problem will get worse.

If the latch it is behind a drawer, you will need to remove the drawer first. (To remove the drawer, pull it all the way out and then lift upward to pull it out the last few inches.)

If the snap keeps popping shut by itself, you can replace it. They wear out over time and this is the primary symptom.

Another cause of this problem can be mis-alignment of the latch, but this is less common since the latch is held in place by two screws and usually doesn't move. If you repeatedly have trouble with doors not closing well and the latch is screwed in tightly, check the alignment of the hinges first (following the procedure above, "Adjusting cabinet door hinges") before moving the latch.

Replacing the latch is a simple matter of two screws. Before you remove it, note exactly where the screws were located on the old latch.

Put the new latch in the same way to ensure correct alignment. A stubby Phillips screwdriver can be helpful for this task, since the latches for drawers are usually in hard-to-access locations.

The latches are available through Airstream dealers and the Airstream Life Store. Every late model Airstream owner should have a couple of spares handy. There are two strengths of this latch. A three-pound version is Airstream part number 381228 and the 10-pound version is Airstream part number 381228-01. The difference is merely the force it takes to open the drawer or door. In my experience it pays to get the 10 pound version so doors and heavily-loaded drawers don't pop open during travel, plus it lasts longer.

Adjusting overhead cabinet spring hinges

The spring hinges on overhead cabinet doors have limited adjustment. There are two screws on the upper (door) part that affect the position of the hinge. Normally this never needs adjustment, but if the screw has come loose it can be tightened. If the screws are coming out and the hole is stripped (meaning that the screw can't be tightened), see "Loose screws" below.

There's a third screw that goes into the spring itself. This has an effect on the tension of the spring, which governs how much force is needed to open the door. Make sure that it is screwed into the spring far enough that it doesn't pop out when the door is opened.

Tambour doors

Vintage Airstreams from the 1970s and late-model Sport series Airstreams have tambour sliding doors on the cabinets. If these get sticky or tend to bind up, you can lubricate the slides with silicone spray. If the Airstream is decades old, you might need to more extensively clean and lubricate the slide tracks. Dust and other particles accumulate in the tracks over time.

If the tambour is damaged, replacement material is available from a variety of sources online.

Loose screws

Airstream mostly uses #8 Phillips head screws in the furniture. This makes repairs easy, as you only need one screwdriver for virtually everything. It also means you only need to carry a few assorted lengths of #8 screws for spares. Sometimes a screw works its way out and disappears, so having a few spares is a good idea.

In some cases, you can convince a repeat offender to stay put with a little Loc-Tite or other brand thread-locking adhesive. This is found at hardware and automotive parts stores. If the hole for a screw has become enlarged so that the screw can't stay put, forget the Loc-Tite. Instead, your solution may be a larger screw, say #10 size.

In wood, you can also try a little trick. Poke a wooden matchstick, toothpick, or golf tee into the screw hole and break it off at the surface. This may provide enough extra material for the original screw to grip. You can also put in a drop or two of wood glue and let it dry before trying the screw again.

In aluminum, an enlarged hole usually is because the aluminum has stretched. While a larger screw may solve the problem, you should stop and ask yourself why this particular screw pulled so hard as to enlarge the hole. Is a second screw needed for additional bracing? Is there a structural problem somewhere that is causing this problem (for example, have other screws fallen out, leaving this one to do all the work)?

Repairing edge banding on countertops

On trailers without solid-surface countertops, there may be edge banding (trim) glued to the wood. A few minor issues may arise with this edge banding, all of which are fairly easy to repair.

If the edge banding is attached well but with a slightly raised edge that protrudes above the level of the countertop, you can carefully trim this off with a single-sided razor blade. Hold the blade at about a 30 degree angle to the countertop. Go slowly to ensure you don't scrape and mar the countertop surface. You can also use a fine flat file at a 20 degree angle, working inward from the edge.

If the edge banding comes loose and the glue is intact on the banding, it may be possible to remelt the glue with a heat gun and re-apply the edge banding. Be careful since the banding will start to warp above 200 degrees Fahrenheit. Hold the banding firmly in place for a minute but don't press so tightly that the glue is squeezed out. A flat piece of wood can be helpful for this task, to push the banding and keep you from burning your fingers.

If the edge banding glue is gone or won't hold, you can use contact cement or wood glue. (Gorilla Glue is not recommended because it expands too much and will leave a mess of excess to clean up.) Do this job when the temperature in the trailer is above 65 degrees, or whatever is recommended by the instructions on the glue. After applying glue or contact cement to both sides, press the edge banding on to the countertop edge firmly and hold it in place with masking tape or a clamp overnight.

Flooring replacement

After many years, you may choose to replace the floor covering of your Airstream. This is a big job that goes beyond the scope of this book, but we'll cover a few considerations just so you know your options.

Generally, it's easiest to replace the floor when all the interior furniture is out, as would be the case during a total renovation. If you try to replace the floor with the furniture in place, there will be compromises and additional difficulty, especially when trying to fit the new floor covering around cabinet bases and walls.

Installation difficulty is one factor to consider. Flooring may be self-adhesive, "floating," glued, nailed, or stapled to the plywood Airstream subfloor. Interlocking floating flooring such as Pergo™ is forgiving, since any piece may be easily replaced and alignment is nearly automatic, but it can be harder to shape around curved cabinet bases. More difficult are materials, such as glued cork tiles, that must be perfectly aligned as they are glued down.

For vintage trailers or trailers with a small useful load (see "Loading"), weight is a key consideration. Engineered wood or laminate products can be heavy; other materials such as cork and vinyl are lighter than the carpet and pad they may be replacing.

Cost is not usually the deciding factor because of the modest floor area in an Airstream. But take package size into account, since many products are only available in full packages. If you must cover 40 square feet and the chosen product only comes in 19 square foot packages, it is expensive to buy a full package for only a plank or two.

If you have a very old Airstream (1940s or 1950s) and the original tiles are nine inches square, they are almost surely asbestos-based and appropriate health precautions must be taken when removing them. When asbestos tiles were banned, the industry changed to 12x12 tiles. It is difficult to find 9" replacement tiles today. Some vintage owners cut down 12" tiles to maintain the original appearance.

The condition of the wood subfloor must be taken into account. Most Airstreams have subfloor seams that may "print through" thin flooring. Sheet flooring, vinyl tiles, and thin cork tiles show more subfloor irregularities than other materials. The bolts that attach the subfloor to the frame may need to be countersunk and caulked. Staples connecting plywood sheets may protrude slightly and require embedding with a hammer. Also, if you discover any rot in the floor (the result of a water leak), the rotted wood must be removed and replaced.

Many glue-down materials require contact cement. Some contact cements emit dangerous and extremely flammable fumes. Water-based contact cements are much safer to use within the confines of a trailer. If you must use non-water based contact cement, plan on wearing a respirator, protective clothing, and using fans to provide air circulation.

Flooring options

Linoleum floor (sold today under the Marmoleum™ and Harmonium xf™ brands) is a "green" material, composed largely of oxidized linseed oil mixed with pine resin and wood flour to form sheets on jute backing. It is available both as tiles and sheets.

Vinyl sheet, like linoleum sheet, is an excellent choice based on both cost and wear. Vinyl is also available in both tiles and planks, both of which are easy to install. Each piece can be individually cut to fit and the majority of patterns can be installed in any orientation so that cutting waste is minimized. Go for a thick vinyl, since thin vinyl will show subfloor irregularities more than many other materials.

Laminate flooring utilizes a printed wood-grain surface on a fibrous backing, and may include a soft backing layer for noise reduction. It is easy to install with basic carpentry tools. Most laminate floors are "floating," i.e., not attached to the floor underneath. A small clearance should be left at the edges for expansion and concealed by the peripheral molding.

Engineered wood products utilize a surface of real wood veneer on a wood backing, and also may include a soft backing layer for acoustic purposes. Like vinyl tile, many engineered wood products are now self-adhesive. Engineered wood is available in many thicknesses. A thickness of 1/4" to 5/16" will very nearly equal the weight of a carpet and pad. Thicknesses of 1/2" or more are quite heavy and are more suitable for your dining room than for an Airstream.

Cork tiles or planks are a natural material and may be cork throughout or a cork surface mounted on a backing. Thin cork tiles will show more subfloor irregularities than any other material except vinyl.

Bamboo flooring has a distinctive pattern from the nodes in the stalks and may be natural, carbonized, or stained. Natural colored or blonde bamboo is as hard as maple and is more stable than oak. Carbonized bamboo, in shades from honey to dark amber, is treated with a steam process that makes it slightly softer than the natural product. Stained bamboo is available in more than thirty colors.

Carpet tiles are easily installed and are easily replaced in case of damage. Commercial quality carpet tiles, such as those used in restaurants, wear like iron and are impervious to most spills. Carpet tiles can be cut with shears or a sheet-rock knife and are perfect for irregular areas.

Carpet is much more forgiving than other flooring options because a bad cut can usually be invisibly repaired. Judicious choice of carpet type and pattern will hide soil; multi-colored carpets such as Berber are especially good in this respect. Carpet that does not have an integral pad should be laid with a separate pad.

Do-it-yourself installation of replacement floor coverings can be tricky unless a rectangular area is being covered or the unit has been gutted. In a gutted trailer, the material can be laid wall-to-wall and the furniture installed on top of the flooring, as in new Airstreams. However, where carpet replaces a thinner floor, there may be clearance problems with doors and drawers.

Trimming out floor edges

When you've finished installing the floor, you'll need to trim the edges. Prefinished moldings to match manufactured flooring are expensive, often equaling the cost of the flooring for small areas. A cheaper option is to stain common hardwood quarter-round stock to match. Prefinished moldings work well with hard-to-match materials such as cork.

Flexible, self-adhesive, plastic moldings are an alternative to wood and are good for handling the curved surfaces in some Airstreams. McMaster-Carr is a good source for moldings.

Exterior Cleaning and Appearance

The aluminum clear coat finish

Modern Airstreams have a durable clear coat finish. Since 1999, Airstreams have come with a fluorocarbon clear coat which is pre-applied to the aluminum sheets by Alcoa before delivery to Airstream. Earlier models used a different formulation called "Plasticote," which was applied at the factory, and older Airstreams (1940s through the mid-1960s) usually had no coating at all.

Trailers from the 1970s and 1980s often have a "sunburned" look when the clear coat has begun to peel, especially toward the top of the trailer where the sun has hit hardest. There's no fix for this other than to chemically strip off the rest of the clear coat. Afterward you can make the surface look more uniform by either polishing the aluminum (very labor-intensive, see the "Polishing" discussion in the Aluminum Body Repair section) or having it professionally recoated at considerable expense. Many people just live with it.

Later Airstreams seem to be holding up better. We don't yet have data on the long-term durability of the current formulation of clear coat, since it has only been in use since 1999, but it should hold up for many years before showing signs of UV deterioration, and longer if you store your Airstream under cover, so it's not something to worry about. Most of the maintenance associated with the aluminum body and clear coat is simple cleaning.

Washing the Airstream

Close all windows and vents before you get started. (Yes, that's obvious, but people forget.) It's best to wash the Airstream under shade or on a cool day. Pre-rinse the exterior to remove debris that might scratch the surface.

A soft car wash mitt and long-handled brush with soft bristles will speed up the job tremendously. Microfiber towels are a good choice for drying and buffing. For application of certain products you will also find a spray bottle is helpful.

If you use a pressure washer, be careful. Set the pressure below 2500 psi and take care to avoid injuries from high-pressure water, electric shock, tripping on the hose, etc. Clear the area of obstacles and be aware of the surrounding environment (landscaping, people, pets). Be careful when spraying around decals, windows, doors, vents, and gaskets, as they can be damaged. Using the smallest possible tip angle will deliver the most powerful stream of water. A 40-degree angle tip is recommended by Airstream. Because of the need for care, washing by hand is often preferable.

Almost any cleaning liquid will clean a new Airstream with undamaged clear coat, but in the process you can damage the clear coat and inadvertently make the next cleaning harder. Avoid harsh detergents (like dish washing liquid) and choose products specifically made for clear coated vehicles.

Airstream recommends various external cleaning products, but really any automotive product suitable for clear coated or painted vehicles will work fine. Waterless and traditional rinse-off cleaners both work well. Waterless formulations have the advantage of allowing you to do some washing while in campgrounds that prohibit trailer washing. Concentrates are convenient because you can minimize the amount of liquid you are carrying around, and mix up what you need in a spray bottle.

Soft towels (microfiber is ideal) and buffing pads are recommended. Also, try to wipe with the "grain" of the aluminum skin, which generally goes horizontally along the body. This way any minor scratches that are accidentally introduced will be harder to see.

After cleaning, be sure to take the additional step of adding a protective layer to prevent bugs from sticking to the clear coat, especially on the front dome. Polymer-based products are preferable to waxes, which are based on paraffin and can eventually build up on the surface and in seams. For older trailers with Plasticote (pre-1999), Airstream recommends Walbernize partly on the theory that it helps maintain the coating.

You may also want to treat metal edges with a protectant to reduce filiform corrosion. For more on that, see the discussion on "Filiform corrosion" in the Aluminum Body Repairs chapter.

If you wash the roof you might see a little chalky white runoff, which is normal. It's from the paint and sealant on the roof.

If want to clean behind the stainless steel front wrap protectors, see the instructions on how to swing them out later in this section.

Airstream Sport and Basecamp trailers have a transparent protective film on the front lower body, instead of the usual stainless steel wraps found on other late-model Airstreams. This urethane film is very tough and will stand up to routine washing very well. If at some point it begins to wear out, peel or crack, check out automobile paint protective film as a replacement.

Cleaning hard-to-remove contaminants

Road tar and tree sap dry very hard and attach firmly to the Airstream's clear coat. Fortunately, any solvent-based cleaner that works for road tar will work for tree sap, and won't hurt the clear coat of Airstreams made after 1999. (Test in an inconspicuous spot on earlier models.) Light mineral spirits, WD-40, or denatured ("rubbing") alcohol are acceptable, as well as products specifically made to remove road tar, obtainable in auto parts stores.

Whatever solvent you are using, give it time to penetrate or soften the contaminant, and then gently wipe in the direction of the aluminum "grain." Don't press hard, or you might scratch the finish. Multiple applications may be needed for large sap deposits. Let the solvent do the work rather than using a lot of elbow grease.

Rinse with a vinegar and water solution to remove the solvent, then wash normally. Always follow up an intensive cleaning like this with a protective polymer-based paint care product to restore protection. Wax is best avoided, since it tends to build-up, making subsequent cleaning and protection more difficult.

Removing hard water deposits

Most common water spots are caused by mineral deposits. A 50/50 solution of vinegar and water does a great job of neutralizing these marks. There are also products such as Nuvite NuGlaze or Duragloss Water Spot Remover #505 which safely remove water spots.

Cleaning the front wrap protectors and front window stoneguards

The wrap protectors found at the front of most aluminum Airstream trailers are made from stainless steel, not aluminum, and they don't have a clear coat like the rest of the Airstream. If ordinary washes don't get the stainless wrap protectors clean enough, try stainless steel cleaner (available in hardware and grocery stores).

The front window stoneguards are the large tinted plastic protectors (usually gray in color). On trailers with front panoramic windows, debris from trees often settles in behind them.

To open them for cleaning, use a screwdriver on the two quarter-turn fasteners at the forward edge of the panel. Be careful—this frees them to swing open, and a gust of wind can send them back against their hinges, putting a crease in the trailer. Use cleaners approved for use on plastic. Scratches in the plastic panels can be remedied with polishes made for airplane windows.

Cleaning after salt exposure

If the Airstream has been parked a location near salt water, you need to take extra care to clean it completely. Salt spray can travel long distances in the air and wreak havoc on finishes and mechanical parts.

Most car washes are too small or have turns that are too tight for a travel trailer, but if you can find a truck wash or just a hose, be sure to rinse the entire body, hitch, A-frame, wheels, and brakes thoroughly. Do this as soon as possible after leaving the salty area, because salt-related damage happens quickly. In particular, salt and humidity will dramatically accelerate filiform corrosion (see the discussion on "Filiform corrosion" in the Aluminum Body Repair chapter).

Getting on the roof

You'll eventually need to get on the roof of your Airstream. Once in a while it's important to clean the roof, perhaps after being parked under a tree that sheds branches, leaves, or flowers. If you have solar panels you'll need to get on the roof to clean them periodically to ensure good performance. About once a year it's a good idea to get up on the roof to check the sealants around roof vents, too.

The Airstream's roof can be a dangerous place. It's easy to slip and fall off. When Airstream service center personnel are on the roof they wear a harness attached to an overhead beam so they can't fall far. Since you don't have such a harness, take care. <u>Never</u> go on the roof when it is wet or snowy. Never stand on the end-caps. If you can work from a stable ladder next to the trailer instead of standing on the roof, that's usually preferable. (Be safe with the ladder, too!)

The strongest place to get on the roof is by the entry door. Place your ladder there if you can. Leave the door open so nobody can open it and knock your ladder over. If you use a straight ladder, throw a towel or some other protective fabric where the ladder contacts the Airstream, to avoid scuffing it.

The awning tube is strong enough for the ladder to lean on, and it will give you a hand-hold when climbing up. But after that, there are few things to hold onto. Keep your body low and try to have a grip on something as you move around.

You'll see rows of rivets on the roof. Those indicate the locations of structural ribs. These are the strongest parts of the roof.

Be careful not to step on anything else, especially the skylight. Take a look around. You'll see a round plumbing vent, a 14" square vent fan or two, the refrigerator vent, possibly solar panels, possibly a skylight, a TV antenna, and (the largest thing) the air conditioner.

While you are on the roof, you should take a moment to do a quick inspection for possible leak points. See the Roof Inspection procedure in the "Leak Prevention, Detection and Repair" section.

Cleaning the roof and solar panels

Cleaning the roof is mostly a matter of cosmetic improvement, but it's a more practical issue for solar panels. Even a single leaf or a thin layer of dust can have a dramatic effect on their efficiency. You'll need to get on the roof to clean the panels well. Any product that works on glass will be sufficient, and even a quick rinse with plain water and drying with a towel will improve their efficiency. If you see brown tannin stains left by decaying leaves, scrub the glass with a little detergent and water until those marks are gone.

While you're working on the roof, consider kneeling rather than standing, to keep your body weight low. Don't let the roof get soapy where you are standing or walking, because it will be dangerously slippery. It's helpful to have someone on the ground to hand up tools and supplies to you to minimize your movement on the roof.

A long-handled brush is great for general roof cleaning tasks. Be careful with water hoses, since they tend to slip off the roof and can drag tools with them, or even trip you up. A bucket of fresh water can be easier for small jobs.

Washing trailer wheels

Since Airstreams come with many different types of wheels, both painted steel and clear coated aluminum, cleaning technique depends on the wheels you have. In general, basic washing with a brush and ordinary automotive soap and water will do a good job. There are many automotive products formulated to remove tough accumulations of brake dust, if that's an issue.

Avoid cleaners with ammonia if you have aluminum wheels, and generally speaking avoid abrasive cleaners or polishes on coated aluminum wheels.

As with the body of the Airstream, it's important to remove salt from the wheels as soon as possible. This includes road salt in the winter and sea spray. Filiform corrosion can occur on coated aluminum wheels even more quickly than on the body.

Zip-Dee awning

For over forty years most Airstreams have been made with Zip-Dee awnings. So that's probably what you've got. The nice thing is that they're all the same, except for the "Relax" powered awning introduced as an upgrade starting in 2013.

Setting up the manual Zip-Dee awning can seem a bit complicated at first. It's best to have someone show you how because there is a definite procedure and it's best to follow the factory instructions to avoid possible damage. Ask your Airstream dealer or whoever sold you the trailer, or check Zip-Dee's instructional videos at **www.zipdeeinc.com**.

The good news is that your Zip-Dee awning is a long-lasting product that needs very little maintenance. Lubrication and cleaning are all it needs for many years. When the fabric eventually wears out, it can be replaced without sacrificing the mechanical parts.

Awning hardware maintenance

The hardware of a Zip Dee awning (everything that's not fabric) should be cleaned and lubricated about once a year. Start with the aluminum arms and telescoping tubes that hold up the awning, whether manual or powered. Wipe them clean or use soap and water for stubborn dirt, and then spray the telescoping arms and tubes with lubricant. You can use silicone spray or BoeShield T9, but not WD-40 or grease because they attract dirt and don't leave a lasting film.

For a manual awning, don't forget to spray the springs near the claws at the end of the upper rafters. If you have a power awning, don't use silicone spray on the two small holes in the support arms. Put a little white lithium grease in those.

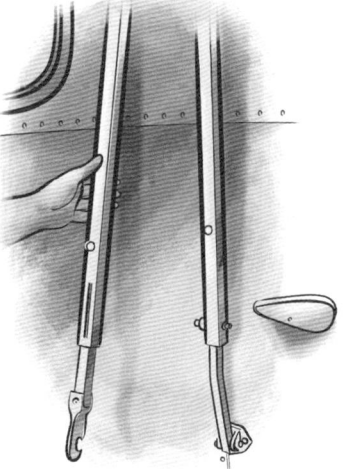

The telescoping bars and tubes of each arm on a manual awning can be slid completely apart, one arm at a time, and wiped off. Flush out the inside of the tubes with water from a hose. No lubrication is needed there but it won't hurt.

Flush with water and spray with silicone any parts that don't come apart. The little spring-loaded snaps on each arm of a manual awning don't come apart, so spray them with silicone. Flush out the springs trapped in the rafter arms (near the claw-shaped casting), then spray with silicone. In general, lubricate everything that moves or rotates, like the ends of the roller tube. Spray into the gaps between moving parts.

It's normal for the bright finish of the aluminum to dull over the years. Chrome polish will help a little for appearance. Silicone spray helps add luster.

Finally, use a 7/16" socket wrench to tighten every nut and bolt you can see. Nothing should be loose.

The manual awning has a spring that helps roll up the fabric when you put it away. If the awning is pulling so hard that it wants to roll up while you are deploying it, the spring roller can be easily adjusted. This procedure is documented in Zip-Dee's document "Adjusting Tension of Patio Awning Spring" and can be found on their website at **www.awningsbyzipdee.com**.

Other repair procedures can be found on the Zip-Dee website as well, including repairing bent arms, repairing a bowed roller, and reinserting the fabric into the case.

Awning fabric maintenance

The fabric of a Zip-Dee is Sunbrella®, a very durable acrylic woven fabric that is treated against UV damage and doesn't support mildew fungus, the main destroyer of woven fabrics. The weave of the fabric lets it breathe, which is why it dries quickly with only air exposure and doesn't drip on you in humid weather. The fabric is treated with a fluorocarbon finish that makes it water repellent. Drips can come through in a hard rain especially at seams and stitching, but with care, the water-repellent finish can last the life of the awning.

You'd think the acrylic fabric would last forever, but organic debris (such as dirt, seeds, pollen, bird droppings, spider webs, etc) can collect in the fibers and that debris <u>will</u> support mildew fungus. So regular cleaning of the awning fabric is important. A monthly hosing off with clear water (no soap) will help prevent dirt from becoming deeply embedded in the fibers, and eliminate the need for more frequent deep cleaning.

Every two or three years, a thorough cleaning is needed. Don't wait for the fabric to look dirty. That gives dirt a chance to set and the stains may not come out.

Deep cleaning is not hard. Brush off the loose dirt, hose the awning down, then scrub the awning with a clean, soft bristle brush using Zip Dee WashOut powder concentrate or a solution of 1 gallon of cold or lukewarm water with 1/4 cup natural soap. Don't use detergents or commercial awning cleaners.

For stubborn stains, add up to 1/2 cup of chlorine bleach. Allow the soap to soak in by rolling the awning closed for 10-15 minutes, then rinse very thoroughly until you are sure all the bleach is gone. The air will dry the awning quickly. Be very careful to avoid getting chlorine bleach on the Airstream body, and rinse off any that gets on it.

If you've got tree sap in the awning fabric, try rubbing alcohol. Use a soapy rag or sponge on the treated area to completely remove any residue. If alcohol doesn't work you can try WD-40, but test first on a small out-of-the-way spot, as it could stain the fabric.

Small holes in the awning fabric (possibly caused by burning embers, carpenter ants, or accidental cuts) can be repaired. Contact Zip-Dee for a swatch of fabric that matches your awning. Cut a patch about an inch bigger than the hole. If you use pinking shears or zig-zag the edges of the patch it will be less noticeable. Zip-Dee recommends attaching the patch with clear silicone sealant, or you can use fabric glue that is rated for outdoor use (found at crafts stores). Follow the instructions on the glue to get the longest-lasting repair.

Awning tips

If you have a manual awning and there's a chance of rain, be sure to set the awning so that one side is higher than the other. This will cause rainwater to drain off one end rather than pooling on the awning fabric.

<u>Always</u> take in your awning when you are away, and at night. Thunderstorms can come through without warning and cause very expensive damage!

Another rule of thumb: If it is too windy for you to sit under the awning, it's probably too windy for the awning to be out, too. Power awnings will automatically retract in a high wind, but you need to take in your manual awning yourself.

Rolling up the awning when wet is no problem if you unroll it later and allow it to dry. If you leave it rolled up, trapped moisture and organic debris (leaves, pollen, bird droppings, bugs, etc.) can allow mildew growth.

Zip-Dee also can supply replacement parts for any piece of the awning that might break and offer advice on how to avoid problems. For example, if the cast metal claw at the end of the rafter arms breaks repeatedly, talk to them about adjustments that may be needed in your awning or a change in the procedure you use to put it away. For more information, parts lists or manuals, call Zip-Dee at 1-800-338-2378.

Belt line trim replacement and front wrap protectors

The lower trim (also called "rub rail") and the upper trim ("belt line") in late model years is a flexible stick-on trim that fits into an aluminum channel around the perimeter of Airstream trailers. On most it's silver in color. After a while the silver goes chalky and then the adhesive lets go and the trim begins to droop or fall off. Replacement of the trim is easy.

You can order rolls of replacement silver trim from Airstream, through your local dealer. You also will need a little bottle of adhesive primer (JPC Primer 94) in a "dauber applicator," available from Airstream as well. This stuff preps the aluminum surface for the 3M VHB adhesive that's on the back of the new trim.

Begin by swinging out the stainless wrap protectors at the front of the trailer (except Sport models, which don't have them). There are three 7/16" nuts to remove on each side, and then they swing out on hinges. This gives you access to the rub rail that goes behind the wrap protectors. It also gives you a chance to clean accumulated debris that gets caught behind them.

Next, peel off the old trim. If it is old enough, it will peel off easily and leave little residue. Then clean up all the dirt in the aluminum channel with soap and water and a sponge. A little scraping of leftover adhesive may be necessary at this point, but the surface doesn't have to be perfect. The final cleaning is done with rubbing alcohol on a rag.

Apply the primer to the cleaned channel, let the primer set up for five minutes, and then stick in the shiny new silver trim. Cut the ends to length with kitchen scissors or another safe cutting tool. The trim is thick and difficult to cut, so be careful of your fingers.

Aluminum Body Repair

Probably the most durable part of your Airstream is the aluminum body. It may get dinged or dented with use, but it will never rust, and with proper care it can last for many decades. There's almost no maintenance associated with the body, other than cleaning.

Most new owners are phobic about the slightest nick or ding in the body, and it's understandable. Nobody wants to see their beautiful Airstream shell blemished. On the other hand, owners of vintage Airstreams tend to regard minor damage as "beauty marks" and leave them alone unless they are major dents or tears.

There's a good reason for that, too: there is little that can be done to repair aluminum so that it looks like new. Minor dents can sometimes be "popped out" but more commonly a dent means the aluminum has been stretched, so even if a repair is attempted there's often a tell-tale crease remaining. Unlike a car, you can't mask damage with body filler and paint over it.

To repair major metal damage (such as from a vehicle accident or large hail), panel replacement is required. This means drilling out the rivets that hold the panel in place as well as removing any doors, windows, hatches, etc. associated with that panel. This is advanced repair beyond the scope of this book, so if you are facing that sort of work and aren't well-equipped for a big job, you would be better off taking the trailer to Airstream in Jackson Center, Ohio, or a good Airstream service center for the panel replacement.

There are two simple and common repairs you can do to the aluminum body, namely fixing leaks and replacing rivets. Leaks are usually fixed with sealant, and the procedure is addressed in the next section, Leak Prevention, Detection, and Repair.

There are three basic types of rivets used in your Airstream: buck rivets, POP® rivets, and shavehead rivets (also called "Olympic rivets" for the popular brand). Let's look at each type and its typical use.

POP® rivets

The POP® rivet is the one you'll most commonly deal with. (These days the brand name POP® has become almost generic, so often people just call them "pop rivets".)

This rivet is applied using a rivet tool (sometimes called a rivet gun), which you can buy at hardware stores. The rivet tool is something that should go into your everyday tool kit, because POP rivets do occasionally fail and replacing them is a very easy job if you have a few spares and the rivet tool on hand.

Most of the POP rivets in an Airstream are holding the interior aluminum panels in place. They are also used to hold some exterior components where waterproofing isn't critical. Sometimes these rivets break in normal circumstances, and it's not a serious issue. You'll know a POP rivet is broken because it will either be obviously loose or missing, or you'll see a little circle of black around the head of the rivet. The black is aluminum oxide, caused by the loose rivet head rubbing against the aluminum panel.

Replacing a POP rivet

If a POP rivet has come loose, it should be replaced. You may be able to pull out the head with your fingers or loosen it with a screwdriver. But if it won't come out of the hole, you can remove it in one of two other ways: drill it out with a 1/8" drill bit (straight into the center of the head) or chop off the head with a metal paint scraper or thin screwdriver.

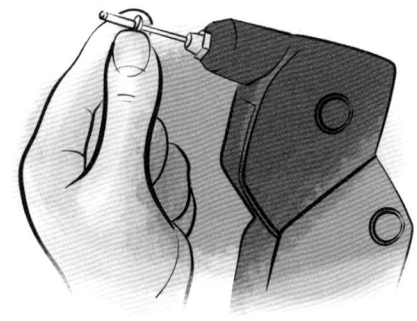

Generally chopping off the head is easy: you just slide the paint scraper under the head from the side, and tap it with a hammer. The head will come off and the tail will fall inside the wall, never to be seen again, and you'll be left with a nice empty hole for the new rivet.

Replacing the rivet is easy, too. You put a new POP rivet mandrel (the thinner end, also called the stem) in the tool, then press the wider tail end into the hole, and hold the rivet tool firmly against the surface while squeezing the handle three or four times. Be sure to keep the rivet tight against the surface as you do this; don't let it slide out at all. After the third or fourth squeeze, the mandrel of the rivet will break off with a snap, and you're done.

Pull the tool away and admire your handiwork. The rivet will have an empty hole in the center where the mandrel used to be, and you'll find that broken-off piece in the rivet tool. Just shake it out and you're ready to install another rivet.

If you are going to replace a POP rivet on the exterior (for example, to re-attach the name badge to the right of the entry door), apply a couple of layers of masking tape around the area first. Sometimes the rivet tool "jumps" when the rivet mandrel breaks, and it's easy to accidentally let it mar the aluminum surface. The tape will protect the surface.

Airstream uses a variety of POP rivets, but most are aluminum and most have 1/8" diameter body or 3/16" diameter body. The 3/16" are usually used in cases where the original hole has become enlarged a little. You can find these common sizes at hardware stores. There are also specialty rivets with extra-wide heads, used for belly pan repairs. It's a good idea to have a few of those in your tool kit too. If you can't find them locally you can order them online from Airstream or a variety of other sellers.

Rivet stuck in tool

Sometimes after you install a rivet, the mandrel gets stuck in the tool. This is sometimes caused by the mandrel being slightly bent when it snaps. It's not usually the fault of the tool. To avoid this problem, try to keep the tool as flat to the surface as you can as you squeeze the handle. It may also help to periodically spray a little silicone into the tool to keep it lubricated.

To remove a stuck mandrel, try working the handles as you tug on the mandrel with pliers. You can also try pushing the mandrel backwards through the tool with another rivet. If all else fails, you'll have to disassemble the tool. Check for information from the tool manufacturer, and note how the parts come out so you can reassemble it correctly.

Solid rivets

Most of the exterior skin is assembled with solid (or "buck") rivets. These very strong rivets hold two panels together or fasten a panel to one of the trailer's internal ribs.

Installing them requires access to both the interior and exterior side of the panel at the same time. The outside installer holds an air-powered rivet gun, which is sort of a miniature jackhammer that pounds on the head of the rivet. He presses this against the head of the rivet, which is sitting in a predrilled hole through the aluminum pieces that are to be fastened together.

The inside installer holds a shaped metal tool called a "bucking bar" that is pressed against the tail (or stem) of the rivet. The rivet gun very quickly hammers the rivet, mashing it inward and squashing the tail against the bucking bar, causing it to get shorter and wider. This fills the hole and locks the two pieces of aluminum together very strongly. Under normal circumstances, this rivet is in place forever, and it seals so tightly to the body panel that caulk is not needed for the rivet to be waterproof.

When bucked rivets fail (which isn't very often) you have to ask yourself what else is going on with the Airstream to put extreme stress on that rivet. Usually this is an indicator of something more seriously wrong, like major rot in the wood floor. The wood floor is essential to the overall rigidity of the Airstream body, and if it has been allowed to rot (from water leaks) the entire body can start to flex excessively and thus break rivets. (For more on this subject, see the discussion on floor rot in the Leak Detection, Prevention and Repair chapter.)

Usually the bucked rivets last the life of the Airstream, and are only replaced when body panels must be repaired. Here's where owners often face a decision point, because replacing the bucked rivets requires removing the interior of the Airstream as well as the exterior, so that two workers can drive the rivets in place. This adds considerable expense to a repair, and so quite often owners (or their insurance companies) opt for a shave-head (Olympic) rivet instead.

"Olympic" or shave-head rivets

The Olympic brand shave-head rivet provides the same function as the bucked rivet but can be fastened from the outside by one worker, so it doesn't require removing the interior to do an exterior panel repair.

The design of this rivet is clever. It is installed just like a POP rivet but when you squeeze the handle of the rivet tool, three legs of the rivet billow outward like petals of a flower, on the opposite side of the panel where you can't see it. These three legs enable a strong bond, not as strong as a bucked solid rivet but adequate for small repairs and patches.

If you need to replace a small number of solid rivets, Olympics are the way to go. If you are replacing an entire panel, it's debatable whether to go with Olympics or do the "full Monty" and remove the interior to install solid rivets.

After an Olympic shave-head rivet is installed, it has an obvious bump in the center of the rivet that doesn't look as nice as a solid rivet. It's a remnant of the rivet mandrel that broke off during installation, kind of like a belly button is a legacy of an umbilical cord. To make the Olympic rivet look like a solid rivet, there's a tool called a "rivet shaver" which cuts off the bumpy part of the rivet stem and polishes the head so that it's much harder to tell it was installed as a replacement. Now you know why these are called "shave-head rivets."

The rivet shaver is an expensive tool and takes some practice to operate, so unless you are going to install many Olympics, it's best to have someone experienced shave the rivets for you. If you only have to install a few Olympics, you can clip off any remaining fragment of mandrel and carefully round off the head with some fine sandpaper.

Like solid rivets, Olympics are watertight when installed correctly, but some people put a thin coat of sealant on the base of the rivet before installing, just to be sure.

If you are looking at a used Airstream to possibly buy, check all the exterior rivets to see if they are solid rivets or have tiny circles in the centers which indicate they are Olympic replacements. If you see a lot of them in one area, it's time to ask the seller about the damage that was repaired and verify that the repair was done well.

Fixing minor aluminum blemishes

A small ding in the aluminum, up to about 1" diameter, can sometimes be disguised by putting an Olympic rivet in it. Before you drill a hole to try this, spend some time envisioning how the rivet will look. Even though it might seem odd, a rivet that isn't in line with a body seam still tends to be noticed less by the eye than a dent.

Another whimsical way to make a small ding disappear is to put a sticker on it. We've seen fake "bullet hole" decals, bumper stickers, red "Texas" stars, and many other ways to make a ding become a decoration.

Holes punched in the aluminum can be patched. You'll need a scrap of matching aluminum (with the same type of clear coat, if your trailer has it) and a way to make clean cuts so that the edges look good. If you are going to try making a patch, consider making it in a decorative shape. We've seen patches shaped like US states, stars, moons, hearts, and many others. Be sure to put a thin layer of sealant under the patch where it meets the existing body aluminum, before riveting it in place. After riveting, some Parbond or Acryl-R along the edges wouldn't hurt either.

Removing decals

If there's a decal on your Airstream that you want to get rid of, do it soon. After years of UV exposure, the adhesive can eventually bond with the clear coat or the aluminum and erode it. This leaves a permanent "ghost" of the decal.

The easiest way to remove decals is with the 3M Adhesive Eraser Wheel. It's basically a polyurethane grinding wheel that you put on a drill, and and it costs about $35. The wheel strips off the vinyl and the underlying adhesive without damaging clear coat. Once it is removed, you can follow up with a few applications of Goo Gone or similar adhesive remover to clean up the remainder.

If they aren't too old, red WBCCI numbers can sometimes be removed by putting a damp towel over them and "ironing" them off with a steam iron. Very old numbers on vintage trailers may leave a "ghost" impression that doesn't come off completely even after polishing.

Filiform corrosion

Other than dents, the most common damage owners will see to the skin of their Airstream is "filiform corrosion." Filiform corrosion can become a cosmetic nuisance relatively quickly if you frequently store or camp in humid areas or near the ocean. It's a white corrosion between the clear coat and the aluminum that looks like spider webs, or worm trails. Moisture gets under the clear coat at a nick, rivet hole, the edge of an old decal, or where the aluminum was trimmed during manufacture, and corrosion begins to worm its way along the surface of the aluminum. When it gets severe, it can lift the clear coat and cause it to peel.

Filiform is strictly a cosmetic problem (not structural), but that doesn't make owners feel any better when they see the white tendrils beginning to appear. It will stop entirely when the relative humidity is very low (as in the southwest desert), but restart whenever the aluminum is exposed to moisture again.

You can dramatically slow its progress by sealing any possible pinholes in the clear coat with regular applications of a polymer protectant, and treating affected areas with a compound designed to prevent corrosion such as Boeshield T-9 Rust and Corrosion Protection, or Lear Chemical Research's ACF-50.

If possible, avoid storing the Airstream near any body of salt water or in a humid environment (such as a dirt-floored barn), and avoid traveling in winter on salted roads. If you camp near the ocean or travel in the winter, be sure to give the trailer a thorough washing before storage.

There's no way to permanently remove filiform damage other than to remove the clear coat, polish off the filiform, and recoat—a laborious process that's overkill for most situations.

Cosmetic treatments are possible. For minor areas, you can carefully sand off the clear coat with fine grit paper, clean with mineral spirits, and re-coat with clear nail polish. This is a good solution for taillight bezels, door handles, and other aluminum parts on the body.

Filiform commonly manifests along the "belt line" of Safari, Flying Cloud, and other Airstream models which have the meeting point of the upper and lower sheets of the body exposed. This area can be treated and then covered with the belt line trim from a Classic series Airstream.

Polishing

You've seen those mirror-like polished Airstreams, and perhaps you're wondering whether that's a route you want to take with yours. Polishing isn't really a regular part of maintenance, but it is a very attractive option for trailers that don't have a clear coat finish, or whose clear coat is peeling off.

Exposed aluminum will oxidize slowly, gradually becoming more gray in color. This is not detrimental to the Airstream, since the oxidized aluminum actually forms a protective layer for the rest of the metal. If there's a clear coat, the oxidization occurs mostly where the coating has failed.

Airstream has changed the type of aluminum it used a few times over the years, but even the newer alloys can take a polish, at least up to the 1999 model year. The catch is that any clear coat on the trailer has to be chemically stripped off first. Typically a product like "Aircraft Stripper" is used. If you do this, be very cautious as some of the chemical strippers can be highly toxic and detrimental to your health.

Since 1999, Airstream has been using a very tough fluorocarbon clear coat by PPG. As of this writing, nobody has yet devised an efficient and safe chemical method for removing it, which makes polishing impractical for trailers made 1999 to present. Of course for those Airstream owners that's good news—the clear coat seems to be exceptionally durable and long lasting.

Polishing can have an economic benefit. Buyers of vintage Airstreams pay more if the trailer is polished. One professional appraiser of Airstreams says a good polish will add about $5,000 in value—which is more than polishing usually costs to do, even if you hire the job out. So polishing is one of those rare improvements you can do that actually has a return on investment.

People commonly think that polishing removes the top layer of tarnished aluminum. Actually, that's the last thing you want to do, particularly on vintage Airstreams made of Alclad 2024 where there's a pure aluminum layer atop an alloy of aluminum and copper. Removing the top layer would permanently damage it.

A professional grade polish converts the oxidized aluminum layer chemically back into shiny aluminum. That layer is "recycled" and redeposited on the surface. Microscopic peaks of metal are worn down to fill scratches and pits, smoothing the surface at the same time that it gains that unforgettable shine. This is called "healing" the surface.

This is why abrasives such as rouge and sandpaper are never used for a good polish. Those methods are destructive because they scrape off aluminum. Getting a great polish on an Airstream that has previously been abraded is much harder.

All kinds of polishes can be used to make an Airstream shine. Your choice of polish should be based on the depth of shine you want. A middling shine can be had quickly with various one step polishes, and you can use elbow grease, a rotary buffer, a Cyclo buffer, or whatever tool works.

If you want the ultimate mirror shine with no cloudiness or haze, the best method is the way the airlines do it, working up through three or four grades of high-quality polish. This takes more time than the one-step polishes but the results are exceptional.

Regardless of the technique you use, if you see twisty reflective "swirl marks" or "strike lines" on a sunny day, you'll need to use a finer grade of polish. The swirl marks are caused by scratches in the surface, left by the rotary buffer. A finer grade of polish will reduce the swirl marks until they are unnoticeable.

If spending a few dozen hours (or even 100-200 hours on a highly oxidized trailer) working on the aluminum is not appealing to you, you can hire the job out. Professional Airstream polishing typically runs $100 to $200 per foot of trailer length. Cheaper services can be found, but if you go for the lowest-cost bidder, don't be surprised to end up with swirl marks and haze that are visible in bright sunlight. It's like painting a car: you tend to get what you pay for.

After polishing, you have a few options. The easiest option is to let the aluminum gradually oxidize again, which will take a few years in most climate conditions. But if you can't stand seeing your hard work slowly fade, then you'll have to maintain the polish by going over it at least once or twice a year. This is not nearly as hard as the first time, because one or two grades of polish will suffice to keep the "mirror shine" in place.

The long-term option is to have the trailer professionally recoated. A new clear coat will preserve the shine (although it does get a little duller from the coating). There are very few companies that can do this, and even fewer have experience with Airstreams, so choose carefully. One company that has considerable experience is P&S Trailers in Helena, Ohio.

Belly pan repairs

The belly pan is the underside of your Airstream. Made of thinner aluminum than the body, it is riveted to the frame and protects the underside, as well as improving the aerodynamics of the Airstream. If you removed the belly pan you'd find insulation, plumbing, the steel frame of the Airstream, and other parts. Below the pan you'll see the propane gas lines and the axles of the trailer.

The belly pan is not normally removed except for repairs that require access under the floor, but after a few years of travel it's common for the pan to become loose where it is attached by rivets. This is because of a galvanic reaction between the aluminum of the pan and the steel of the frame, which it touches. (This is also known as "electrolysis" or "dissimilar metal corrosion.") Water and road salt will accelerate this process.

When the galvanic corrosion becomes severe around the belly pan rivets, the rivet holes in the pan can enlarge and allow the pan to fall down around the rivet. If this happens at several rivet points, the pan can drag on the ground. There's not much an owner can do to prevent this issue, so the usual approach is to maintain the belly pan by replacing rivets as the pan corrodes, and eventually replace the belly pan when it becomes too corroded (perhaps after a couple of decades of use).

The rivet replacement procedure is simple. The rivet that was holding the pan in place will probably still be embedded in the steel frame, so first you must drill it out with a 3/16" drill bit. Then, replace the rivet with one that has a much larger flange (head).

This larger flange will grab a bigger circle of the belly pan and thereby make up for the enlarged hole. A "large flange" style rivet with a 3/16" body, POP part #AD68ABSLF, is available (see Resources at the end of this book). Alternatively, aluminum washers or even strips of aluminum sheet can be used to simulate a large flange.

It's a good idea to keep a handful of these rivets in your traveling tool kit, along with a cordless drill, drill bits, and rivet tool, in case you need to make a quick repair on the road. Replacing a rivet on the belly pan can be done in just a couple of minutes if you have everything with you.

By the way, you should also consider bringing along a junk beach towel. A junk towel is surprisingly useful. Throw it on the ground when you've got to slide underneath the trailer to replace a belly pan rivet, and you'll be glad you brought something to protect you from sharp gravel and road debris. Or if you are changing a tire, kneel on the towel and protect the knees of your pants. During a dirty job the towel is ideal for wiping off your hands, or cleaning up bits of grease that you picked up from the hitch. It is handy for cleaning dirt off some exterior part before you start to work, or dusting inside the refrigerator or water heater compartment. You can also use it to wrap up a heavy object so it doesn't smash into other things while traveling. My junk beach towel is one of the "tools" I use most often.

Larger tears in the belly pan caused by road debris aren't usually an emergency, but should be repaired after your trip to make the trailer less inviting to rodents that might want to nest in the belly pan. Patches made of aluminum sheet are commonly riveted over holes and tears.

Belly pan aluminum varies over the years, and it's not critical that you patch it with exactly the same type and thickness of aluminum sheet. Thinner aluminum is easier to work, while thicker aluminum is more durable. A common choice for replacement is .024 5052-H32 aluminum sheet, which can be ordered in full sheets from aircraft supply stores such as Airparts Inc and Aircraft Spruce, or found in smaller sheets at some local hardware stores.

There are a few places where plumbing goes through the belly pan. Gaps around these holes can easily be sealed with a product called "butyl tape." This can be purchased at RV supply and some hardware stores. It's a soft gooey tape that can be molded to fill larger gaps than caulk can fill.

Finally, if you start to see strips of rubbery stuff hanging from the underbelly wraps (the rounded edges of the bellypan where it meets the side walls), that's peeling sealant. Sikaflex 221 in black is used here—see the discussion on "Sealants" in the Leak Prevention, Detection, and Repair section.

Leak Prevention, Detection, and Repair

Water damage is one of the top destroyers of Airstreams. Water causes the wood subfloor to rot, allows the growth of mold, destroys upholstery, ruins electronics, rusts the steel frame below the floor, and stains almost everything. Water leaks can cause thousands of dollars in damage in a short time. If you do nothing else to maintain your Airstream, merely keeping it dry will allow it to last for decades.

One of the best ways you can do this is to keep the Airstream under cover. If you rent a storage spot, consider paying extra for covered storage. Not only will you prevent the possibility of a rainwater or snowmelt leak doing damage while in storage, but you will dramatically cut down the damage the UV rays of the sun do to roof sealants, clear coat, and plastic parts. UV damage leads to leaks.

Another way to prevent leaks from taking hold is to get a periodic pressurized leak test. This is done only by a handful of Airstream service centers and dealers. A large blower is set up inside the trailer to suck air in through a roof vent and thereby pressurize the trailer slightly. It doesn't take much pressure to do this, just one or two pounds per square inch. With all doors and windows closed, a technician can then go over the trailer from the outside with a squirt bottle of soapy water. Where air is leaking out of the trailer, soap bubbles will form, indicating a potential leak point.

The pressurized leak test is not a guarantee. Some leaks can still be missed, while bubbles may show up at places that wouldn't have leaked in a typical rain. Don't get hung up on chasing every "leak" revealed by this test. But it is a good annual or biennial preventative maintenance procedure, in addition to a good Roof Inspection (see discussion below).

Of course, rainwater is only one source of water damage. Leaks in the plumbing can also be damaging. The "Storage inspection" discussion talks briefly about finding plumbing leaks, but we'll dig further into that subject here.

Leak detection techniques

There are many reasons you might suspect a water leak in your Airstream. For example:

- Excess humidity inside the trailer (which may show up as condensation on the windows)
- Stains on wall coverings, floors, or curtains that have no obvious explanation
- Drip marks in the dust (during storage)
- Strange smells caused by the growth of mold
- Rusty steel parts like screw heads
- Black streaks coming down from interior POP rivets
- Water dripping from beneath the trailer, or the water pump cycling on repeatedly when no water is being used
- Any interior spot that seems damp or wet after a rain
- A musty or mildewy smell inside the trailer after it has been closed up for while. (When buying a used trailer, remember that a musty or mildewy smell is not normal. Sometimes people think, "all old trailers smell that way," but they don't. Only the leaky ones do.)
- A soft spot in the floor.

A drip from the air conditioner on the inside of the trailer is likely caused by a clogged air conditioner drain tube or cracked drip pan, and is not a rain water leak. (See "Air conditioner maintenance" in the Climate Control section.)

Any sign of water or excess moisture is cause for concern and should be investigated promptly, before serious damage occurs to the Airstream floor or other components.

Large leaks are easy to spot, but you want to catch them while they are still small, so at the first hint of a problem, start inspecting. Your first step is to determine whether the leak is from rainwater penetration or from the trailer's pressurized plumbing system. If your clue was that the water pump cycles even when the faucets are closed, and you are sure there's no air in the lines, it may be a plumbing leak. (This can also happen when the check valve of the water pump has become compromised by sediment or mineral build-up. See "Water Pump" in the Plumbing chapter for more information.) Or, if water is leaking out of the trailer's belly pan on dry days, it's a plumbing leak. Rainwater leaks, of course, only happen on rainy days—although the moisture might be present for quite a while afterward.

Plumbing leaks

Now your job is to find the exact source of the water. Plumbing leaks are easier because you can focus on the plumbing. Leave the water pump on so the system stays pressurized, and check that all of the faucets and fixtures (including the toilet) are closing off completely. Check the water heater for drips outside. Check the city water fill (outside) to make sure it's not leaking.

Then look at the plumbing connections in the cabinets under the kitchen and bathroom sinks. The most likely leak location is at a fitting (where two pieces join), or where the copper line of a faucet may have developed a slight crack. A flashlight and some paper towels are great tools for finding leaks in those places. Often cold metal will fool you by feeling wet to the touch, but the paper towel will reveal if water is really present, and you can stuff a piece of paper towel in places you can't get your hand. Water droplets and stains on the floor are much easier to spot with a flashlight as well.

The plumbing tends to run in tight spaces behind drawers, inside cabinets, and inside storage compartments, so be prepared to pull out drawers and remove everything from beneath the cabinets until you find that leak. In particular, locate the fresh water pump and check all the fittings near it.

Also, check the winterization bypass valve plumbing located near the water heater. The PEX plumbing in modern Airstreams is very durable, so the most likely leak points are at fittings, valves, appliances, or places where the plumbing has been chafing or modified.

If the leak is at a threaded fitting, you may be in luck. Often these sorts of leaks can be resolved by disconnecting, cleaning the threads, and reassembling with a healthy amount of plumber's tape (see "Basic Leak Repair" in the Plumbing section). Drips at the water heater are also usually easily repaired (see "Dripping Drain Plug" and "Dripping P/T Valve" in the Appliances section).

Other plumbing leaks might require some PEX tools or a replacement part. Even if you aren't equipped to repair it, at least you can point a service tech to the exact problem and save some diagnostic time that way. In the meantime, shut off the water pump and do what you can to mop up the moisture so the damage is contained.

Rainwater leaks

Rainwater leaks are harder to isolate, because water can enter at one point outside the Airstream and wick through the insulation to a completely different place inside the Airstream. The levelness of the Airstream can cause the water to run forward, backward, or sideways.

The frames of the windows and doors (and internal ribs of the Airstream's body that you can't see) will also cause water to change its path. A leak directly above a door or window won't usually emerge at the top of the door or window, but instead travel around the edges to emerge lower down at the sides. Where you see the water inside often has little relation to the location of the actual leak.

For that reason it's often an exercise in frustration to try to deduce a leak's source by tracing it backwards. It's simpler and quicker to either get a pressurized leak test or address all the likely leak points on the roof and body using the experience of other Airstream owners before you.

The top rainwater leak locations on an Airstream are in the sealant or plastic flanges around roof vents, plumbing vents, and skylights. Although everyone always suspects the air conditioner first, it's rarely the cause of water in the trailer because the air conditioner has a drain pan that allows condensate water to drip out by the wheel well. (The exception is when the drain line becomes clogged, which will cause water to drip out from the air conditioner panel in the ceiling when it is running.)

In trailers built before 1994, a wet spot in an exterior storage compartment or along the edge of the floor can be caused by water penetrating at the lower rub rail, if the sealant has failed there. This type of leak will wick directly to the subfloor edge and may be unnoticeable on the inside until it's too late, so even if you haven't seen a wet spot, it's good routine maintenance to carefully check the entire perimeter of the lower rub rail for failed sealant. Gaps, cracks, or an absence of sealant at the rub rail are big red flags and should be addressed promptly.

Other common leak points include the rear bumper compartment seal where it meets the body, the main awning attachment points (sometimes the weight of the awning will pull the attachment away from the body and stretch the screw holes enough to allow a leak), and the clearance lights. The clearance lights, stove vent, and some other spots may have gaskets, but when in doubt you can put a bead of sealant along the top edges just to be sure.

Finding a rainwater leak might be easier if you notice when leak happens. Is it only during towing, or on windy days? Only when the trailer is leaning a particular way?

If you want to try reproducing the leak with a garden hose, start low and work up. That way it will be easier to tell where the leak starts. You can tape over a suspected leak point and see if that stops the leak.

Most likely your rainwater leak comes from a roof penetration, so unless it's clearly coming from the stove vent, window, or the lower rub rail, head to the roof.

Roof inspection

First, read "Getting On The Roof" in the Exterior Cleaning and Appearance section. Make sure you understand how to safely get on and move around the roof.

The primary goal of inspecting the roof is to find possible leak points. Usually this is in the form of failed sealant around roof vents and other roof penetrations. Failed sealant may be cracked, deteriorating, or starting to pull away. Good sealant is solid, slightly flexible to the touch, and free of gaps or holes. Only certain types of sealant will work well on aluminum, so if you spot household silicone caulk up there it should be removed and replaced in favor of the right stuff. For more on the correct sealants, see the discussion "Sealants" later on.

Another possible cause of leaks is loose or missing rivets, but this is much less common than people often assume. Still, it's easy to check for this, so no harm in looking. A loose rivet will move, and usually that leaves a ring of black aluminum oxide around the rivet head. A missing rivet will just leave a small hole.

A more common cause of leaks is a broken flange around a roof vent or plumbing vent. The roof vent flanges are made of plastic and can easily crack if the installer tightened the screws a little too much. Often this mistake is covered up with a lot of sealant, which only masks the problem temporarily. If you suspect a leak around a roof vent, it's best to remove all the sealant to check. That procedure is described below.

Where steel screws are used to hold down something on the roof (such as a plumbing vent, Fan-Tastic Vent flange, or TV antenna) look for orange marks indicating that rust is coming up from the screw heads through the sealant. If rust is coming up, it's because moisture is seeping down, so that sealant should be removed completely and replaced with fresh.

Also check the sealant along the top edges of the entry door and windows. It's much easier to see gaps or cracks in those places when you are looking from the top down, and those places are often overlooked.

A secondary goal of roof inspection is to find broken parts on the roof, like perhaps a cracked air conditioner shroud, a broken TV antenna, or cracked solar panel. The air conditioner shrouds tend to start to crack after a few years in the sun and are easily replaced in a few minutes with just a screwdriver. In particular, check the skylight (if your Airstream has one) for hairline cracks that could lead to a leak later.

Most other components are longer lasting, but everything eventually fails under the assault of ultraviolet radiation from the sun. Also, if you've "trimmed" a few trees while towing, there's a chance you might have some damaged parts as a result.

Solar panels are pretty tough, so the only major problem you are likely to see on them is cracked glass or a disconnected wire.

The most durable part you'll find on the roof is the roof itself. Later model aluminum Airstream trailers have white painted roofs to help keep them cool. The white paint is long lasting and rivets rarely come loose, so you don't have to spend a lot of time checking it out.

You also don't need to worry about resealing the seams where one sheet of aluminum overlaps another. Airstream seals these extremely well at the factory and the majority of the sealant is underneath where the sun can't get at it. The sealant lasts for decades. The seams need only be checked when there's obvious damage (perhaps a dent) or you've exhausted all other possible causes of a roof leak.

While you are inspecting the roof components, check for leaves or other debris that might be in the refrigerator vent. This is a long metal vent directly over the refrigerator. Reach inside carefully and see if there's anything clogging it. The vent needs to be clear so that the refrigerator can cool effectively.

Sealants

There are many sealants you can use on an Airstream, and a few that you shouldn't. The common silicone sealant that you find most often in hardware stores should be used only in the kitchen and bath, never on the exterior. Stick with the recommended polyurethane sealants for exterior use, because it's a tough world out there and sealants that aren't UV stable or can't provide a watertight seal for years really aren't worth applying.

Note that we aren't talking about "caulk." Caulk isn't flexible, whereas the sealants used on an Airstream are elastomeric, meaning they can stretch without breaking their seal as the travel trailer moves down the road.

In the old days the general-purpose sealant of choice was called Vulkem, and you'll still hear vintage Airstream owners talk about it. Like the modern sealants, it had a marvelous ability to seal gaps tightly, stick to aluminum, and remain slightly tacky beneath the surface for many years. These days it has been supplanted by a more modern formulation that carries the same name, as well as a few other new products. All the sealants we're going to discuss here are good choices, so it's really just a matter of choosing the one that works the best for your needs.

None of these recommended sealants are commonly found in hardware stores, so check the Resources section of this book if you want to buy some. If you are tackling a job that may require replacing sealant, plan ahead and place your order.

Although there are at least half a dozen products you can use, in four different colors (black, silver/gray, white, and clear), it's overkill for the average owner to have all those sealants for routine maintenance. You can get by with just one or two, if you choose carefully and aren't fussy about color mismatch on the roof.

The most common maintenance job is sealing a gap on something that failed your Roof Inspection (above). Typically this is around a plumbing vent, vent fan, or skylight. Airstream recommends AdSeal Premium Quality Sealant for this job. It comes in white and gray color, and for roof work most people would choose white. But since AdSeal is hard to find, other UV-stable, exterior-grade, non-silicone sealants that are recommended for aluminum and plastic can be used instead.

The same AdSeal in gray color is good for sealing the "eyebrows" of the riveted frame windows (the aluminum-framed Airstream windows, not the black-rubber-framed Hehr windows found on Safari and Sport models) and the main door. It's useful anywhere a thicker bead of gray sealant is required.

For sealing openings on the sides, Airstream recommends acryl-R Seam Sealer, which works well and forms a very tough bond. When Airstream is assembling new trailers it makes sense to use acryl-R, but again for routine maintenance it is usually more than you need. It requires a special dispenser and dries into something a hammer and chisel may be needed to separate. Clean up should be done as soon as a mistake is noted, or else it may be there forever.

Instead, for small general repairs you might choose a tube of Parbond. Parbond is thin enough to fill small gaps and it's very easy to apply from a squeeze tube. Parbond is ideal for restoring seals around the top edge of windows, furnace, water heater, the top edge of the lower rub rail, and other penetrations on the sides of the Airstream that don't have gaskets. Late model Airstreams use gaskets around many of the exterior penetrations like marker lights, cable/TV outlet, water fill, stove vent, etc. and those do not require sealant. If any of those gaskets are leaking, they should be replaced.

To apply Parbond, simply remove the cap and slowly run the end along the seam or gap at an angle while gently squeezing the tube. This stuff is pretty liquid in its raw state, but after it dries, it becomes a tough rubberized seal.

Sikaflex 221 Multi-Purpose Polyurethane Sealant is a good general purpose choice and a worthy alternative to Vulkem 116 (and the very similar TremPro 635). Sikaflex is a little thinner than Vulkem but otherwise very similar. The nice thing about Sikaflex is that it is easier to find in RV stores.

All three of these come in large tubes for caulk guns, and can be used for just about any sealant job on the Airstream. They are thicker than Parbond and better for larger gaps and bigger jobs.

Sikaflex 221 comes in white, black, and gray. White is good for roof work such as vents, while black is a good match for the underbelly wraps (the edges of the belly pan) and around Safari windows.

Most sealants have a definite shelf life, so carrying around tubes "just in case" is not a great idea. Often you'll find the sealant has cured in the tube after a year or two, rendering it useless. Buy it when you need it. If you are in a pinch (having noticed a leak that needs immediate attention, for example) you can check hardware stores for a construction sealant that is guaranteed waterproof, UV stable, approved for outdoor use and which adheres to aluminum, painted surfaces, and plastic. Similarly, you can pick up a small tube of kitchen/bath silicone sealant for interior repairs at any hardware store when you need it, so there's no need to carry that around.

Once you've opened a tube of sealant, take some care to reseal it well for storage. There are many techniques to try to seal the tube, such as putting a golf tee in the opening, covering with the tip of a rubber glove, using food saver vacuum bags, hot glue on the tip, and commercially-available storage caps of various designs. Don't freeze it: that method can cross-contaminate other items in the freezer (your ice cream might taste funny after a while) and the manufacturers of the sealants generally don't recommend storing at that temperature.

Whatever you do, don't expect an opened tube of sealant to still be usable in a year. Even if you take tremendous effort to close up the tube against outside air and moisture, it will probably go bad in a few months. Parbond seems to be the exception. It lasts for years just by replacing the cap. If you want to carry one sealant in your tool bag for small fixes on the road, Parbond is a good choice.

The sealants discussed here are fairly safe, but you should take a moment to read the fine print on the tubes before using them. Wear vinyl gloves when working with sealants, and avoid skin contact or breathing of the vapors in a confined space. (That also goes for the chemicals used to clean up afterward.) Pay attention to the manufacturer's recommendations for the temperature at which you apply the sealant, as well as application techniques, cleanup, and storage.

Sealant replacement technique and tools

By now it should be clear that maintaining the sealants is a key part of keeping your Airstream dry and happy. Generally the sealants last a long time, so the old days of climbing on the roof to "recaulk the seams" every year are over, unless someone has put an inferior product up there.

In extremely sunny and hot climates like Phoenix, Arizona, the sealants will not last as long. The best thing you can do to extend their life (and the life of the entire Airstream) is keep the Airstream under cover when it is in storage. If you can't do that, make a point of inspecting the sealants on the roof and sides at least once a year.

As mentioned in the "Roof inspection," failed sealant may be cracked, deteriorating, or pulled away. Good sealant is solid, slightly flexible to the touch, and has no gaps or holes. Don't be intimidated if it's time to replace sealant. The procedure is pretty easy and gratifying once it's done.

Before you begin make sure the area you'll be working on is squeaky clean. Sealants don't stick well to dirt, and the dirt will allow water to flow past the sealant. Soap and water and a soft bristle brush will do fine. If you are working on the side, remember to brush with the "grain" of the aluminum. That way, any minor scratches will blend in.

In addition to your tube of sealant and a caulk gun (if you are using a large tube) to apply it, you'll want some mineral spirits or isopropyl alcohol, masking tape, a soft cloth or towel, paper towels, vinyl gloves, and a plastic scraper. Don't use sharp tools as scrapers, as they can remove fingers as well as old sealant.

The only slightly hard part of the job is removing the old sealant. It has to be completely removed, because some sealants won't adhere to others, and even parts of the old sealant that look "good" probably aren't. You've gone to the trouble of starting this job, so remove every bit of the old sealant. Replacing only part of it is like replacing only half the oil during your car's oil change.

Mineral spirits or isopropyl alcohol will help soften the old sealant. Sometimes people recommend WD-40 for this job. (Don't use lacquer thinner or anything that strips paint or is harmful to plastic.) To protect the aluminum sides of the trailer from scratches in case you slip, you can put down a wide stripe of masking tape.

Scrape until the surface is completely clean, then follow with the isopropyl alcohol. Finally, you need to make the surface chemically clean because remnants of the alcohol will interfere with the new surface, so wash the surface again with soap and water and dry it completely.

Now you've got a clean canvas and the fun part begins. Apply the sealant with the caulk gun, moving slowly with a steady pressure on the trigger. After you've run the bead, wet your gloved finger with mineral spirits and smooth out the seam. It's a good idea to start somewhere that isn't really noticeable until you get the hang of it. Have some mineral spirits and rags or paper towel on hand to clean up mistakes.

Sealants like Sikaflex, TremPro, Vulkem, and AdSeal generally stay tacky for quite a while—sometimes for days depending on humidity and temperature. Read the label for specifics. This gives you plenty of time to make corrections and get the job done neatly, so there's no need to rush. When you are done, there should be absolutely no voids or gaps, and the bead of sealant should be fairly smooth so it doesn't catch and hold water.

Identifying floor rot

It's a phrase that strikes dread into the hearts of owners of vintage Airstreams: floor rot. You may have heard of it, but do you need to worry about it? Yes, if water has been allowed to get inside the trailer for an extended period of time, floor rot is an inevitability. This can be from rain or from leaking plumbing.

Although it is sometimes called "dry rot," it's anything but dry. Moisture in the wood subfloor (below the carpeting or vinyl) allows living organisms such as bacteria to "eat" the fibers in the wood, weakening it. The microscopic critters that eat the wood need moisture in order to thrive, which is why wet wood rots. The process stops when the source of water is removed.

Floor rot is a serious issue, because in an Airstream the floor is an integral part of the overall construction. A weak floor can allow the entire aluminum body to flex more than it should, causing many long-term problems. So even though replacing sections of floor is difficult and potentially expensive, it must be done to protect the integrity of the trailer.

Keep in mind that a slight amount of "give" in the wood subfloor is normal. It will flex under your weight as you walk on it, and that's OK.

If you have just recently purchased a used Airstream trailer, or you already have it, you may be concerned about potential problems lurking under the vinyl or carpeting. Before panic sets in, you should verify you actually have a problem, and if so, how bad the problem really is. Many, if not most, incidents of floor rot are relatively minor if caught in time, and can be repaired by replacing small sections of the floor instead of the whole thing.

Start by estimating the extent of the damage. The first stage of rot is really just the warning signs discussed above on the discussion on "Leak detection techniques." You may see signs of a leak or smell strange odors, but a brief period of wetness will not be enough to rot the floor. Stop the leak, and you may not need to do anything else, except possibly spray on a mold and mildew killing solution to stop any odor.

If you suspect more serious water damage, you'll have to remove the floor covering (vinyl or carpet) to inspect the condition of the underlying wood. If the underlying subfloor has discolored and smells punky but is otherwise intact, a spot repair is indicated. Depending on the size of the area and its location, you may be able to get away with wood strengthening epoxy, such as Rot Doctor.

If you choose this method of repair, you need to follow the directions on the package, and in addition kill any mold in the floor before using the epoxy. You don't want to epoxy over live mold, because eventually the mold will grow out from under the epoxy. Mold brings potential health problems.

If the rotten spot is along the wall, the rot almost certainly extends under the wall, and therefore has damaged the structural connection between the floor and the aluminum body. This connection is crucial to the overall strength of the trailer, so in such a case wood replacement may be a better strategy.

A hole in the floor means you definitely need to replace at least a section of floor. A pointed object such as a screwdriver or awl will go straight through the floor—which is an inspection test used by some buyers of vintage Airstreams. A hole is the result of a long-term unattended leak, so if you find one you will likely find more spots that need help. Most of the time the hole will be along the edge of the floor, in a corner, under some complex plumbing, or under the toilet or fridge, all of which will require quite a bit of disassembly.

If the trailer has this level of advanced floor rot, it probably has other significant problems. Most people attempting this level of repair know of other issues to fix at the same time, so the interior may already be gutted, making the work easier. If you are going to go to the trouble of taking out large parts of the interior in order to fix a hole, consider what other upgrades or repairs can be done, such as replacing plumbing lines or fixtures, checking electrical connections, new flooring, etc.

Windows, Doors, Locks, and Vents

Unlike most other travel trailer brands, Airstream makes its own doors and windows. The main entry door on an aluminum Airstream is a complex part which takes over eight hours to manufacture. It matches the curvature of the Airstream shell, and it's almost entirely made of aluminum. A flat door made for the "white box" RV manufacturers just wouldn't work. Because of its specialized design, the door and screen have unique adjustment procedures which are discussed in this section.

If you have a late model aluminum trailer with aluminum-framed windows and two latches at the bottom, those windows were also made by Airstream. You can see that they curve to match the body, like the entry door. This window design has passed the test of time, working reliably for decades with little maintenance.

Some Airstreams in recent years, including the Safari and Sport lines, have windows made by Hehr. These are identifiable by their black rubber trim on the outside, a flat design (when viewed alongside the body) and smaller operable openings. The Hehr windows aren't as reliable (see the discussion later entitled "Repair Hehr window crank") or as easy to clean, but with some minor maintenance they can last the life of the Airstream.

The compartment doors on the exterior are also made by Airstream, of aluminum of course. Small parts, like locks, latches and handles are made by other companies.

For the most part, the windows, doors, locks, latches and vents only need routine cleaning and lubricating. Adjustments and repairs are rare.

There is one important safety procedure related to the windows. Every late-model Airstream has an Emergency Exit window. This window generally has red handles and a label identifying it as the Emergency Exit. At least once in your ownership, you should practice opening this window and figure out how how you're going to squeeze out through it if you really have to. Make sure anyone else who travels with you knows how to open this window, too.

Lubricants

An Airstream trailer has only a few moving parts, and most of them are in doors and windows, which is why we're discussing lubricants here. The other major moving parts are the wheel bearings, brakes, and hitch parts (see "Running Gear and A-Frame"). Cleaning and lubrication are 90% of maintenance for windows, doors, locks, latches, and vents.

Let's get one thing straight right up front: WD-40 is not lube. It's amazing how many professionals, websites, and even manufacturers will recommend WD-40 in place of a true lubricant. WD-40 is a useful solvent, cleaner, and water displacer, and it will temporarily lubricate but it's not the product you want to use on a squeaking hinge or anything else that needs long-term lubrication.

Instead, the best general-purpose lubricants or our purposes are silicone spray and Boeshield T-9. Both are easy to apply, penetrate tight spaces reasonably well, add water-repellency, and provide lasting lubrication (although nothing lasts forever). Boeshield is a little more durable because it leaves a clean waxy film that is less likely to wash off, and it can be dripped into a lubrication point with precision. Silicone spray is easier to apply when shotgunning large areas like the stabilizer jacks. Either way, you'll find many places in the Airstream where a quick shot of silicone spray or a few drops of Boeshield solves a problem. Carry some of your preferred lubricant in your Airstream for lubricating hinges, locks, latches, stabilizers, and just about anything else that moves and doesn't require grease.

After applying lubricants, work the part back and forth a while until the lube penetrates and the object moves smoothly and silently. Have a few paper towels on hand to clean up overspray and drips.

As useful as these lubricants can be, they are no substitute for grease in high-pressure or high-temperature applications. Grease mostly goes on the hitch parts, wheel bearings, and tow ball.

There are purpose-made hitch ball lubricants on the market, which are a little less messy to apply than grease and which seem to last a long time. (This type of lube is just as good as grease at ruining pants if you brush up against it.)

Regardless of which lube you choose for the tow ball, the important thing is to have some sort of heavy lubrication on it at all times so it doesn't make noise and wear out quickly. Light lubricants such as silicone spray, 3-in-1 oil, petroleum jelly, etc., won't do the job because of the high pressure exerted on the lubricant during use.

Most people will do well with a can of silicone spray in their tool bag as their primary lubricant and some grease for the hitch parts. If you have a specialized need, it's easy to acquire most lubricants along the road from hardware and auto parts stores, so there's little reason to carry a lot of lubricants on a daily basis.

Cleaning and lubricating gaskets

Roof air vents and windows have rubber seals that often stick shut after a while. Generally, the procedure to resolve this is to first clean the rubber seal with a sponge dipped in mildly soapy water, then dry it with a towel. After it's dry, spray some silicone spray or Aerospace 303 Protectant on a paper towel and wipe that liberally onto the gasket. This lubricates the gasket and keeps it from sticking. Do this annually and you'll never have a vent or window stick shut.

Stabilizers (squeaking)

Do your stabilizers make an awful screeching sound as you wind them up and down? This can be worse when you are using a cordless drill to set them, rather than the manual wrench.

Fix this by adding lubrication to the threaded jack screws and the metal frames that the screws go through. You'll need to get under the Airstream a little to see these spots, so break  out your junk towel and lay it on the ground for padding, then lie on your back and take a look. Once you see how the jack works, slide out of the way a little (so you don't get lube dripping in your eyes) and get busy with your silicone spray. Run the jacks up and down a few times to make sure the lubricant is well distributed.

Door hinge maintenance

The most common problem with the main door hinge is squeaking at the hinge. Regular lubrication will alleviate this. Even if it isn't squeaking, it is important to lubricate regularly, otherwise the pin may start working out. Open the door and spray the hinges as you move the door in and out to distribute the silicone inside the moving parts.

If your main entry door hinge pin keeps working out, you can replace it with an upgraded model (Airstream part number 381552-100) that has a groove in it for a C-clip (part number 381552-101). The C-clip keeps the pin from moving out of place.

Entry step maintenance

Airstream has been installing swing-down steps since 1955. Before that, people used little step stools at the entry door. In 1972, Airstream began offering aluminum fold-out steps on some models. Steel and aluminum steps are both still installed today, depending on the model of Airstream.

Regardless of whether your steps are aluminum or steel, you should wash dirt out of the hinge areas periodically and lubricate with your handy can of silicone spray. Don't use grease here, since it will just attract a lot more dirt.

Be careful when applying silicone spray to the hinges of the entry step, because the overspray can make the steps slippery! You can use a piece of cardboard as a shield when spraying to control the overspray. If you've accidentally lubricated the surface of the steps, wash it down with soap and water until all the slipperiness is gone (this might take a few passes), and then lube the hinges again more carefully.

Other than lubrication, the steps only need attention when they begin to wear or are damaged. If they start to feel loose, check the attachment points. If the no-slip surface on the treads begins to wear out, you can replace it.

The aluminum steps have a few screws and bolts which could come loose. If they do, use a little thread locker (like Loc-Tite) on the threads to keep them from working out again. If the aluminum step gets damaged, you can buy replacement parts from an Airstream dealer.

Steel steps can of course be repainted with primer and good quality high gloss paint, if needed, but that won't be for several years.

I saved the Number One maintenance tip for any type of folding step for last: Always make sure your steps are up before pulling away from your campsite! Put it on your Departure Checklist because it's a commonly-forgotten item.

Locks and latches

There's a lock on every external compartment (sometimes two), and two latches on every Airstream aluminum-framed window, so that's a lot of little points to lubricate. Fortunately, with your handy-dandy can of silicone spray, it's a quick job.

Just go around the trailer methodically and give each latch a tiny squirt of silicone, then work the latch back and forth until it's nice and smooth. Squirt a bit of silicone into each lock through the keyhole (using the thin straw that comes with most cans), or spray the key and work it in the lock repeatedly.

If you use silicone spray for this job you'll end up with silicone on your fingers, which is smelly until it dries, so a pair of gloves wouldn't be a bad idea. Definitely also bring along some paper towels to clean up excess spray, or use Boeshield instead. There will also be a bit of a smell inside the trailer until the silicone spray dries, and this job is best done at the same time as the window gaskets, so do this on a day when you can open the windows and air out the trailer.

Entry door and screen door adjustment

Over time, the main entry door on an aluminum trailer may become hard to close. If you sometimes have to slam the door to close it, check that you aren't over-tightening the four stabilizer jacks on the Airstream.

Believe it or not, the Airstream body is flexible, and it will twist enough under some circumstances that the entry door and/or compartment doors can become difficult to open or close. This is normal. Try setting the stabilizer jacks a little less tightly to see if this alleviates the problem.

Another cause of a door going out of adjustment can be a loose main door hinge. Check the hinge to see if there are any problems there. A loose hinge is hard to fix; get an expert opinion on this problem.

If the hinge is OK and the main entry door or screen door are still hard to close when parked on level ground, you can adjust them yourself with a few tools. Start with the screen door first, since it can affect the main door.

Check the fit of the screen door by closing it and looking where the frame of the screen door passes by the deadbolt in the main door frame. If the screen door is hitting the deadbolt, the screen door needs to be aligned.

Open the screen door about 12 inches and gently push it from the outer edge towards the upper and lower hinges. You're trying to move the screen door frame away from the deadbolt of the main door frame by gently bending the screen door hinge.

Next, open the screen door about two feet, and swing it gently to close it. If the fit is correct, the screen door catch should engage and hold the screen door closed. You can stop here.

If the screen door catch does not engage easily and the door springs back out, then you need to take the additional steps below.

Insert a small wood block measuring approximately 1" x 1" x 4" behind the S-shaped upper and lower screen door hinges (do one at a time). For each hinge, close the screen door on the wooden block to adjust the 90-degree bend in the hinge.

Next, close the screen door fully. <u>Gently</u> tap the screen door hinges against the main door frame, so they follow the profile of the door frame. A square mallet or hammer protected with tape is the ideal tool for this.

Finally, if the bottom of the screen door is catching on the bottom of the door frame, open the screen door a few inches and grab the bottom of the screen door. Bend it outward slightly until it closes without hitting the door frame.

If your main door is now closing well (without slamming), you can stop here. Otherwise, you may need to take additional steps to adjust the main door. This procedure gets a little more advanced, so read through it before beginning.

Start by checking the striker bolt alignment. The entry door has a lock with a pair of "jaws" that trap the striker bolt. You're looking to see if the striker bolt in the door frame is centered on the jaws of the main door lock when the door is closing. If the striker bolt is not exactly centered, you can adjust its position.

To do this, loosen the striker bolt (which has a hexagonal head) by turning it counter-clockwise with a wrench. If the striker bolt needs to be moved more than 1/8", you'll have to drill out the POP rivet below the striker bolt, because it holds a plate that the bolt is screwed into.

Tap the striker bolt up or down as required. Airstream recommends using a cold chisel with a notch ground out to fit over the striker bolt. Once the striker bolt is centered on the jaws of the lock, retighten the striker bolt. If you removed the POP rivet, redrill the hole for the POP rivet (if necessary) and install a new aluminum POP rivet.

Finally, lubricate the jaws of the main lock using silicone spray.

Fan-Tastic Vents

Airstreams have been supplied with Fan-Tastic Vents for decades, so your Airstream probably has one or two. There are numerous varieties of the Fan-Tastic Vent, with different speed controls, powered and unpowered lifting mechanisms, rain sensors, reversing mode, wireless remote, etc. It's also possible that the original fan has been replaced with another brand (MaxxFan is popular), but at the core they're all similar.

Cleaning is the only routine maintenance a Fan-Tastic Vent needs. For instructions on cleaning and lubricating of the vent seal, see the discussion earlier in this section called "Cleaning and lubricating gaskets."

The fan blades and screen also get coated with dust over time. To clean those parts you first have to do some easy disassembly.

The screen is easy. Just remove all eight painted flat head Phillips screws from around the perimeter of the ring insert. If you have a "Pop n' Lock" type screen there won't be any screws to remove. (This is an upgrade you can buy for your vent to make cleaning easier in the future.) Pop n' Lock screens have a raised tab where you can get a grip in the screen to pull it out. It takes a good strong pull.

It's important to get the screen and fan squeaky-clean. Particles of oil, usually from cooking, stick to them and attract dust. To help with this, wash with dish detergent, then dry the parts, then spray on a thin coating of Aerospace 303 Protectant and buff with a clean cloth. The Aerospace 303 Protectant adds a slippery layer to help prevent dust from sticking.

You can try to clean the fan blades in place, but it's hard to get to the top sides of the blades, and many areas surrounding the screen will be impossible to reach. For better cleaning it's easier overall to remove the fan blade and wash it in the sink at the same time as the screen.

To remove the fan blade for cleaning, first remove the fuse by pushing up and turning the black fuse cap 1/4 turn counter-clockwise. That way you won't accidentally short out anything with your screwdriver. If you haven't yet taken out the screen, do so now.

If your fan is a manual crank type, remove the center screw from the black lift knob.

If your fan is an automatic type, remove the two screws that hold the lift motor in place. The motor will dangle by a pair of wires. Optionally, you can unplug the lift motor.

Next, remove the three screws that are flush with the face of the screen assembly. Gently wiggle and guide the entire screen assembly down and let it hang by the wires.

If your fan is equipped with a rain sensor, locate the two 20-gauge black wires that feed down from the top side of the fan through the T-slot in the base. Trace the wires back to the red connector on the circuit board and carefully unplug it.

On newer models, you'll need to remove a Phillips-head screw from the center shaft to remove the blade. On older models look for a small set screw on the fan blade core, and loosen it with a 3/32" Allen wrench. Now grab the fan blade with two hands on opposite sides and wiggle it up and down and side to side until the fan blade comes off the motor shaft.

Clean the screen and fan blades as described above and also wipe down the inside edge of the screen assembly wherever there's dirt. Be careful to support the assembly as you clean it so you don't rip out any wires.

At this point you can also reach up to clean the underside of the vent dome (lid), or you can save that job for some day when you are on the roof.

All done? Go ahead and reverse the steps to reassemble everything. Note that the fan blade is keyed where it slides onto the shaft (in other words, there's a flat spot on the shaft that has to match up to the hole on the fan), so you'll need to spin the fan blade around a little before it will go back on. Make sure the wiring is tucked away properly and not crimped or jammed when reinstalling.

MaxxFans, which are popular replacement vents, are similar in design. On some MaxxFans the fan blade comes out after removal of an acorn nut on the bottom. Then carefully pry the fan downward (it's a tight fit on the center shaft).

Replacing window and door screens

On aluminum-framed Airstream windows, screen replacement is just like many household screens. There's a rubber spline in a channel that holds the edges of the screen in place. Remove any window dressings (blinds, shades, curtains) so you have working space first. This may require removing a screw at the end of a curtain track (or drilling out a rivet, which you can easily replace later).

Then pull the gray rubber spline out of its channel. Needle nose pliers are good for this, or you can use any thin prying tool. The screen will come out and you can use it as a rough template to cut a new one from screen material bought at a hardware store. Cut the new screen about two inches bigger all the way around. New spline is available too, if you need it.

To reinstall, get a window screen roller. This tool pushes the spline and screen back into the channel.

Start at a straight section, and once you've got it going, continue working around the remainder of the frame. Don't stretch the spline material. Keep some tension on the screen mesh as you go, making sure not to cut the mesh with the roller.

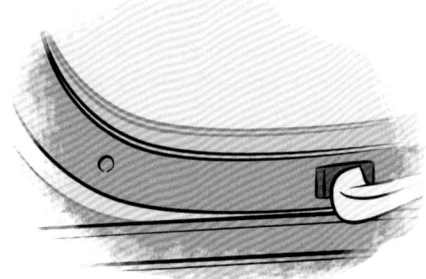

Don't spline the screen too tightly, since this will cause distortions. If the screen begins to bunch or distort, you can pull the spline out and start over, as long as you have not damaged the mesh. Once it is in and you are satisfied, you can trim the excess screen material away.

On black-framed Hehr windows with small screens, remove the black operator knob (one screw) first. Then pry the screen frame from the back frame carefully using a thin, stiff putty knife. Be careful not to mar the window frame.

Hehr recommends ordering a new screen assembly rather than trying to reuse the old screen frame because it looks nicer and the job is easier. But if you want to replace the screen you can, following the same instructions as above.

The entry door screens on late model Airstreams use the same basic procedure. The spline is on the outside of the screen door, and may be in three or four separate pieces.

Replace Hehr window crank

Safari, Sport, and some other models of Airstream trailers use a type of Hehr window that opens only at the bottom third of the glass. This is the type of window with a large black rubber gasket around the outside perimeter of the window.

The window operators (cranks) in these windows are made of a soft metal and they eventually strip and fail. You can delay this failure by not cranking them too tightly when closing them. You'll know when they are going bad, because you will have to spin the window crank quite a while before it finally "catches" and starts to move the window.

Replacing the operators is not a fun job but is feasible for someone with a few tools and lots of patience. It's not a job for beginners. (Strictly speaking, this is a repair rather than maintenance, but it's included here because it comes up fairly often.)

New replacement window operators typically have to be ordered online. Hehr calls them "torque operators" and they are part #008-192 if you've got the window knob on the right (as seen from inside the trailer). The emergency escape window takes a "center" operator, part #119-331 and is somewhat more difficult to replace. Double-check the location and appearance of the operator in your windows against pictures online before you place your order.

Replacing the torque operators only requires two tools, a Phillips screwdriver with a narrow handle and a regular (flat-bladed) screwdriver. For the escape window operator, you may need a horizontal bit driver and an extra long Phillips bit to get some of the screws out. A flexible screwdriver extension and magnetic bits will help.

Inside the trailer, open the window fully if it still works. Remove the black knob by removing the screw in the center.

Outside the trailer, remove the two small black screws in the hinge just above the movable part of the window glass.

Open the window (if it didn't operate by the knob) and carefully pry out the E-clips on the arm hinges, one on each arm. Be careful not to lose the E-clips, as they tend to go flying off. (Replacements can be found at most local hardware stores.) Then pop the arms off using the flat bladed screwdriver.

Now you can lift the window all the way up and either wiggle it out of the hinge or slide it sideways until it comes out of the hinge.

Again using the flat screwdriver, pry the lower end of the spring off the upper arm so that the arm can move freely. Be careful not to puncture the screen with the spring. Do this on each side.

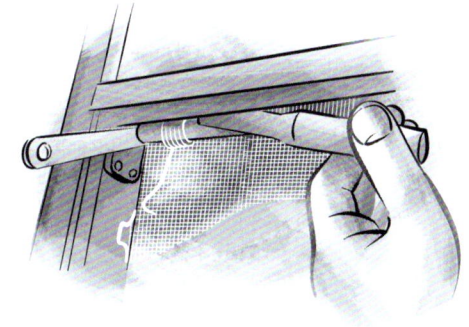

On the right side, remove the screws that hold in the mount for the round bar. The top one will be hard to get to, so this is where the narrow handle of your screwdriver is crucial. On the left side, remove the three screws that hold in the torque operator. Again, the top one is a pain to get to. Take your time and don't strip out the screw heads.

Drop the round bar down on the right side, then the left. It should come out now, with the torque operator attached. It might take some wiggling. Don't let the springs and arms fall off, because that will just make your life harder.

Remove the torque operator and replace with a new torque operator, and wiggle the whole assembly of bar, springs, arms, and operator back into place.

As they say, "installation is the reverse of removal," but getting the top screw back in on each side is tricky. Try taping the screw loosely to the driver or using a magnetic bit. Getting the window back in the hinge is a hassle too, and usually takes quite a few tries to get right.

Plumbing

The plumbing system on an Airstream is much like in your house, just smaller. The fresh water pipes, faucets, and drains are exactly the same as modern household versions. The major differences are that the Airstream has an RV-specific water heater and holding tanks for fresh, gray, and black water so you can camp without hookups.

All Airstreams since the 1960s were built with water pressure regulators, so you don't need to carry an extra pressure regulator for the campground spigot. On later model trailers it is integrated into the Shurflo city water fill. It's preset for 65 psi to prevent damage to the Airstream's plumbing from excessive water pressure.

Plumbing system maintenance is pretty simple. There are only three routine tasks:

- Sanitizing the fresh water system
- Winterizing the plumbing in the fall
- De-winterizing the plumbing in the spring

The other plumbing-related tasks are more in the category of repairs or cleaning, so they get done as needed. This includes things like:

- Fixing a leak
- Cleaning the toilet seal
- Cleaning the water pump strainer
- Clearing a drain clog
- Calibrating the tank monitors
- Replacing the air gap in the water heater

Most of those procedures are explained in this section. Water heater-related maintenance is covered in Appliances section of the book.

Plumbing tools

For routine maintenance you don't need many special tools. Mostly you'll use things like screwdrivers, a small bucket or pan, a towel—things that are readily obtained when needed or which you already have lying around.

Plumber's tape, also known as PTFE or Teflon® tape, is very handy. This tape is wrapped around the threads of fittings to make them watertight. It's your first line of defense against slow drips. Use it everywhere you see a threaded fitting (except flared fittings) including the water heater drain plug.

Most of the drain plumbing on modern Airstreams has hand-tightened plastic fittings, but sometimes a tool is helpful, so have large pliers, an adjustable wrench, or vice grips that can open to at least 2" wide.

Finally, a few plastic or rubber hose gaskets are good for the occasional dripping water hose. Sometimes the gasket (O-ring) falls out of the hose and disappears, and at other times you need to double up to accommodate a funky water spigot. They are cheap and small, so have one or two in your plumbing kit just in case.

Later in this section we discuss PEX plumbing. You really don't need to carry around tools for working on the PEX since it's a generally trouble free system that doesn't require maintenance. You will need some special PEX tools only if you are going to modify the plumbing system or replace parts.

Sanitizing the fresh water system

People often ask if it is safe to drink from the fresh water system aboard the Airstream. The answer is "Yes, as long as you maintain it."

The entire fresh water system should be sanitized at least once a year. The procedure is easy and doesn't require any specialized tools.

Even if you prefer to bring bottled water for drinking you should still sanitize the fresh water system regularly. After all, you're still using the trailer's water for washing dishes, brushing teeth, and cooking. Also, failure to sanitize can allow bacteria to multiply in the water system, causing odors and other unpleasant results.

To sanitize the system, look up your fresh water tank capacity in the Owner's Manual, and add six gallons for the water heater. Multiply the total by 0.13, and that's how many ounces of household bleach you will need. Dilute that bleach in a jug of water, pour it in the fresh water fill, then fill the tank with water.

Turn on the water pump and run each of the faucets (including the shower head) until you can smell bleach. Be sure to run both hot and cold water separately so that the sanitizing solution reaches both the hot and cold pipes, and fills the water heater.

Let the water stand in the system three to four hours at a minimum. Then drain the system and refill with fresh water. You can drain the system most quickly by opening the fresh water tank's drain valve. See your Owner's Manual for the specific location of the drain valve.

Don't forget to drain the water heater, too. Instructions on how to remove the water heater's drain plug are in the discussion "Removing and reinstalling the drain plug" in the Appliances section of this book.

If bleach taste or odor remains, you can rinse the system by pouring a solution of 1 quart of vinegar to 5 gallons of water into the fresh water tank and running that through the faucets with the water pump. There are also commercial products to make the water taste better, which you can find in RV and camping stores. Drain the water out again, and refill with clean water. That's it!

Common water supply problems and solutions

Because your Airstream travels, it is going to be filled with water from a wide variety of sources. Some water will be hard, others soft. Some water will be heavily chlorinated, other sources may have sand or other contaminants. You will likely encounter a range of temperatures from freezing to scorching. Amazingly, the Airstream can handle all of this. But there are a few things you can do to help out, or solve the occasional (rare) problem.

Water filtration

Using a water filter is a matter of personal choice. Campground water has to meet the same standards as any other public water system, so it should be safe. But you might not like the taste, or your body might be sensitive to different water than what you are accustomed to drinking at home. If so, a good filtration system is the solution.

The simplest and cheapest filters are activated-carbon, which help with taste and clarity. They are good at reducing chlorine taste, sediment, pesticides, and Volatile Organic Compounds (VOCs). These are readily available at RV supply stores.

From there, you can upgrade to filter out even finer sediment, bacteria, protozoa, chemicals and metals with other types of filters. You can also soften the water, de-ionize it, and even sterilize the water with a UV light. Of course, every added element means more expense, more weight, more stuff to carry, an ongoing maintenance cost, and (in the case of external filtration systems) more setup time at the campground. So before you buy, consider carefully how far you are willing to go for extremely pure water.

When traveling in Mexico, if you don't want to drink the local water because you're afraid of "Montezuma's Revenge," you have several choices. You can buy and use a water purifier that makes the water bacteriologically safe (it should filter down to between 0.45 to 1.0 microns and be labeled as a "purifier," not just a filter), you can super-chlorinate your drinking water, you can try a Reverse Osmosis system designed for RVs, you can use an ultraviolet light purifier, or you can buy 5-gallon jugs of *agua purificada* from a local supplier. All of these options have their advantages and disadvantages, so do some research and decide what will work best for you.

Hard water problems

Ordinary filters won't effectively counteract prolonged use of hard water, which is very common in the desert southwest. Eventually, mineral deposits will begin to settle in the water heater and cause leaks or clogging in faucets and other fixtures. To prevent mineral build-up from hard water, look for special RV water softeners. They can be easily installed in-line to reduce the impact of minerals as needed.

To offset the impact of hard water build-up, annual flushing of the water heater is recommended. See that procedure in the Appliances section. If deposits are clogging the faucets, you can usually unscrew the screens at the faucet openings and clean them easily.

There's also an inlet strainer attached to the water pump. In severe cases of mineral build-up you might find that the screen inside this strainer needs to be removed and cleaned. It's attached directly to the water pump and usually just unscrews.

Freezing weather

The Airstream should be winterized whenever temperatures are expected to drop below freezing and there is no source of heat in the trailer. If not, even a partial freeze can cause problems.

Normally you winterize in the fall before the freezing temperatures arrive, and de-winterize in the spring once the danger of freezing at night has passed. But what about those times when you are using the Airstream and temperatures dip below freezing just for a few hours, or a day?

On many modern Airstreams, the furnace of the Airstream directs a small amount of warm air to the holding tanks to keep them from freezing. (Some models use a 12 volt heating blanket instead.) So, with the furnace running, you need not worry about burst pipes or frozen tanks even when temperatures dip into the 20s. During a light freeze, if you are comfortable inside the trailer, your Airstream's plumbing is too.

If you are traveling on a day when temperatures will be below freezing for a short time and the trailer is not winterized, you may be able to temporarily fight back by letting the furnace run as you tow. But this strategy comes with risks.

First of all, you'll need to leave the gas bottles on while towing, and a gas appliance (furnace) running while towing. Most safety experts would be aghast at this, and I'm not recommending it.

Second, the furnace will run much more than normal, because of the cooling effect on the trailer's body as a result of being towed. You may run out of propane or kill the trailer battery (the power supplied by the 7-way cord from the tow vehicle is usually not enough to keep up with the draw of the furnace). If that happens, the trailer may freeze while you are feeling toasty warm in the truck—and with a dead trailer battery, your options will be limited.

Third, even with the furnace running and the rest of the trailer warm, the city water fill might freeze because it is exposed to the outside.

Hairline cracks can form in the plastic body of the filler, which is not visible from the outside. This can cause a leak inside the Airstream, which you might not notice until later.

So, as a rule of thumb, if temperatures will be below freezing when you tow, the trailer should be winterized. You can de-winterize when you get out of the cold weather and set up your campsite in Florida. Once you learn the procedure and do it a couple of times, you'll find it's really not all that hard.

In serious cold—down to the single digits Fahrenheit, for example—even the furnace won't be able to keep up for long, and some bit of plumbing may freeze even while the furnace runs constantly. The damage may not be apparent until later, when the plumbing thaws out. Keep your Airstream as warm as possible if you are caught in this condition, or carry RV antifreeze and be prepared to do a "field winterization" right where you are.

If you suspect some light freezing may have occurred when the Airstream was not winterized, proceed cautiously. The dump valves are among the first spots to freeze. Don't force a frozen valve. Wait for it to warm up again, or use a hair dryer on it. Tugging on the dump valves while frozen could tear the seals, which will cause an unpleasant leak and require replacement of the valve.

A major freeze could mean multiple failure points, including the water pump, low-lying sections of pipe, faucets, appliances, city water fill, etc. If the Airstream has suffered a major prolonged freeze without winterization, it will need a complete plumbing system inspection before it can be used again, otherwise you may find you have an indoor sprinkler system. Compressed air, if available, is a good way to test the system. You can find and install "blow-out plugs" easily.

Overflowing fresh water tank

If your Airstream was not properly winterized, small amounts of water might have remained in the water pump and frozen. One failure mode resulting from this is a broken "check valve" in the water pump. This check valve prevents water from flowing backward into the fresh water tank.

The symptom is obvious. On the first camping trip of the season, the owner connects to a campground water spigot. A short time later, water starts to pour out from the fresh water tank fill. The campground water has flowed past the water pump's check valve, filled the water tank, and is now overflowing.

Sediment build-up in the water pump can cause this problem too. In either case, a new water pump is usually needed. In the meantime, if the water pump still pumps, just use water from the fresh tank rather than connecting to city water. Double-check in the area of the water pump for leaks, too.

Other water tank issues

New owners of late model Airstreams are sometimes disturbed to see that the fresh water tank beneath the trailer bows downward when it is full. It looks like it is sagging. In fact this is completely normal. The tank is secured by metal bands and bolted up to the frame, but it is designed to sag down a little when full. Don't worry, it's not going to break.

When you do your periodic inspections, you should study the metal bands that hold the water tank, as well as the tank itself. If the metal bands come loose, that's more of a problem, although it rarely happens. Tapping a larger threaded hole for a larger bolt will resolve it. (This requires a tool that most people don't own, but it's an easy fix for a properly equipped shop.)

Most vintage Airstreams have the water tank above the floor. For many years Airstream installed them toward the front of the trailer, sitting on the floor. If you have one of these older greenish-colored plastic tanks, check for algae growing inside it (using a flashlight), and also for cracks or weeping of water. If the tank has contamination, the water system should be sanitized. If it is leaking, it should probably be replaced. Even if you repair one leak, more are likely to occur due to age.

Draining the water tank

On newer Airstreams with underbelly water tanks you can find a drain valve at the base of the water tank. Usually it's on the side of the tank near the wheels. Sometimes it is protected by a metal cover. Your Owner's Manual will help you find it. Vintage Airstreams with inside tanks sometimes have a drain valve next to the tank, which leads to plumbing going through the floor.

It's useful to know where this valve is, because you'll want to use it when winterizing the trailer. It's also good to know its location so that you can quickly glance at it when doing your pretrip inspection, and verify that it hasn't been damaged by some piece of road debris. This valve can be difficult to open, and if it is, some food-grade silicone spray will help lubricate it.

When draining the fresh water tank with this valve, it will help if you open the faucets to let air into the system. If you don't want water all over the ground, you can alternatively drain the tank by turning on the water pump and running a faucet (thus putting all the water into the gray tank, where it can be quickly dumped). Of course, it will take a while to empty a full tank that way.

Water pump

The water pump is a pretty simple device. It runs automatically, using 12 volt DC power from the battery, to keep pressure up in the water lines when you are using the fresh water tank supply. A pressure switch senses when the pressure is going down and turns on the pump.

Most newer Airstreams have a "variable speed" pump that runs as fast as needed to keep up with the demand for water. Some Airstreams have a pump that has just one speed and cycles on and off as needed.

A check valve keeps the water from flowing backwards. Flexible hoses are connected to both ends (input and output) of the pump to reduce transmission of vibrations through the water pipes, and the pump is mounted on rubber feet to reduce vibration through the floor too.

Variable-speed water pumps can be run while the Airstream is connected to campground water to help boost the pressure, if the campground water pressure is weak, which is nice for showers. Of course, if you do this, keep in mind that you're using water from your fresh water tank in addition to water from the campground.

Normally a water pump needs no maintenance other than winterization or cleaning the strainer. If the pump fails it is generally just replaced rather than repaired, but some models can be disassembled and rebuilt.

If the pump seems noisy, or won't stop running, you may have air in the water lines. Try running all the faucets for 30 seconds to let the air out. You may have to also open the outside shower faucets, if your Airstream has them.

Restrictions (such as kinks or clogs) in the water lines near the pump can also make the pump noisy. Check the area around the pump and also notice if your pump has a clear or translucent plastic cup attached. This is the strainer, which can be removed and cleaned if it is getting clogged up.

Getting air in the lines when switching between campground water and the fresh water tank is normal. This air bleeds out when you use the water. But if air is getting in the lines while you are camped, something in the plumbing system could be losing pressure. This might be a leak in the plumbing or perhaps dried out internal parts in some of the faucets.

If the water pump runs randomly when nothing is on, it's almost a certain sign that water is leaking from the plumbing somewhere. Investigate this using the techniques described in the Leak Prevention, Detection, and Repair section. If no leak is found, the problem might be the pump itself. If the pump's internal check valve is failing, the plumbing will gradually lose pressure and cause the pump to run periodically.

Types of plumbing

Newer Airstreams use PEX plumbing for the fresh water system. PEX is a type of flexible plastic tubing joined to brass or plastic fittings with copper clamp rings. If you look under the bathroom or kitchen counter at your plumbing and see red (for hot water), white, or blue (cold water) pipes, that's PEX. The copper rings used to secure the pieces together may look black but if you scratch them slightly you'll see the copper shine through.

PEX is a very durable type of plumbing that is certified for use in homes and even in places where it won't be readily accessible, so usually it doesn't need repairs. It's ideal for Airstreams because of its flexibility, which helps it "go with the flow" as the Airstream rolls down the road.

Older Airstreams may have a mish-mash of plumbing types, usually because a prior owner has modified the original copper plumbing. That's right, in the early years of Airstreams, well into the 1970s, Airstream installed rigid copper pipes. In the late 1970s and 1980s Airstream used polybutylene (gray plastic), but that turned out to be an unreliable system and was abandoned. Many owners have upgraded their "poly" plumbing since.

Some vintage trailer enthusiasts maintain that copper remains the best choice, but in most older Airstreams you'll find the copper has been partially or entirely replaced over the years. You may find copper, 1/2" PEX, PVC (rigid white plastic), clear vinyl, polybutylene (gray plastic pipe), and a variety of clamps and fittings. But there are two simple bits of advice:

1. Don't mix different types of plumbing if you can avoid it. In particular, clamps or adhesives meant for a specific type of plumbing will generally not work on others. When dealing with a vintage system that has mixed types of plumbing, it's often best to just replace it with a single new type, either copper or PEX. This is particularly true if you have an older trailer with gray polybutylene plumbing—which at this point is overdue for replacement.

2. If you are going to repair or modify PEX, you'll need PEX-specific tools. This includes a good tool for either the copper clamp rings that are used in modern Airstreams, or the stainless steel crimp rings that can alternatively be used. You will also need a cutter for plastic pipe, a PEX crimp or clamp tool, a crimp remover, some extra PEX tubing, brass elbows, tees, and other fittings for your project. Push-fit fittings that are hand-installed (like "Sharkbite" brand) are good for quick repairs, especially in hard-to-access locations, but are much more expensive.

If you are planning to modify or repair your PEX plumbing (perhaps to install a new faucet or shut-off valve or to correct freeze-related damage), you'll find that learning to work with PEX is easy. You can find instructions on how to work with PEX on various Internet sites, YouTube videos, and in hardware stores that sell PEX.

Neither copper plumbing nor PEX requires routine maintenance, so in the rest of this section we'll focus on fixing more typical problems that occur with plumbing, such as minor leaks.

Basic leak repair

Before starting any repair to the pressurized (hot and cold water) plumbing, shut off the water at the pump and disconnect the city water connection outside. Then open any faucet and bleed off the water pressure. Have a towel and a drip pan or bowl ready to collect the remaining water that will come out when you open up the system.

Threaded fittings

The most common leaks occur at threaded fittings, and they are usually the easiest to fix. Identify the part that's leaking with a little paper towel and a flashlight so you're sure you are tackling the right job. Unscrew the leaking fitting. You may need some pliers, vice grips, or a large wrench to get it apart. If so, be sure to wrap the jaws of the tool with a rag so that you don't mar the surface of the fitting.

A little plumber's tape wrapped around the threads of the fitting is usually all that's needed. Wrap the tape tightly around the threads three or four times, stretching it a little as you go. Screw the fitting back together and test it. If it still oozes or drips water, you can try repeating the job with a little more plumber's tape. If the fitting is badly corroded, it's probably better to replace it.

Dripping hose connection

It's fairly common to connect to the water in a campground and get a slow drip at the campground's spigot. Sometimes this is the result of a pressure regulating or backflow prevention device installed by the campground, and you can't do anything about it. But if the leak seems to be at the threaded connection of your hose, there are a couple of things to try.

First, don't over-tighten the hose. This usually makes things worse. Remove the hose and check for debris in the screw threads (check both ends: your hose and the campground's spigot).

If that doesn't work, inspect the rubber O-ring that is typically found inside the threaded end of your hose. If the O-ring is missing or damaged, it can be quickly replaced with a spare from your toolkit. Just pry out the old O-ring with a screwdriver and pop the new one in.

If the O-ring isn't the problem, the threads on either your hose or the campground spigot may be damaged. You can try another hose, or use a temporary work-around to this problem by wrapping the threads of the campground spigot with some plumber's tape from your toolkit.

In some cases nothing works, and you just have live with a drip at the spigot. It's not unusual to find this issue because those campground spigots have been heavily used every day and eventually they begin to wear out. You'd think that the campground owners would be vigilant about finding the ones that drip so that they can cut their water bill, but I guess they figure the cost of a plumber will be more than the cost of the lost water.

If temperatures are going to dip below freezing at night, be sure to disconnect your water hose before bedtime and reconnect it in the morning. Otherwise you'll have a block of ice preventing water flow in the morning, and your hose could burst. Electrically-heated water hoses are available through RV stores, if you are going to be spending a lot of time in a campground at below-freezing temperatures.

Leaking sink

It's rare to get a leak at the sink, but if you do, it's going to be from the putty around the drain. This is easy to replace after a few years of use. You'll need a small tub of plumber's putty, which is a clay-like substance found at any hardware store.

Beneath the sink you'll find a threaded fitting with grips that you can probably unscrew with your hand. This holds the drain plumbing in place. With that unscrewed, the drain itself will come loose (just pull the plumbing down and press the drain upward). Remove all the old putty.

You reseal by rolling out a length of plumber's putty into a rope about six inches long and 1/8" diameter. Press it around the drain opening where the old putty was, and then press the drain back into place. Screw the plumbing drain back into place and clean up the excess putty that squeezes out.

Leaking faucet

A leak at a faucet usually means the faucet's internal gaskets are wearing out or clogged with minerals. Sometimes the faucet parts can be disassembled and cleaned, or rejuvenated with new washers and gaskets, but for other faucets replacement is the only practical solution.

Before you consider replacement, check all the connections to the faucet and the sink sprayer (if equipped). Sometimes they loosen just from ordinary vibration during travel.

Drain system maintenance and cleaning

The showers used in modern Airstreams require little maintenance. Cleaning is described in the Interior Cleaning and Appearance section of this book.

To avoid problems with the shower drain, use a drain screen to catch hair, avoid using chemical drain cleaners, and periodically pour a little enzyme-based RV holding tank chemical down the drain to help break down organic debris.

Sand and dirt will clog the shower drain, and can't be removed with drain cleaners, so use the exterior shower or a garden hose outside for washing dogs, sand off your feet from the beach, etc. Don't store dirty entrance mats, etc., in the shower pan during travel—or if you do, put them in a plastic bag. If dirt does clog the drain, try flushing it out with a hose and high-pressure water. It's far better to avoid the problem in the first place.

Don't use any products for cleaning household plumbing that contain harsh chemicals, acids, etc. The only cleaning agents that can be used without causing harm to the system are household ammonia and tri-sodium phosphate (TSP) in small quantities. Do not use any product that contains petroleum distillates. This attacks the rubber seats of your toilet and dump valve. Likewise, don't use abrasive cleaners. All products should be approved for ABS plastic drainage systems.

If you have a clog in a sink, clear it by unscrewing the P-trap under the sink (have a bucket or pan handy to catch the water that will come out!). Clear it out with a small plumber's snake or other tools, rather than trying to dissolve it out with chemicals. It's not unusual to find the bathroom sink draining slowly because of a build-up of toothpaste or hair, but you can resolve this in a few minutes of work. If it creeps you out to work on the drains, wear gloves and grit your teeth — you'll get through it.

Toilet maintenance

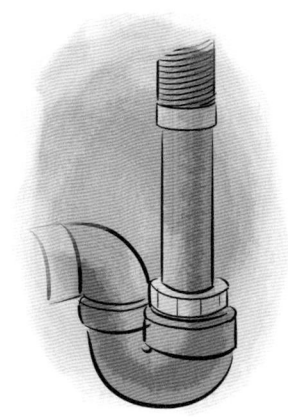

For decades Airstream has used Dometic RV toilets that are dead simple. They have a round "flush ball" or slider at the bottom of the bowl that opens when you press a pedal, and an automatic flush. Press on the pedal, a little water flushes the bowl, and gravity does the rest of the work. The waste simply falls into the black tank below.

In recent years Airstream has begun offering a fancier "macerating" toilet in some models. This device is kind of like the waste disposal often found under kitchen sinks: it chops up the waste, which makes it easier to dump later, and allows the waste to be pumped to a black tank mounted somewhere else on the trailer other than directly below the toilet. This is helpful to RV designers, but more complicated for users, since now instead of a familiar foot pedal, there are two switches to use with modes for flushing, adding water, and removing water. It also requires electricity to work.

Nobody likes repairing the toilet, so maintenance is particularly important here. Most problems can be avoided by simple choices.

Most importantly, **the black tank should only contain things you've previously eaten, easily-dissolved toilet paper, water, and a bit of tank chemical to help things along.** Nothing else. (You don't need the special "RV Toilet Paper" that is sold in RV stores, as long as you stick with a single-ply toilet paper that disintegrates in water fairly quickly.)

This is particularly critical for the macerating toilets, because the macerator can be clogged by almost anything else. Luxurious four-ply toilet paper that feels like high-thread-count bedsheets will quickly become cotton rope if allowed to tangle with the spinning metal of a macerator. This will clog the mechanism and probably blow a fuse.

Toilet seal maintenance

A small amount of water should always cover the black seal at the bottom of the toilet bowl. This seal shouldn't be allowed to dry out. If the water constantly leaks through the seal, the seal either needs cleaning or replacement.

A leaking seal can also allow sewer gases to get into the bathroom. If you smell sewer gas inside the bathroom (and you're sure it's not coming in through the open window or roof vent), the seal is the likely source.

Usually the cause of a slow water leak through the seal is mineral deposits from hard water that have built up on the flush ball or seal. You can clean the seal with a soft bristle brush (an old toothbrush works fine) and toilet bowl cleaner. Put on some gloves and scrub the top of the flush ball and under the seal where it contacts the flush ball. Then apply light downward pressure on the top of the seal while brushing around its perimeter.

You can also make a little tool for cleaning the underside and edges of the seal by sticking some adhesive Velcro to a wooden tongue depressor.

If it still leaks after cleaning, you're probably going to have to replace the seal, but first try a simple trick. Empty the bowl and pour a little vegetable oil over the seal. You may see bubbles indicating where the seal is leaking, and you can give that area of the seal a little extra cleaning. If not, let the oil sit for a while. The oil will probably swell the seal just enough to stop the leak temporarily.

If all else fails, seal kits can be purchased from RV stores, Airstream dealers, and eBay. Make sure you get the correct part for your model of toilet. The model number should be in the mass of Owner's Manuals that you got with the Airstream, or possibly imprinted somewhere on the toilet itself.

Although this job sounds scary, sometimes the seal can be replaced without removing the toilet (depending on the model you have), and the kits are only about $15-25. For other models, the entire toilet must be unbolted from the floor and the replacement seal kit gets more expensive because you'll also need to replace the seal at the base of the toilet. This job isn't fun but it's not terribly hard, either. If you can't bear the thought of it, you can always take it in to the helpful RV technician at the dealership, who is paid to suffer through jobs like this.

Sewer hoses

Sewer hoses don't last forever. To avoid disasters of the worst possible sort, replace that hose at the very first sign of cracking, pinholes, or any sort of wear. You might just set up a schedule of replacement every few months or annually, depending on how often you travel.

People who wait for the hose to fail usually regret their choice. After a few years watching fellow RV'ers at the dump station, you will undoubtedly see a dramatic example of this. Chuck that questionable sewer hose and economize on something else.

Black tank maintenance

There's really not much to maintaining a black tank. There are just a few guidelines to keep it working well. The main thing is to have a good ratio of water to solids in the tank, in order for it to empty properly. This is not really something you have to think about much. Normal use will take care of it.

Tank chemicals (often called "sanitizers" or "digestants") should be added to the black tank every time after it is dumped, along with a gallon or so of water. These chemicals help break down and liquify the next tank of waste, which is what you want for trouble-free tank dumping.

We recommend you choose tank chemicals that don't use formaldehyde. Formaldehyde kills the beneficial bacteria that help break down waste. Essentially, it "pickles" the poop. Not only is that counter-productive for you, but it can prevent septic systems from working, which is a big problem for campground owners. Formaldehyde is also a known carcinogen. Products labeled "bacterial digestant," "enzyme based," or "septic safe" are the best choice.

For long term stays in campgrounds, you should leave the black tank valve closed until the tank is at least half full, so everything in it will flow out readily. Dump it and close the valve again.

Many Airstreams have a black tank flush feature. Using this once in a while helps clean out the interior of the tank. If your trailer doesn't have a black tank flush, don't worry. Regular use of enzyme tank chemicals and plenty of water will work just fine.

If you want to really clear it out, dump the tank, then fill it with warm water and a triple dose of enzyme chemicals and let it sit overnight. Then tow the trailer a few miles to let the contents of the tank slosh around and dump again. It won't be pristine inside (it never will) but this treatment will help prevent buildup over time.

Leaking dump valves

If you open the dump valve cap and find that liquid waste comes out before you've pulled the valve, it's because one of the dump valves is leaking. Most often this is caused by something caught in the valve itself, so the valve can't seal properly. You can try a good tank flush as described above, plus working the valve back and forth a little, to see if the contamination can be washed out.

If the problem persists, it may be time for new valve seals. They do wear out in time, usually after several years of use or if they've been damaged by a freeze. Replacement valve seals and complete replacement valve assemblies are readily available through RV parts stores, and they are usually not expensive or hard to install (typically just four bolts). Late model Airstreams use black Valterra valves, and vintage trailers have Thetford unless they've been replaced. They are slightly different.

People understandably don't enjoy this job, but if you flush out the black and gray tanks repeatedly with plenty of tank chemical and water before beginning it will be a lot less unpleasant.

Gray tank maintenance

The gray water tank really requires no particular maintenance, but if you want to keep it as clean as possible it is a good idea to periodically treat it with the same enzymatic tank chemicals that you use on the black tank. These chemicals will help "digest" the food particles that tend to accumulate in a gray tank and may help prevent some clogs in the drain pipes.

As with the black tank, when staying in a full hookup campground you should leave the gray tank valve closed until the tank is at least half full, so everything in it will flow out readily. This also leaves some gray water to flush the sewer line after you dump the black tank. Close the valve again after dumping.

Calibrating the tank monitor
(Catcon Micropulse System Monitor)

Airstream used the Catcon Micropulse™ System from the beginning of the 2004 model year to mid-2013. In 2013, Airstream began installing the Garnet Technologies SeeLeveL® gauge (monitoring system) in some models, and by early 2014 Airstream was installing SeeLeveL in all of its trailers. These instructions are only for the MicroPulse System (it's the one that seems to give people the most trouble).

Theoretically the Micropulse Systems Monitor shouldn't need recalibrating. However, sometimes it does anyway. If you are observing inaccurate readings, recalibrating the system is a good first start. If recalibrating doesn't help, the system may have one or more bad sensors, which can be replaced. For help with that, get directly in touch with Airstream or Catcon Products (techsupport@catconproducts.com, 817-590-8718).

The MicroPulse System uses remote pressure sensors to gauge the amount of liquid in your tanks. The system is easily calibrated but requires filling the fresh, gray, and black tanks with water so the sensors can report their precise levels to the system's memory. (The "battery" sensor is determined by battery voltage and is therefore not part of this calibration process.)

Normally the LED display is used to report the status of each tank and the battery. However, when in the calibration mode the lower LEDs are used to report a particular function of the calibration process. These functions are not printed on the faceplate of the monitor so you will need to refer to the illustration here during the calibration process.

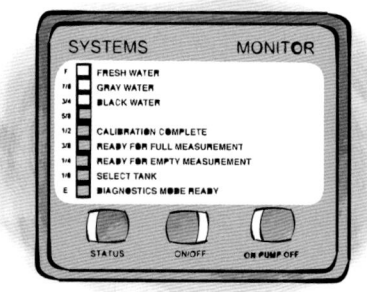

The tanks can be calibrated individually or all at one time. Calibrating one tank at a time reduces the chance of error (and sometimes you only need to calibrate one tank), so these instructions are given for one tank at a time.

The recalibration procedure is as follows:

First, turn the Micropulse control panel off. Then remove the faceplate of the monitor by inserting your fingernail between the upper edge of the faceplate and the surrounding plastic bezel.

Carefully pull the upper edge of the faceplate towards you about ½" and lift the faceplate up and then out. The faceplate is held in place with a small spring clip at the top and two small metal fingers at the bottom. You must lift the panel up until the bottom fingers clear the bezel.

Next, remove the RJ-11 "telephone style" plugs from the back of the monitor for the tanks you are NOT calibrating. For example, if you are calibrating the fresh water tank, remove the BW (black water) plug and the GW (gray water) plug from the back of the panel. FW means "fresh water."

Completely drain the tank being calibrated. If you plan to calibrate each tank, it is easier to drain all of the tanks now.

The sensor needs to read some water pressure in order to measure the "empty" condition, so add fresh water to the tank being calibrated, as follows:

- **Black Water Tank: 1 gallon**
- **Gray Water Tank: 1 gallon**
- **Fresh Water Tank: 2 gallons**

Putting two gallons of water in the fresh water tank provides a reserve when the fresh water LED indicates empty (LED flashes red).

Now you can set the Micropulse to enter diagnostics (calibration) mode. Push in and hold the STATUS switch while you turn the ON/OFF switch to ON. Continue to hold the STATUS switch until the LEDs flash yellow once and then flash green.

Press and release the STATUS switch one time to begin the calibration process. A green LED will appear next to the corresponding tank being calibrated. The bottom LED ("Diagnostics Mode Ready") will illuminate to indicate this step is complete. (A green LED next to the tank name will not appear if the tank sensor is not found; e.g., the RJ-11 jack is not plugged into the back of the monitor).

Press and release the STATUS switch one time to move on to the next step.

Wait until the second-from-bottom LED ("Select Tank") goes out. The "Ready For Empty Measurement" LED (third from the bottom) will illuminate. You are now ready to set the amount of water in the selected tank for the empty condition. Press and release the STATUS switch once. The system will calculate the empty level of the tank, and the "Ready For Empty Measurement" LED (third from the bottom) will go out.

Now the "Ready For Full Measurement" LED (fourth from the bottom) will go on. Fill the selected tank so it is almost full. The ideal liquid height is just below the top of the tank, but this cannot be detected from outside so use the following as a guide:

Fresh water tank: Fill it to just overflowing at the fill port. Using a one-gallon container like a milk jug, remove one gallon of fresh water by running the water from your sink or outdoor shower. This ensures that there is no water in the filler pipe or overflow pipe.

Gray water tank: Fill the gray water tank until water begins to appear at the shower drain. Using your waste drain valve (and hose) drain off approximately one gallon of water. To do this, open (pull) the gray water drain valve and count slowly to five before closing.

Black water tank: Fill the black tank through the toilet until you can see the water level about one inch below the bottom of the pipe leading down from the toilet bowl (from inside the bathroom).

Once the tank is full, press and release the STATUS switch one time. The system will calculate the full level of the tank and the "Ready For Full Measurement" LED will go out.

At this point the calibration of this tank is complete, and the "Calibration Complete" green LED should now be illuminated. There's one more critical step: to save and store this calibration, press the STATUS switch once. The LEDs on the monitor will turn red from "E" (empty) to "F" (full) one time, then turn green from "E" to "F" one time, and then flash green one time.

(Note that if the "Calibration Complete" LED lights red instead of green, the calibration has failed. The most likely cause for a failure is that the full level was not set the minimum of 4 inches above the empty. In that case you'll need to turn off the system, adjust the water level in that tank, and start over.)

Now turn the system off. If you plan to calibrate another tank, disconnect the tank wire you just calibrated, plug in the wire for the next tank you wish to calibrate, and repeat the procedure. When you have completed all calibrations, reconnect all the wires.

Finally, place the lower edge of the faceplate against the plastic bezel so the two prongs in the back of the monitor can slide down behind the lip of the bezel. Allow the faceplate to slide down to the rim of the bezel and then snap the upper edge into place. You might have to use a fingernail or small screwdriver to carefully push the top spring on the faceplate down so it snaps back into place.

Getting out of calibration mode

If you follow the procedure above exactly, the monitor will end up in normal mode at the end. But if you wish to exit calibration mode early, turn the power OFF, then ON. All LEDs will light green. (If not, it is not in calibration mode.)

Toggle the status switch once. The unit will light green for all installed functions, and the bottom LED will light green. This signals the unit is in diagnostic mode.

Toggle the status switch once again. As soon as the 1/8 LED is illuminated, toggle the status switch four times in a row. The display will go blank and then start up in normal mode.

Running Gear and A-frame

This section applies only to aluminum and fiberglass travel trailers (including Nest and Basecamp). If you have a motorhome like Interstate or Atlas, only the general discussion on tires applies to your rig. By "running gear" we are talking about the parts of the Airstream that keep it rolling. That includes the tires, wheels, axles, brakes, shock absorbers, and wheel bearings, as well as the hitch coupler.

From a safety and reliability standpoint, these are among the most important areas of your Airstream, because a failure in the running gear can mean a big problem during a trip. So we'll spend some time reviewing all the parts that make up the running gear and focus on safety.

Hitch coupler and ball maintenance

At the front of your Airstream, the part of the chassis that sticks out and holds the propane tanks is called the A-frame. Other parts that reside here include the batteries (on non-Classic models), propane tanks and lines, hitch jack and the hitch coupler. We'll discuss the batteries and propane items in separate sections of this book.

The hitch coupler is a pretty simple item but obviously very important, because if it lets go your trailer can suddenly become an independent traveler. The normal maintenance is to inspect the coupler to see if it is getting rusty, damaged, or loose.

You can check for looseness by hitching up to your tow vehicle and then raising the hitch jack until the back of the tow vehicle begins to come up. There may be some small amount of play in the ball/coupler connection, but the ball should stay firmly locked in the coupler. If it doesn't, you may need to have a new coupler welded on.

The coupler will last longer if you give it a shot with your silicone spray above and below once in a while.

In the past, Airstream has used two different size hitch couplers that accepted either a 2" or 2-5/16" hitch ball. Airstream trailers 1970 and later have couplers that require a 2-5/16" hitch ball.

The hitch ball should be lubricated with a dedicated hitch lube like Reese's Hitch Ball Grease, other white grease, or another durable greasy lubricant that won't wash off. Sewing machine oil, petroleum jelly, and WD-40 do not qualify for this job. If you can find a jar with a wide enough mouth, you can put grease in the jar and then rotate the jar over the ball to neatly lubricate it—then just cap the jar for next time.

Lubrication not only limits wear on the ball and quiets the hitch, but it also helps prevent rust and wear in the coupler. It is fine to lubricate the coupler itself by putting a little grease in it from the underside. There's a myth that says grease will attract dirt and accelerate wear; don't believe it. Even dirty grease is better than no grease in this case.

If the hitch ball shows signs of wear, replace it, and make a mental note to lube it more often in the future. You can buy replacements in many hardware and RV parts stores. A large wrench will be needed to remove and replace the ball. When you do your Pre-departure inspection, check that the ball is tight. It shouldn't move or turn at all. If it does, tighten it again with that big wrench.

A tow ball kept properly lubricated will last many years. When you are parked, you can cover it with a plastic bag or similar so it doesn't jump out and grease your pant leg, as they like to do.

Hitch receiver inspection

Technically the hitch receiver is part of your tow vehicle, not the Airstream, but it's such a critical part of maintenance that we've included it in this book.

Few people ever look at this part of the connection between trailer and tow vehicle, even though it's the thing that keeps the trailer from becoming an unguided aluminum missile. The hitch receiver is an arrangement of welded metal bars or tubes underneath your tow vehicle to which a tow ball is typically attached.

The hitch receiver gets bolted on either at the factory or shortly before you buy your first trailer, and then generally it never gets examined again. Most of the time people get away with ignoring the receiver because they don't do much towing. But you really need to take a look at this thing once in a while, because what you haven't noticed can hurt you.

Receivers do fail, usually as a result of metal fatigue and rust caused by salted roadways, and sometimes because of poor design. The receiver has to manage thousands of foot-pounds of torque from the torsion bars and goes through thousands of stress cycles every time you tow. Receivers often fail at low speed because the stress encountered from sharp turns, dips, and potholes on secondary roads is greater than the stress on the receiver when cruising on the highway.

Because hitch receiver failure can be catastrophic, it's a good idea to take a few minutes every year to conduct a simple hitch inspection on your tow vehicle—or have it done on a lift by a mechanic.

It's very easy and the tools are simple. You'll need some wire brushes and/or a cordless drill with a brass wire brush attachment, to clean up rusty spots. A bright LED headlamp or a shop light is needed to closely examine the corners and crevices. Once the inspection is complete, you'll need a can of black spray paint to make the receiver look new again.

When getting under a car, always take some safety precautions. Make sure the parking brake is set. If you are jacking up the car for more clearance underneath, use jack stands and follow the procedures suggested by the manufacturer of the jack and jack stands. Never get under a car that is supported by a jack alone.

When studying the receiver hitch, look for shiny lines on welds that would indicate a recent crack, rusty lines against painted areas that might indicate an old crack, broken welds, bent metal, and loose or rusty mounting bolts. Large patches of rust flaking off are cause for concern. Put a wrench on the bolts to make sure they are tight.

Take your time—a good inspection will probably take you more than ten minutes of methodical probing and examination. A magnifying glass can be helpful if you have trouble seeing things up close.

Lots of cracks or heavy rust are a good reason to replace the entire hitch receiver, rather than trying to fix it. They do wear out sometimes and they aren't terribly expensive to replace, so don't risk towing with a marginal hitch receiver.

During your inspection be sure to examine the receiver box itself (the place where the tow ball or hitch stinger slides in). On most receiver boxes you'll see a strengthening collar (additional metal thickness) on the rear end of the box. However, receiver manufacturers seem to rarely put a strengthening collar on the front end of the receiver box, even though both ends endure the same stress. For this reason it's a good idea to take a close look at the front end of the receiver box to ensure that the box itself is not stretching, or cracking at the corners. If it is, a welding shop can fix and reinforce it for you.

Assuming everything looks good, it's time to clean up the receiver hitch. Use the wire brushes to remove all the surface rust, until the metal is shiny. A wire brush attachment on a cordless drill can make quick work of this job. Wipe the surfaces clean, then inspect the spots you've cleaned once again, just to be sure you haven't missed a possible crack or broken weld.

The final step is to mask off the surrounding area with tape and paper, and spray the receiver with black paint. The paint will help you notice if a weld breaks or a fatigue crack forms in the future.

Breakaway switch

This switch, which is mounted on the A-frame near the hitch ball coupler, is designed to engage the trailer brakes at the moment the trailer separates from the tow vehicle. It works when the safety cable attached to your tow vehicle yanks a pin or key out of the breakaway switch. Once the pin is removed, the 12 volt house battery power is applied to the trailer brakes, which makes them stop the trailer quickly.

Maintenance is simple: just check that it works, and lubricate the pin. To test, just pull the pin out. It will usually take a good hard yank. Have a helper kneeling near the brakes. Your helper should be able to hear a click and hum from the trailer's drum brakes. With disc brakes, you'll have to listen for the hydraulic actuator (usually located somewhere up front) to make some noise. The brakes should be locked full on, and the trailer should be immoveable.

While the pin is out, lubricate it with your handy can of silicone spray. Don't leave the pin out for long. Extended removal time can drain the batteries and possibly cause damage to drum brakes by overheating the magnets.

(For the same reason, don't use your breakaway switch as a parking brake. However, in the extreme event that you unhitch your trailer on an incline and your trailer begins to roll, the breakaway switch cable pin can be pulled out and your trailer will come to a dead stop.)

Check the cable as well. It should be in good condition, without fraying or rust. Finally, plan to replace the breakaway switch every five years. They don't last forever. Replacements are cheap, easy to install, and easy to find at RV parts stores or Airstream dealers.

That's it for maintenance. But since we are here, let's consider good operational practices. For such a simple device, there's an amazing amount of conflicting opinion about how the cable of the breakaway should be connected to your tow vehicle.

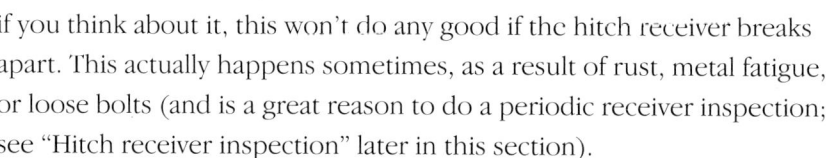

The primary thing is to consider where to put the cable end while you are towing. Most often people attach it to a point on the tow vehicle's hitch receiver, but if you think about it, this won't do any good if the hitch receiver breaks apart. This actually happens sometimes, as a result of rust, metal fatigue, or loose bolts (and is a great reason to do a periodic receiver inspection; see "Hitch receiver inspection" later in this section).

So ideally you should connect the cable somewhere else. An easy solution is to put a large bolt through the loop at the end of the cable, with two large fender washers and a nut. This makes a nice chunk that you can put inside the tailgate of a pickup truck, or inside the rear liftgate of an SUV. If the trailer separates, even as a result of hitch failure, this part will stay with the tow vehicle and activate the breakaway switch.

Another common practice is to loop the breakaway cable through the safety chains and terminate the attaching point at the chains' hooks. But if the chains break away from the tow vehicle, or if they stay intact but the breakaway cable is longer than the chains, the breakaway switch will not activate.

Similarly, if you've replaced the breakaway cable with a coil-type expandable cable, check the length when it is fully stretched out. If there is a failure of the hitch and the chains pull tight—but not the coiled cable, the switch will not activate.

Finally, keep in mind that the breakaway switch will not work if the batteries are disconnected in the Airstream. This could be the case if you tow the Airstream after a long period of storage and don't remember to reconnect the batteries.

Power hitch jack

The power hitch jack needs little attention. If you want to check it, remove the cover (you'll need a screwdriver) and check the condition of the grease on the gears. If the grease is missing or dirty, you can use lithium grease on the metal gears. There's no need to put grease on the nylon timing gears.

With the jack fully down, give the inner tube of the post a quick spray with silicone spray. Check the tube to make sure it isn't bent.

If your hitch jack repeatedly blows fuses, check for damage, and then check that you are using the right fuse type. It should have a 30 amp "slow blow" fuse. This is required because of the initial power draw when you activate the hitch jack.

Tire maintenance

Your tires do a big job, and they don't ask much of you in return. Just keep them inflated, inspect them periodically (more on what to look for in a moment), and replace them when they get too old or worn.

Ignoring your tires can result in really expensive damage. When a tire blows out or is run flat, it often throws off chunks of tread which whack the Airstream and damage the body and wheel well. It's not uncommon for an on-the-road tire failure to cause thousands of dollars in secondary damage. So let's get to know our tires and prevent that.

Inflation

The maximum air pressure you should pump in is marked on the side of each tire. Typically it's either 50 psi or 65 psi. The weight rating printed on the side of the tire assumes maximum air pressure; any less and the weight rating goes down.

The tire pressure should reflect the loaded weight of the trailer. Running incorrect tire pressure can cause uneven tire wear and/or poor handling. If you have Goodyear tires, see Goodyear's Load/Inflation tables online at **www.goodyear.com/rv/pdf/rv_inflation.pdf** to determine the air pressure you should use. If in doubt, you can run the highest rated pressure, but keep an eye on the tread wear pattern (more on that later in this section).

Get an accurate tire gauge and keep it with your trailer tools. A 12-volt DC air pump with an extension cord is handy for on-the-road tire top-ups. It's a nuisance trying to find an air pump at a gas station when you need one, and often difficult to get close enough to it with your trailer. Having an AC-powered air compressor at home is a convenience, too.

Because ambient temperature affects tire pressure, and because tires naturally leak a little air (1 to 2 psi a month is considered normal), check the tire pressures once a month. During a trip, check them weekly. Typically you'll need to add air when the weather gets cold, and you might need to take a little out when summer heat arrives. If your tires always seem to lose more than 1 to 2 psi per month, inspect the valve stems for cracks or damage, or have a tire shop replace the stems and valve cores as a preventative measure.

Be sure to check the pressure and inflate when the tires are "cold," meaning first thing in the morning before you start towing. The pressure will increase as you go down the road, and that's normal—there's no need to remove air because the tire pressure has increased during the day. Tires on the sunny side of the trailer will read a little higher, and that's OK too.

Using a Tire Pressure Monitoring System (TPMS)

One of the best ways to keep track of your tire inflation is to install a TPMS. These systems typically use sensors screwed onto the valve stems or placed inside the wheel. A remote monitor in the tow vehicle will alert you if the tire becomes dangerously underinflated, or overinflated (usually from overheating of brake or wheel bearing parts). Some will also monitor the tire temperature, which is useful to help you understand what's going on as you travel.

You want to know what's going on with your tires because often you won't feel or see a change in tire air pressure. In fact, on multi-axle Airstreams it's possible to lose a wheel entirely and not feel any change in towing characteristics. Knowing immediately what's going on can save you a lot of trouble.

If you get a TPMS, buy a quality one. Cheap ones are often marketed under different names by different resellers, and this is a case where you will get what you paid for. Truck Systems Technologies (TST), Pressure Pro, and Doran are all known for producing quality TPMS units. Look for one that provides accurate pressure and temperature for each wheel, and read reviews from owners before you choose.

One nice aspect of having a TPMS is that you will know the pressure of each tire moments after you get in your tow vehicle, every time you tow. No more bending down and checking each tire one at a time, no more getting your hands dirty, and less time spent getting ready to tow. Don't forget to buy a spare monitor for the spare tire, so you don't have to slide under the Airstream to check it before every trip. If your tow vehicle doesn't have a built-in TPMS, consider getting enough tire monitors for it, too.

Rotating the tires

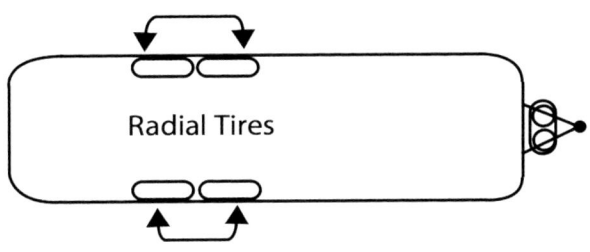

The term "rotating the tires" seems a little odd; don't the tires rotate all the time? Actually, it refers to the practice of removing the tire and wheel assembly and remounting it in a different wheel position on the Airstream. This has the effect of evening out the wear, because of slight differences in the axle alignment and the weight on each wheel.

Rotating isn't strictly required but if you choose to do it, every 5,000 to 10,000 miles is a common recommendation. Keep the tires on the same side of the trailer, so move the front right tire to the rear right position, and vice versa. Then swap them back the next time.

When to replace the tires

Think of your tires as a consumable asset. Miles, heat, sun, ozone, underinflation, punctures, hitting curbs or potholes, and time consume the tire even if you can't see any change from the outside. Replace a trailer tire when you see any of the following problems:

1. The tread is less than 3/32 of an inch. You can use the famous penny test, where you stick Abe Lincoln in the tread upside-down. If you can see the top of Abe's head, the tread is too thin.

2. The tire has worn strangely or unevenly. If the tread didn't wear evenly and you have a thin spot at any point, the tire is done. Worn edges indicate chronic under-inflation. A single worn outer edge can be a sign of overloading or an axle alignment issue. A worn center band suggests over-inflation. Other types of uneven wear can be the result of an alignment problem, a wheel bearing problem, or an out-of-balance wheel. An oval or circular worn patch anywhere suggests an internal belt separation, which is a serious problem that can doom a tire in a matter of 100 miles. If you find any of these issues, talk to a tire professional about the possible causes and corrections.

3. If the tire is over five or six years old, even if there's plenty of tread left. Tires "age out" after a while, and if you are using a long-wearing tire like the Michelin LTX you will probably find they age out before they wear out. You can tell the age of the tire by reading the date code imprinted on the sidewall. (It may be on the side facing under the trailer, so you may need to crawl under with a flashlight to read it.)

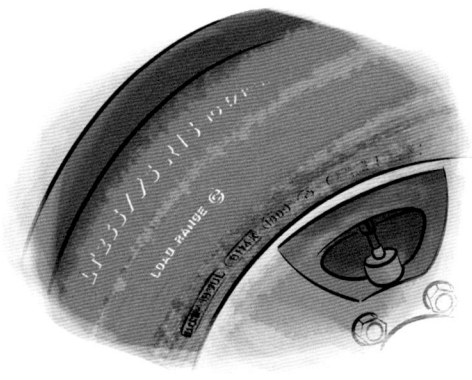

The date code is 4 digits printed on the sidewall in a little box. The first two digits are the week the tire was manufactured, the second two digits the year. For example, "2812" means the tire was manufactured in the 28th week of 2012. If your tire only has a three digit code, replace it ASAP, because it was made before the turn of the century.

4. If a tire develops a bulge in the tread or sidewalls. A bulge means something broken internally in the tire's structure. It's no longer safe to use.

   If you remove a tire and it seems strangely out of shape compared to the others, that's an indication of internal failure. You can get it checked by a professional to be sure, but it's probably in need of immediate replacement.

5. If the tire gets a puncture in the sidewall or on the tread within one inch of the sidewall. Typically when you bring such a tire in to a tire shop for repair, they'll give you the bad news and you'll be buying a new tire.

6. If the tire has been run while seriously underinflated (less than 75% of the rated max. pressure). Even though it might look OK, that tire has been stressed and is far more likely to have a rapid failure.

7. If the tire has "checking," meaning cracks. After a lot of time and UV exposure, especially if it sits a lot, the rubber will begin to break down. This will be most noticeable on the sidewall. Checking is a clear sign that you need fresh rubber on your Airstream.

When you replace the tires, don't forget the tire stems! Get new stems every time you buy tires or whenever they start to show cracks. Natural rubber stems are the cheapest choice but they deteriorate quickly so we don't recommend them. EPDM is a synthetic rubber which is used in most quality valve stems. It has a broader temperature range and resists ozone and chemicals that attack natural rubber.

If you have Load Range D tires (which take 65 psi) or higher, ask for "high pressure stems" that are reinforced with brass.

All-metal stems are also available, and are often recommended for users of tire pressure monitoring systems that screw onto the stems. Airstream Classic models with Alcoa wheels require a clamp-in style all-metal valve stem with a threaded metal nut.

Preventing tire damage

Between trips, cover your tires if they are exposed to the sun. You can buy simple tire covers at most RV stores or make them yourself. Using a tire cover cuts UV radiation (think sunburn on your tires) and heat, and your tires will last longer as a result.

Hidden tire damage is caused by using leveling blocks that aren't wide enough, so that part of the tire tread is hanging over the edge. Make sure that the leveling blocks you use are wider and longer than the tire "contact patch" (the part of the tire that touches the ground), and use ramped blocks if ascending more than a few inches. This distributes the tire load evenly.

Accessing and maintaining the spare tire

The spare tire for Airstreams is located under the front of the trailer body. There's a 1" square tube that serves as a handle, protruding from beneath the front of the body below the A-frame. It is secured by a bracket and a bolt with a cotter pin.

To access the spare tire, first lower the hitch jack to lift the trailer, so that there's plenty of clearance under the A-frame. Make sure the trailer tires are chocked if the trailer isn't on level ground. Pull out the cotter pin and hold up the handle while removing the bolt. Slide the bracket off and the full weight of the tire will be on the handle at that point. Lower the handle to the ground and the tire will be available to be slid out from under the trailer.

If you have trouble handling the weight of the tire, you might find this easier to do while sitting on the ground.

If the trailer is hitched up, be sure to raise the hitch jack fully once you're done, so you don't accidentally drive off and damage it.

Spare tire maintenance

Everyone forgets to check the pressure on the spare tire. Check it when you check the pressure on the other tires. If you keep the spare mounted so that the valve stem is facing downward, you can check the pressure without actually taking the spare out of its holder, although you will have to crawl under the trailer a little.

Check the date code and condition of the spare whenever you have the chance. For more about checking date codes and tire condition, see "When to replace tires," earlier in this section.

It's also a good idea to wash the spare tire and wheel once in a while, to remove build-up of road chemicals (fuel, salt, etc.) that might cause gradual damage to the tire or wheel. You can put the same polymer protectant that you use on the Airstream on the wheel to help preserve it.

Changing a tire

Everyone calls it "changing a tire" but what you are really doing is changing a tire and wheel assembly. The wheel is the metal part, the tire is the rubber part, and you are going to remove them as one piece. Later, a tire shop will remove the tire from the wheel to patch or replace it.

Airstreams don't come with the tools you need to change a tire, so it's up to you to obtain the necessary tools and carry them in the Airstream. The lug nuts on most Airstreams require a 13/16" socket, but some may need a 3/4" socket. You'll also need a 1/2" drive wrench (also called a "breaker bar") and a 6" or longer extension, or a cross-type lug nut tool. To put the lug nuts back on correctly, you should have a good quality torque wrench, also in the 1/2" drive size.

If you are working by the side of the road, it's a good idea to put out some flares, orange cones, or whatever you might have to warn people zooming by. At the very least turn on the hazard lights on the tow vehicle—they'll flash the Airstream's taillights too. Make sure you're visible too, by throwing on a reflective safety vest or shirt.

Get the spare tire and wheel out of its carrier. The procedure for that is described above. Check the air pressure in the spare. If it's low, you should add air to get it up to the recommended pressure. A tire that is low on air is likely to blow out, which could make things a lot worse. If the pressure in the spare is more than 15% low and you can't add air, you might consider three-wheel towing for a short time (see discussion below).

Next, loosen but do not remove the lug nuts of the wheel you need to remove. This is because it will be difficult to loosen those nuts once the wheel is off the ground. If you can't get the nuts off with your arms, try positioning the wrench so you can put your foot on it.

Jacking up the trailer

Jacking up an Airstream can be done in two ways. If you have a two or three axle Airstream and you just want to get the Airstream up enough to change a tire, you don't need a jack. Make a stack of leveling blocks in front or behind of the wheel you aren't removing (on the same side of the trailer), then pull the Airstream up on the blocks. This will allow the other tire to hang free in the air. If the tire isn't free to rotate, try again with a taller stack of blocks.

Jacking up a single axle Airstream is a little more involved, but not much. The difference is that you will need a hydraulic jack to lift the trailer. Airstream places a label that says "JACK" on the belly pan, just rear of the wheels. An arrow on the label points to a plate riveted to the main frame rail where you can put the jack. If you can't find the label, you can put the jack under an exposed section of the trailer's frame near the axle.

Don't use the axle or the belly pan for jacking. Your jack can damage the axles internally, and it will just punch through the belly pan.

No matter which method you use, set the parking brake on the tow vehicle and/or chock the wheels that are still on the ground so that they can't roll.

Remember, any jack is just for raising and lowering the trailer, and you shouldn't go crawling around under it when supported just by the jack. **Jackstands must be used if you need to work under the trailer.**

After jacking up the trailer and setting the parking brake on your tow vehicle, you can remove the lug nuts from the flat tire/wheel. Take the wheel off and put the spare on. Tighten the lug nuts until they are snug before you back the trailer down off the blocks, then continue with the procedure below.

Using a torque wrench

Once the tire is back on the ground, you must finish tightening the lug nuts to the factory spec. The correct torque is extremely important. Under the right amount of tension, the wheel is drawn to the brake hub face and the lug bolt will be well mated with the lug nut. Too much torque and the lug bolt will be stretched, and eventually break. Too little tension and the lug nut can work off.

You can't judge the correct tightness accurately by feel, so you need to carry a torque wrench. This is in the recommended equipment list in this book. Instructions on how to use your torque wrench should come with it. For most torque wrenches you set the target torque in foot-pounds and the wrench will "click" when you've tightened the nut to that setting. Remember to reset your torque wrench to zero when you are done with it.

On late model Airstreams, aluminum and steel wheels have torque specs running from 95 to 115 foot-pounds. Older trailers or those with replacement wheels may have other torque specifications. For example, a mid-1970s trailer with lug bolts (not lug nuts) would have a torque spec of 85 ft-lbs. Check the Owner's Manual or documentation for the wheels to verify the correct torque and make a note somewhere of that number so you have it handy when you have to replace a wheel.

Don't let tire shop personnel put your wheels on with an air wrench. Air wrenches can put out far too much torque and overstress the lug bolts. Instead, insist they use a manual (hand) wrench, or get a "torque stick" rated for 60 ft-lbs and have them use that. Then tighten the nuts to the correct torque specification with your torque wrench.

Better yet, just tell the tire shop to give you the wheels when they are done, and you can put them on yourself. That way you know it will be done right.

Use the torque wrench only to tighten the lug nuts, never to remove them. It's a calibrated instrument that can go out of whack if you use it to remove nuts.

It's very important to check the lug nuts after the trailer has been towed for a while. This is because the lug nuts need a little time to "seat" properly. A common recommendation is to check the lug nuts with your torque wrench after 25 miles, then again at 50 miles, and one last time after 100 miles from when you changed the tire. If you don't check and retighten the lug nuts to proper torque, they may loosen over time, which can lead to losing a wheel.

Instead of just going around the wheel doing each lug nut in sequence, use this pattern when tightening the nuts. The left sequence is for wheels with five lugs, and the right sequence is for wheels with six lugs.

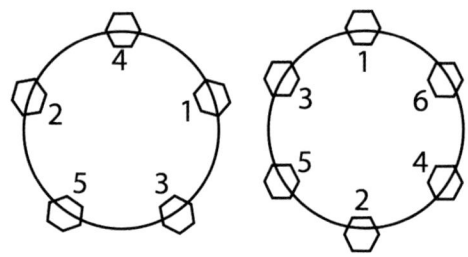

Three wheel towing

Perhaps you don't have a spare, or the spare is too low on air to be safely used, or you somehow managed to get two flats at the same time. If you have a two or three axle Airstream, you have another option. You can simply remove the flat tire and continue towing to the nearest service center.

Believe it or not, you can drive a short distance on three wheels (Airstream says up to 100 miles). But keep in mind that this will stress the remaining tires. You must reduce your speed to 30 MPH or less. Check the air pressure in the remaining tires before proceeding, and don't go farther than necessary.

Patch, plug, or replace?

That flat tire needs to be addressed. Take it to a good tire shop and have them check it. If the problem is just a clean puncture, it can be repaired.

These days the gold standard repair is a mushroom-shaped patch-plug. This seals the outside of the tire against water that could cause the tire's internal belts to rust and also seals the inner liner of the tire so that it will not leak. Ask the tire shop if they can do a patch-plug, and take your tire elsewhere if they can't.

If the tire damage is too severe or in the wrong place, you'll need to replace the tire. Don't hesitate. A tire blow-out can do major damage to your Airstream, and it's a false economy to try to "save" a tire that should be sent off for recycling.

Replacement tires

Long ago, most travel trailers owners simply used whatever truck tires were available. Then the tire industry invented the Special Trailer (ST) designated tire, which was supposed to have superior design for the needs of trailering. This designation has been the standard for travel trailers for decades.

These days, a lot of Airstream owners have become disenchanted with the ST tires, claiming that they are poorly built and prone to failure. So the pendulum has begun to swing back toward Light Truck (LT) designated tires.

While Airstream still outfits most of its trailers with ST tires, it has offered LT tires as standard equipment on Eddie Bauer edition trailers as well as the Panamerica trailer. Airstream also currently offers a 16" wheel upgrade that makes it easier for trailer owners to switch to LT tires.

Whichever you choose, keep in mind that quality matters. Don't just search for a cheap tire, thinking that it doesn't really matter much on a trailer. Look for a brand and model with a good reputation. For example, well-respected brand names such as Michelin produce excellent LT tires that have been used with success by many Airstream owners.

Also, when you buy tires be sure to check the date codes on them. Instructions on reading date codes are in the discussion "When to replace tires," earlier in this section. Sometimes tires have been sitting on the store shelves for months or even years, and you should reject old tires in favor of newer inventory. After all, the clock on that tire's life starts ticking when it is manufactured, not when you install it.

Wheel balancing

Have the tire shop balance the tire/wheel combination after they put on a new tire or patch an existing one. Some shops don't balance trailer tires unless specifically asked, but your Airstream will ride better with balanced wheels.

There's some debate about the best way to balance Airstream wheels. At the very least, the standard method of applying lead weights to the wheels will help. The shortcoming is that the axle hub may still throw the assembly off-balance a little.

If you want to go a step further, you can look into Centramatic wheel balancers. Centramatics are regarded highly because they are maintenance-free and will always dynamically balance the wheel even as the tire gradually wears out.

However, Dexter does not recommend use of Centramatics or any product that causes the wheel to be offset from the brake hub if your trailer is equipped with Dexter Nev-R-Lube bearings, because the change in wheel centerline position could result in bearing failure. Starting in the 2010 model year, Airstreams 25 feet and longer have been factory-equipped with Nev-R-Lube bearings. If you aren't sure whether yours has the conventional type, check with Airstream or your local Airstream dealer.

Brakes

Airstreams come with either drum or disc brakes. Both are operated by an electrical signal from the brake controller in tow vehicle. More voltage (DC) from the brake controller makes the brakes apply harder.

That's where the similarity ends, however. Drum brakes, which are the most common on Airstreams, use simple electromagnets to drag the brake shoes into contact with the brake hub. This causes friction and slows down the wheels.

Disc brake systems rely on a hydraulic actuator, which is a type of pump, to put pressure on brake fluid just like your foot does when you step on the brakes in the car. This brake fluid runs through lines to the wheels and is used to squeeze brake pads against a disc. The disc system is more complex and expensive, but it also provides better braking quality and power.

It's a good idea to keep a record of mileage and date when you do service on the brakes. This will give you an idea of how quickly your brakes are wearing, so you can plan replacement. Annual inspection is recommended for both drum and disc brake systems.

Drum brake adjustment

If you've got an Airstream from model year 2010 or later, there's no brake drum adjustment required. Those Airstreams have Nev-R-Adjust brakes from Dexter, which automatically adjust themselves as you use them.

Other Airstreams with drum brakes need periodic adjustment to keep the brake shoes in the optimal location as they wear. Dexter recommends that manual adjust brakes be adjusted after the first 200 miles of operation (for new brakes), and at 3,000 mile intervals thereafter or whenever you notice a change in performance. It's pretty easy.

First, jack up the trailer and secure it (see "Jacking up the trailer" in the Running Gear and A-frame section). The wheel that you are adjusting should be off the ground so that it can rotate freely. Remove the wheel and tire.

Remove the adjusting hole cover—a small rubber plug—from the adjusting slot on the bottom of the brake backing plate.

With a screwdriver or a brake adjustment tool (available at auto parts stores), rotate the star wheel of the adjuster assembly to expand the brake shoes. Adjust the shoes outward until they are in light contact with the hub. The wheel should turn freely with a slight drag. When you're done, replace the adjusting hole plug.

All of the brakes should be adjusted at the same time, so continue around the trailer to the rest of the wheels.

Drum brake inspection

Airstream recommends cleaning and inspection of the drum brakes once a year. This requires disassembling the brake drum to see all the internal parts, so it's a good job to do combined with the annual wheel bearing packing. See "Wheel bearing and brake service" later in this section for instructions on how to disassemble the brake drum.

Note that brake shoes typically contain asbestos, so be careful about inhaling dust or creating dust. Clean brake parts using a damp cloth, not compressed air or a brush.

With the drum brake hub removed, check the brake shoes to make sure the friction material doesn't have any cracks and that the lining is still at least 3/32" thick. Any brake shoes with paper thin linings should be replaced. Always replace the shoes in axle sets, meaning that if you have to replace the brake shoes on one wheel you should replace the set on the other wheel that shares the axle. That keeps the braking force equal side to side.

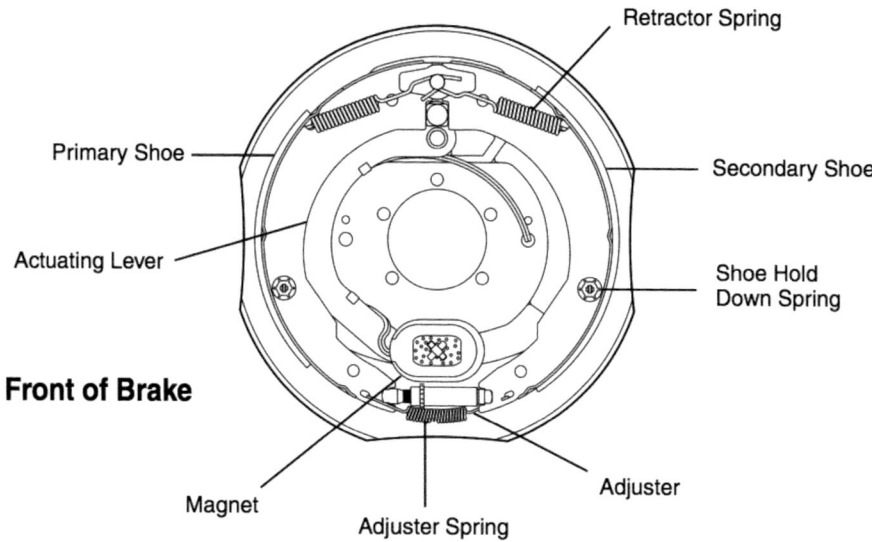

Front of Brake

While you're inspecting the brake assembly, look for loose or worn parts, broken or stretched springs, broken or chafed wires to the brake magnets, or anything that doesn't look "right." Magnets have friction surfaces, which must be intact, and the magnets should not be unevenly worn.

Any parts that you replace should be replaced on the other brakes as well. Most drum brake assemblies (complete shoe/backing plate/magnet/hardware) are inexpensive enough that often people will simply replace the entire thing, rather than deal with dismantling and reassembling the brakes.

Disc brake maintenance and inspection

With disc brakes, DC voltage from the tow vehicle is being used to signal the disc brake actuator (a hydraulic pump) how hard it should push the brakes. Unlike drum brakes, the disc brake actuator isn't powered by the voltage from the tow vehicle. It only uses that voltage as a signal, and instead relies on 12 volt power from the trailer's battery for its own operation.

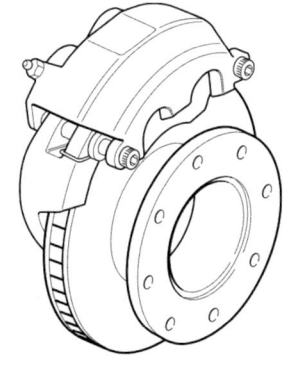

When you press the brake in your tow vehicle, the actuator pumps hydraulic fluid, and this fluid presses the disc brake pads against the sides of the rotors. Friction between the pads and the rotors slows down the trailer. The picture shows a typical disc brake assembly.

Disc brakes give a much smoother braking action, but the actuator introduces a small delay in their reaction time. That's because the hydraulic pump takes a moment to get up to speed. Typically this is only a fraction of a second. If you are experiencing a large delay, a common cause is air in the brake lines. The brake lines can be bled just like those on a car, so if you have the knowledge of how to do that, you can do your own.

You should check the fluid level in the brake actuator regularly, and certainly after a long period of storage. The brake actuator manufacturer (often Dexter or Carlisle, although there are several others) will have recommendations for how often to do this and what type of brake fluid to use.

Usually the fluid level should be between 3/8 to 1/2 inch from the top of the filler tube, but follow the manufacturer's recommendation. Use care to prevent contamination of the fluid with dirt, water, or other foreign material when removing the filler cap, checking the fluid level, or when adding fluid to the reservoir.

Disc brake inspection can be done any time the wheels are being removed from the Airstream. It's a good idea to check the disc brakes every year and whenever you notice a change in braking performance.

Inspection should include checking the disc pads for wear (thin pads should be replaced) or uneven wear. The rotors should be checked for wear, scoring, signs of excessive heat build up, cracks, and warpage. All bolted connections should be tight, and there should never be any fluid leaking near the calipers or the brake lines. The hydraulic brake hoses should be flexible and free of cracks or nicks. Any of these conditions are reason to get a professional brake assessment and repair.

Wheel bearing and brake service

Wheel bearings are arguably one of the most critical parts of your Airstream's suspension, but also one of the most overlooked. Wheel bearings are reliable and low maintenance but they do require regular attention. Airstream recommends cleaning and repacking them annually. Spring is usually a good time to perform this task, and you can add it into your "getting ready for camping season" routine.

Note that this procedure is for drum brakes; owners of disc-equipped Airstreams will follow a slightly different procedure.

Currently, there are two types of bearings available on Airstream trailers, which are sized to the configuration of the brake system. The most common are the standard, or "serviceable" bearings, and the other is a relatively recent arrival on the scene, the Dexter Nev-R-Lube. The Nev-R-Lube bearings have been standard equipment on all Airstream trailers 25 feet and longer since the 2010 model year. Classic trailers with disc brakes may have Nev-R-Lube bearings from as early as July 2005 (date of manufacture).

Nev-R-Lube bearings

Nev-R-Lube is designed to be just that, requiring no lubrication for the life of the bearing, which is warranted for five years or 100,000 miles. Still, Dexter recommends inspection every year or 12,000 miles.

To check the Nev-R-Lube bearings simply jack up the trailer as described in this book. Check for play in the hub/wheel assemblies by holding the top and bottom of the tire and attempting to wiggle the assembly in and out. A good Nev-R-Lube bearing will have almost no play laterally.

Next, simply rotate the tire around, as if it were rolling down the highway. A good Nev-R-Lube bearing will rotate smoothly, with no roughness or "growling." A Nev-R-Lube bearing that has internal damage may feel "rough" as the wheel rotates around.

Finally, check for excess lube seeping out of the seals on the bearing. A slight amount of seepage is normal, but enough oil to lube the ball on your trailer hitch indicates a problem.

Replacement of a Nev-R-Lube cartridge is not difficult, but requires a bit more equipment than the average Do-It-Yourselfer has on hand. Most people should take their Airstream to the dealer to replace a Nev-R-Lube bearing.

By the way, you can't switch from Nev-R-Lube to conventional bearings without also swapping out the axle.

Standard bearings

Maintenance of the standard, or "serviceable" type wheel bearings requires a bit more mechanical ability but tools and equipment the average DIY-er can easily obtain. This job will require a can of quality wheel bearing grease, one grease seal for each wheel on your Airstream, a supply of shop towels (paper towels), new cotter pins to replace the ones you are going to remove, and an adjusting tool known as a brake spoon.

First, you need to raise and support your Airstream as described in "Jacking up the trailer". Next, spin the wheel, feeling for roughness while the assembly rotates. Listen for any odd noises. A metallic rattle while spinning a wheel generally indicates something in the braking system has come loose, so beware of flying and falling objects when you get to the point of removing the brake drum.

Next, remove the dust cap from the hub, which will expose the castle nut, which is secured in place by a cotter pin. The castle nut is so named because it resembles the walls of a medieval castle, with ramparts and turrets, when viewed from the side.

The cotter pin will be bent over the end of the spindle (threaded part of the hub) to keep the castle nut from moving while traveling. To remove the cotter pin, simply bend it back straight so it will slide out of the hole it has been inserted into at the end of

the spindle, and slide it out. Unscrew the castle nut. Usually you will only need your fingers, but sometimes a small pair of slip joint pliers will be needed to get things moving.

Once the castle nut has been removed, you should be able to lift slightly on the hub and drum assembly and pull it straight off the spindle. After you remove the hub and drum, you will be able to examine the brakes. Follow the instructions above for drum brake inspection or disc brake inspection.

After your brake inspection is complete, pry the grease seal out of the hub either using a special tool for prying out grease seals or a stout screwdriver, and remove both the inner and outer bearings. Check the bearings for pits in the barrels, cracks, missing chunks, and discoloration of the bearings. If you see anything like that, replace the bearing.

After you've looked them over, clean them in a solvent (not gasoline) and let them dry. While they are drying, take a shop rag and wipe all the old grease out of the hub. After you do that, look carefully at the races (the surface the bearings ride on inside the hub). Check them for the same issues as the bearings themselves, paying particular attention to the race where you have noticed a damaged bearing. If you see any scoring or roughness, you will need to replace that race.

While you're at it, take a look at the surface the magnet rides on, inside the wheel drum. This is the flat surface inside the drum, parallel to the wheel. If it has a lot of grooves worn in it, or it has one or two deep grooves, you will need to take the drum to be machined or replace it. If machining, make sure the shop performing the work can machine the magnet surface as well as the friction surface. If the surface of the drum is badly grooved or scored, you should also replace the magnet.

Now that everything has been taken apart and examined, it can be cleaned up, the bearings packed and the hub reassembled and reinstalled. Clean the area the magnet rides on with a quality brake cleaner. Avoid breathing the brake dust, as it can contain asbestos.

Once everything is clean and dry, you can pack the bearings. "Packing" means forcing the bearing grease into the bearing. The common method is to take a palmful of grease, and work it into the bearing. Add some grease to the race, then install the inner bearing, and then drive the grease seal into the hub, with the spring on the rubber part of the seal facing the bearing. Apply a little grease to the lip of the seal, reinstall the hub assembly on the spindle, then repeat the process with the outer bearing.

Along with the outer bearing, you should find an odd-shaped flat washer with a tab sticking inward, which goes on after the bearing is placed on the spindle, with the tab going into a slot in the spindle. Reinstall the castle nut, tightening it just past snug, then backing it off to the point where the lowered part is aligned with the hole in the spindle for the cotter pin.

Install a new cotter pin, bending it over the end of the spindle, then make sure the drum assembly rotates freely. If it does, replace the dust cap, then adjust the brakes as described earlier under "Drum brake adjustment."

Pull the pin on the breakaway switch and attempt to rotate the drum. If it won't move, you're done. You can reinstall the pin in the breakaway switch and reinstall the tire.

After you get all your bearings taken care of and tires reinstalled, check the tires for proper inflation and take your Airstream for a test drive. When you're done with that, you can bask in the glow of having performed this task yourself, and saved some cash by doing it.

Don't forget, since you've removed the wheels, you need to re-torque the nuts at 25, 50, and 100 miles as described in "Using a torque wrench" earlier in this section.

Troubleshooting electrical problems with brakes

Your trailer brakes must be inspected and serviced immediately if there's any loss of performance. Onlxy qualified persons who know about brakes and brake systems should perform brake installation or repair. However, if you are having trouble with your brakes, there are a few basic things to check before you bring your Airstream into the service center.

If only one of the drum brakes seems to be malfunctioning, it may be a mechanical fault (broken parts, worn brakes, poor adjustment, etc.) or an electrical fault (electrical short, broken wire, loose connection, etc.). Many problems are electrical, so check for loose or damaged wires, and follow the instructions given earlier under "Drum brake adjustment".
The problem may become obvious during your visual inspection and adjustment.

If all of the brakes are not working, then you need to start at the tow vehicle. First, verify that the brake controller in the tow vehicle is correctly adjusted and operating, using the procedure outlined by the manufacturer of that controller.

Most modern brake controllers can detect some types of faults in electric brakes. If your brake controller indicates a short circuit, suspect chafed wires or shorted magnet coils in the brakes themselves. Once again, it's time for disassembly and repair.

There are a few more things you can check. The 7-way plug is the most common trouble area, as it is exposed to the elements and the wear of frequent plugging and unplugging. This causes corrosion and bad electrical contacts. There can also be fatigue breaks in the wires, with short circuits or open circuits depending on whether the broken wire is touching another one. Since the ground wire is next to the brake control wire in the plug, any errant strand of wire can touch and ground (short).

Inspect the 7-way connector at both the tow vehicle and the trailer's cord, to ensure all the contacts are clean and making good electrical contact. See "Maintaining the 7-way trailer cord" in the Electrical section for details on how to clean the contacts.

Once the contacts are clean, you can check the voltage. You'll need a DC voltmeter. Make sure the tow vehicle is switched ON (even if not actually running) so that there is power to the brake controller. The discussion on "Maintaining the 7-way trailer cord" includes a diagram showing which pins to check for voltage. Have a helper slowly move the manual brake lever on the tow vehicle's brake controller while you monitor the voltage at the tow vehicle's 7-way connector.

As your helper moves the lever, you should see the voltage increasing at the 7-way connector on the tow vehicle, simultaneous with the read-out on the brake controller.

If the 7-way connectors on both the tow vehicle and trailer look good, and voltage is being applied, but the brakes still don't work, you'll have to start checking the brakes themselves and/or make a deeper inspection of the brake wiring in the belly pan of the trailer. This gets into disassembly and repair, so at this point we'll recommend you take it into a service center, unless you have the tools and knowledge to repair the brakes yourself.

You've ruled out the tow vehicle as the cause of the problem, so at least the service center technician can focus on the trailer itself. The brake drum will likely have to be removed for further diagnosis. The technician can also run tests on electrical amperage and voltage to identify problems like a short or open circuit inside the brakes.

If you want to do more yourself, Dexter Axle has extensive downloadable information for installation, service, troubleshooting, and much more (all free) on their website at **www.dexteraxle.com**.

Axles

Torsion axles have been installed on Airstreams since 1961, and they haven't changed much since. A torsion axle has rubber cords inside it, to which arms are attached on both ends of the axle. The trailer wheels are attached to the arms and can flex up and down, using the rubber cords of the axle like springs. This is a key part of what gives an Airstream a smooth ride.

For decades these axles were made by Henschen, but through corporate acquisitions the Henschen brand eventually became part of Dexter Axle. Regardless, the basic construction of the axle has remained the same—a highly reliable design that has survived the test of time.

The axle is pre-bent to have the correct alignment specs needed by your Airstream. If you look underneath the trailer near the center you'll probably see something like a "dent" in the middle of the axle, which is a bend put there during manufacturing to give the axle the correct camber (the angle of the wheel relative to the ground). It is also bent in more subtle ways for toe-in.

If you are seeing rapid and uneven tire wear on new tires that can't be explained by something like underinflation, it could be the result of a misalignment of the axle. The alignment can be adjusted by a shop that aligns trailer axles. Otherwise, the axle is maintenance-free.

An axle goes out of alignment as a result of rough travel. Potholes, curbs, and rough roads contribute to this problem. To get it back into spec is basically a matter of simply applying force to the axle to bend it very precisely.

This is why you should never jack up the Airstream using the axle tube. Although it looks like tough steel, you can bend it out of alignment or even damage the inner rubber cords. Also, never allow heat (from a torch or welder for example) to be applied to the axle, for the same reason. Other than normal realignment, torsion axles are not repairable; they are replaced when damaged.

After about twenty years or so, or sooner if the trailer has sat for many years, plan to replace the axle. The rubber cords inside the axle start to stiffen and deteriorate with time and lack of use, so even though there may be no apparent change in the Airstream, the axle is giving less "spring" and transmitting more shock to the trailer body. It's not a very expensive part considering how long it lasts, and many people do it themselves with a little instruction from the axle dealer.

Shock absorbers

Shock absorbers are installed on most Airstreams (exceptions include Sport models and some Bambi models). Just like the ones in a car, their function is simply to reduce "bounce" and limit transmission of shocks from bumps and potholes.

Shocks will need to be replaced when they are worn out or damaged. Oil leaking out of the shock is the result of a bad seal on the shock and definitely means it's replacement time. Damage such as a lot of rust, a broken sleeve, or worn out mounting bushings is another indicator.

If you've decided it's time for replacement shock absorbers and you own an Airstream built after about 1968, when Airstream switched to a horizontally mounted shock absorber, you really have only two choices for replacement shocks. The first option is to get them from your friendly Airstream dealer. The shocks used on those Airstream trailers are designed specifically for horizontal mounting and are only available through Airstream dealers.

The second option is to substitute a shock that fits and is known to perform well in horizontal mounting. Colin Hyde of Colin Hyde Trailer Restorations in Plattsburgh, New York, has tested various shocks and recommends the Monroe Gas Magnum, part number 555003 as a suitable replacement.

If you own an Airstream trailer built from the late 1960s and earlier, you can use an automotive style vertical-mount shock. A trip to your local auto parts store should net you a set that will work just fine on your Airstream. It helps to go to one of the small, locally-owned auto parts stores, rather than one of those national DIY-oriented stores. A trip to the latter will usually result in the younger, not-so-savvy parts person looking at you like you just stepped off a UFO in the company of Elvis, rather than getting a set of shock absorbers.

Replacing the shocks is not always simple, so attempt it only if you have good DIY skills and tools. To start, first raise and support your

Airstream safely, either one wheel at a time, by pulling it up on ramps of wood or stacked leveling blocks, or one side at a time using a jack. (See "Jacking up the trailer" in the "Changing a tire" discussion, earlier in this section.)

Before crawling under the trailer or removing any tire/wheel assemblies, place a jack stand under the frame of the trailer. With the trailer raised and at least one wheel off the ground, remove that wheel and tire assembly so you can access the shock. If it's been a while since you last checked your brakes and wheel bearings, this is the perfect time to take care of that. (See "Wheel bearing and brake service" for details.)

Use penetrating oil liberally on the exposed threads of the shock mounting bolts and give it some time to work. Then unscrew the nut on the frame of the trailer (usually 3/4" hex), remove the flat washer behind that, and pull the shock off the mount.

Here's the tricky part: Grasp the loose end of the shock, and pull it toward you until the mounting ear on the trailing arm of the spindle mount bends outward slightly. You want just enough bend so the rubber grommet on the end of the shock will clear the threaded end of the mounting ear and frame. When you accomplish this, remove the 3/4" nut and flat washer from that stud and remove the shock.

Installation is the reverse of removal, but you shouldn't have to bend the mounting ear back into place when you're done.

Sometimes this procedure doesn't go well, so be forewarned. For example, sometimes either the threads on the studs are damaged or the entire stud breaks off while trying to remove the nut. While inconvenient, this is not the end of the world. You will need to head back to your local auto parts store and get a replacement shock stud kit. This kit consists of a stud like the one you just broke off, plus a nut-and-bolt replacement mount on the back side of it. You drill a hole in either the frame or mounting ear, slide the nut-and-bolt replacement mount through the hole you just drilled, and tighten the nut.

Another "bad day" problem: In some cases (generally on replacement axles with higher-than-stock starting angles on the trailing arms) you may find the shock is either not quite long enough to reach both mounting studs, or the shock will not align with both studs due to interference with the trailing arm's extreme angle.

The solution to this is to install the end of the shock on the trailing arm, install the tire and wheel assembly, and lower it to the ground. The weight of the trailer will move the trailing arm so you can reach under the front edge of the tire, slide the shock on the mounting stud, and reinstall the nut and flat washer.

Loading

Loading an Airstream for travel is pretty easy. By design, if you put things where they are convenient (food and kitchen tools in the kitchen, clothes in the closets, etc.) the Airstream will usually be set up about right—not too heavy in any particular spot, and with the proper "tongue weight" at the front.

But since everyone carries different things, you still need to verify that the trailer and tow vehicle are carrying the right amount of weight in the right proportions. For example, North American spec Airstreams should have 10-15% of the weight of the trailer at the hitch ball ("tongue weight"). (For European spec Airstreams the percentage is considerably lower and it is called "nose weight.")

When loading your Airstream, heavy items should be placed low and as close to the axles as possible, for stability. Exceptionally heavy items at the front might increase the tongue weight above what your tow vehicle can carry. If too much weight is located at the rear the tongue weight might get too low, which can seriously de-stabilize the trailer and encourage dangerous sway.

The industry and government use a long series of acronyms to define various weight ratings and they can get very confusing, so for the purpose of this discussion we'll focus on the most critical ones. Here's a table to explain what they mean:

	NORTH AMERICA	EUROPE
"Empty" weight of your Airstream as built	Unloaded Vehicle Weight (UVW)	Mass in Running Order (MRO), or Unladen Weight (includes propane and fresh water)
Weight at the hitch ball	Tongue weight	Nose weight
Maximum allowable weight of the trailer when loaded, including propane and liquids in holding tanks	Gross Vehicle Weight Rating (GVWR)	Maximum Technically Permissible Laden Mass (MTPLM), or Maximum Authorized Mass
Maximum weight of your truck and trailer combination	Gross Combination Weight Rating (GCWR)	Gross Train Weight (GTW)

On some late-model Airstreams the weight limits are printed on the serial number plate that is attached to the body on the lower front street side. Trailers manufactured starting in 2009 will also have a sticker on the screen door showing the maximum cargo carrying capacity. On earlier trailers the weight limits are printed on a sticker that is attached inside the first wardrobe closet on the curbside, about 60" off the floor.

Vintage Airstream owners can find weight ratings on a chart published by Airstream on their website. Owners of trailers made in the 1960s and 1970s with front fresh water tanks often find that their trailers tow better with a full tank of water because it adds the correct amount of tongue weight.

Note that the difference between the maximum allowable weight and the unloaded weight is your net carrying capacity. On some trailers this can be over 1,500 pounds, which is quite a lot of stuff, while on some smaller trailers it can be as little as 300 pounds. You should know this capacity and keep it in mind when you are packing for a trip.

Weighing before your next trip

You should verify that your Airstream when loaded is under its maximum allowable weight, that the tongue weight is in the range of 10-15%, and that those loads are safe for the tow vehicle you are using. Technically this isn't a "maintenance" topic but it is included here because **failure to observe weight ratings can result in severe damage to the Airstream, an accident, or death.** In other words, it's a form of maintenance for <u>you</u> and everyone who travels with you.

Further, even if the Airstream is below its maximum weight rating, you need to verify that the distribution of the trailer's tongue weight on both axles of your tow vehicle is correct. It doesn't matter how big your truck is. It doesn't matter if you "can hardly feel the Airstream," or if you "never had a problem." You need to get this right.

Why? Because one day it will make a difference. That will be the day that you have to do a panic stop, or a sudden avoidance maneuver on the highway, or when the wind is blowing 30 knots off your starboard bow, or when you accidentally let the trailer drop a wheel off the edge of the pavement, or any number of other unexpected situations. One day, you'll have to ask your rig to do something extraordinary, and you'll want it to behave.

Without proper weight distribution, that rig you thought was so great when it was towing straight down the road might do something really unexpected. Perhaps the rear brakes will lock up prematurely in a hard stop. You might not be able to control a sway, or stay on the road in a turn. You might feel the trailer "wag the dog." Quite likely you'll have an accident and afterward only know that something bad happened and you're not sure why.

Yet, relatively few travel trailer owners bother to go through the simple exercise of weighing the tow vehicle and trailer. Here, we'll discuss how to weigh it and the numbers you're looking for.

The best and easiest way to verify the correct weights is by visiting a truck scale. The most common ones are CAT Scales, but you can also find truck scales at trash and recycling centers, independent truck stops, and roadside weigh stations. For locations, check catscale.com or do a web search for "weigh station locations."

Typically a truck scale will provide three separate weights: front (or "steer") axle, rear (or "drive") axle, and trailer axles (all counted together). To get started you will need a baseline, which means the weight of your tow vehicle as it is normally configured for towing (including passengers, fuel, and cargo) without the trailer attached. So your first trip through the scale should be without your trailer.

You'll end up with a report from the scale showing the amount of weight on each axle of the tow vehicle. (The trailer axle amount should be zero.) Pull out the Owner's Manual for your vehicle, or check inside the driver's side door jamb for a sticker, and get the Gross Axle Weight Rating (GAWR) for both the front and rear axles. The weights you got from the scale should be well below the GAWRs.

Now hitch up the trailer as you normally do, and go through the scale again. The Airstream should be loaded for travel and it should have full fresh water and empty black and gray tanks (because this is the configuration you'll most often travel in.) This time you will get a report from the scale with all three axle weights shown: front, rear, and trailer.

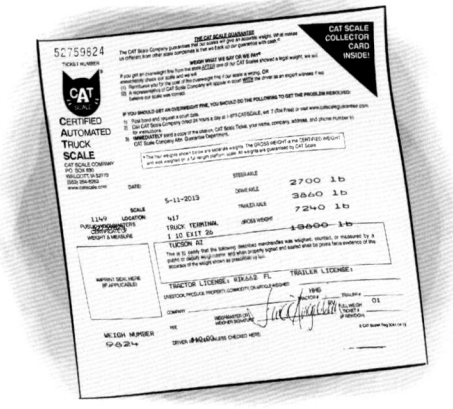

Compare the two reports, line by line. First, the trailer weight should be below the GVWR stated by Airstream. If it's not, the trailer is overloaded and you must reduce your cargo before going further. Go home and take a hard look at what you are packing.

More likely, you'll find that the Airstream is loaded below the GVWR, so you can move on to the front and rear axle weights of the tow vehicle. Here's where people often get confused.

The tongue weight of the Airstream presses down on the rear of your tow vehicle. If you don't have a weight distributing hitch, all of this weight will be added to the rear axle, and the front axle will get a little lighter. Imagine a playground teeter-totter, with the rear axle of your tow vehicle as the fulcrum (center). If a kid sits on the hitch ball end of the teeter-totter, the other end will go up. The other end is the front axle of your vehicle.

Reducing weight at the front axle of the truck is not good. Less weight on the steering wheels can cause a condition called "understeer" where the wheels don't grip the road enough to control the vehicle. In severe cases, it feels like driving on ice. In less severe cases it can be hard to notice until you have to make an emergency maneuver—then you discover at the worst possible moment that the vehicle doesn't want to go where you command it. A light front axle also affects the braking adversely, giving the front tires less ability to slow you down.

That's why we use weight-distributing hitches for heavy trailers. Weight-distributing hitches transfer some of that tongue weight to the front axle of the vehicle, thus restoring the correct performance of the steering.

Very light trailers don't put enough weight on the rear to cause much lifting of the front axle, so weight distribution isn't really needed, but for any Airstream made for the US market after the 1960s (and even some from earlier years) weight distribution is highly recommended or even mandatory. It doesn't matter if you have a vehicle with a strong leaf-spring suspension, rear air bags, or full air suspension. All those do is make it impossible to see the impact of the weight on the rear. They don't correct the reduction of weight on the front axle.

Similarly, if when setting up your hitch initially you used the old technique of measuring the corners of the truck to see how much each corner dropped, you still need to go to a truck scale. That method is really obsolete today, with modern vehicles that have different suspensions front and rear. At best, it's a rough estimate.

The scale will tell you the real story. First compare the GAWR provided by the tow vehicle manufacturer to the actual front and rear axle weights from the scale. If either GAWR is exceeded, that's a problem. It's surprisingly common for the rear GAWR to be exceeded when a weight-distributing hitch is not used or set up correctly. The big danger here is a rear tire blowout, so you want to take this seriously and adjust your weight-distributing hitch to try to move some weight off the overloaded axle.

If there's too much weight on the rear axle, the hitch is probably not set up correctly. Consult the owner's manual for your hitch and follow instructions to adjust the torsion bars. <u>Don't attempt to lighten tongue weight by moving your cargo to the rear of the trailer.</u> The tongue weight needs to run no less than 10% of the total trailer weight, so trying to lighten it can be dangerous.

Next you should compare the unhitched weights of the front and rear axles to the hitched weights of those axles. Most likely you'll find that one axle increased in weight by much more than the other. This is not necessarily a problem, because some tow vehicles (like pickup trucks and some SUVs) are light in the rear end, so they have more net carrying capacity available on the rear axle. The important thing here is that they are both carrying a share of the load and that overall balance of the vehicle (front vs. rear) is still as close as possible to 50/50. Few vehicles will be able to hit 50/50 exactly.

The exact mechanism for adjusting the weight distribution depends on the hitch system you're using. It may be a matter of just shortening the weight bar chains one link (on a Reese), or tightening the strut jacks (on a Hensley). On some vehicles it may also help to angle the tow ball rearward, modify the ball mount to get the tow ball closer to the rear axle, or any combination of these things.

Some hitches are better than others at weight distribution. Regardless of the type of hitch you use, check with someone who knows hitches if you are having trouble. Sometimes the hitch receiver on your vehicle will flex so much that it acts like a spring, bending rather than distributing the weight stress. Reinforcement or repair may be necessary.

Towing with safe loads and getting the weight distribution right pays off in safety and driving pleasure. You'll find it much less stressful when you aren't fighting the steering every time you encounter rough pavement, or get passed by a truck, so it's well worth the investment to fine-tune your hitch system.

Carrying bicycles

Carrying bicycles has always been a challenge for Airstream trailer owners. There are several ways to do it, and all of them have compromises, so pick your favorite.

Front of truck: Many trucks can be outfitted with a front hitch receiver. This is handy if you ever need to push an Airstream into a tight spot, but most people use them for hitch-mounted bike racks. The downside is that your bikes will be on the vanguard of any road debris or fender-bender you may encounter.

Roof of tow vehicle: Usually a Thule or Yakima roof rack on a tow vehicle is a little too high to be convenient, so you'll want to bring a folding step with you. The advantage is that you have your bikes with you when you drive away from the campsite (perhaps heading to a mountain bike trail).

Truck bed: This is the easiest solution for pickup truck owners. A simple fork mount can be purchased that holds bikes securely. If you have a truck cap your bikes will be protected from weather and theft, and it's easy to get a bike out of the truck bed when you want it. The major downside of this is that bikes take up a lot of space, so you may have to clear other stuff out of the way.

Riding inside the Airstream: You can just dump them inside the Airstream hallway, but you'll want to take some precautions against getting bike grease on the furniture, and find some way to keep the bikes from sliding around. Some people remove the wheels and toss the bike frame on a sacrificial sheet on the bed. This is not as convenient as it sounds, since you still have to get the bikes out of the way when you want to use the Airstream.

Rear receiver on the Airstream: It is feasible to have a hitch receiver welded on to the rear of an Airstream as long as it is attached to more than one structural member. You wouldn't want to put a lot of weight on it, but the weight of two bicycles and a rack is acceptable for any late-model Airstream with no structural issues (like floor rot or frame rust). This is a custom job that can be done by welding shops.

Fiamma rack: There is an Airstream-approved bike rack available that bolts to the bumper and body of the Airstream. It's about $500 and requires some installation. This is a nice aluminum rack, but it may restrict access to rear compartment and bumper storage, and may block the rear escape window when loaded.

Storage and Seasonal

Choosing a place to store

The location you choose to store your Airstream can be one of the most important decisions you make for its long-term health. Don't jump at the first place that occurs to you—take some time to think about the best location, both for you and for the Airstream.

There are five major factors to consider:

1. **Security.** As improbable as it seems, Airstream owners have their trailers stolen just like cars, even from supposedly "secure" gated RV storage lots with 24-hour security. Vandalism and break-ins are not uncommon either. Depending on where you live, your Airstream may be safer in your driveway, carport, back yard, or garage where it's not among a sea of other RVs, and where you and your neighbors can keep an eye on it.

   In any case, storing the Airstream out of sight, as in a barn or indoor storage facility, decreases the likelihood that someone will decide it's a good target.

   If you're not confident about the security of your parking location, consider installing a security system (adapted from car security systems) with motion sensor, glass breakage sensor, impact sensor, and a loud alarm. At a minimum, install the sturdiest hitch lock you can find or block the Airstream with another vehicle. We recommend Megahitch Lock "Coupler Vault". To make life harder for thieves, lower the power hitch jack down below the normal level and take the fuse out.

2. **Access to hookups.** It's a huge advantage to have access to electricity at your storage location. Having an electric outlet near your parking site means you can plug in the trailer for recharging or running a vacuum for

cleanup (or other tools). If 30-amp is available you can even run the air conditioning when needed.

It's a bonus if water or a dump are available. Then you have the convenience of dumping the trailer tanks after a trip, and you can more easily winterize the trailer or wash it.

If electricity is not available at your storage location, consider installing a solar panel or two to maintain the batteries between trips. (See "Solar panels" in the Electrical section for details.)

3. **Proximity to home.** Having your Airstream at home means you don't have to travel to a storage lot every time you want to check on it, do maintenance, or get something you left in it. If you can have utilities installed near the trailer (water, electric, sewer) then the Airstream can serve as a guest house, and you have a spare refrigerator and freezer, too!

Having the Airstream close to home also gives you a complete "spare" home in the event of a major power, water, or gas outage. Keep it ready to go, with full propane and water, and you've got the best tool in the world to escape natural disasters or other emergencies.

4. **Cover.** As discussed in the Leak Prevention, Detection and Repair section, keeping your Airstream under a roof is one of the best ways to delay UV damage and possible rainwater leaks. If you have the option to keep your Airstream under cover, even if it's just a roof with no side walls, seriously consider it. If you are parking your Airstream at home, you might want to erect a roof or storage barn.

If you store in a barn, make sure that humidity is controlled. There should be good ventilation and some sort of vapor barrier in the floor. Don't store the Airstream inside a sealed vinyl tent. High humidity can be just as damaging as rainwater leaks, as humidity is a factor in filiform corrosion and mold growth. (See "Filiform corrosion" in the Aluminum Body Repair section.)

Don't put a tarp on your Airstream! It's very hard to prevent a tarp from flapping or shifting in the wind, and the abrasive effect will leave permanent marks on the trailer's clear coat. It can also trap moisture next to the trailer body, accelerating corrosion.

5. **Rodents, insects and birds.** Two of the worst places to store your Airstream are out in a field and in the woods. Another problem area is out in the desert where pack rats are abundant. Find a hard-surfaced area away from clutter, tall weeds, and damp ground.

   It's also better to avoid storing the Airstream under trees. Bird droppings from overhead nests and decaying leaves can accumulate on the roof, and their acidity is tough on the painted surface.

Short-term storage

For short-term storage (less than 30 days), assuming the trailer is not plugged into power, the USE/STORE switch by the entry door of your aluminum Airstream should be put in the STORE position. This disconnects the house batteries from everything in the trailer except the propane leak detector, which means the batteries won't go dead as quickly. The batteries will still naturally drain down a little during this time, but if they are in good condition it should not be a problem. On Basecamp, Interstate, Atlas, and Nest, there's a Battery Disconnect switch that provides the same function.

For 2017 and earlier aluminum trailers, the batteries will not charge even if the trailer is plugged in, when the switch is in the STORE position. Starting in 2018, Airstream changed the wiring so that the batteries will charge when the trailer is plugged in, regardless of the position of the USE/STORE switch.

A checklist for short term storage is a good idea. You don't want to forget that you left a roof vent open, for example, or forgot to turn off the water pump. Checklists can be adapted from *"The Newbies Guide To Airstreaming,"* if you want a starting point.

Rodent and insect problems

You're not the only one who thinks an Airstream is a comfortable place to live. Wasps and bees love to make nests in furnace and water heater vents. Mice and rats like to burrow and spend the winter in the warm insulation. Snakes sometimes follow the rodents, and pretty soon you've got a food chain going.

If you live in a rural area and have little choice about storing your Airstream amongst the wildlife, consider putting in a gravel pad to get the

Airstream on firmer ground, and a roof overhead. Then, make sure you clear the trailer completely of anything that might attract rodents or ants, and consider setting out some traps too.

Despite your best efforts, it's not uncommon to find signs of rodent or insect infestations during your Storage inspection. Don't feel too bad, it's an easy problem to fix as long as you catch it early.

First, clean up the damage. If there are droppings inside a cabinet, for example, pull everything out of the cabinet. Clean it all out carefully, because rodent droppings can carry diseases, and wipe down the area with a weak bleach and water solution to disinfect. Check for further damage such as chewed holes and patch as needed.

Next, get rid of any food sources the mice have been able to access. Rodents can chew through just about anything, but they will go for the easy pickings first. A wrapped chocolate bar is just as easy for them to open as it is for you, so store such items inside stronger containers or in the refrigerator. Breakfast cereal and other bulk food items are best stored in plastic resealable jars.

With their obvious food supply sealed away or removed, you can focus on evicting your unwanted houseguests. The easiest way to get rid of mice is to just hitch up the trailer and go. They hate traveling, and will usually abandon ship at the first opportunity. But a few baited traps placed inside cabinets where the mice have been searching for food will do the job eventually too. Don't use poisons, because you will likely end up with a rotting rodent carcass inside the wall or under the floor, and you won't like the smell of that. If you trap them alive, release them miles away from your Airstream so they don't return.

Finally, take some time to do a good underbody inspection of the Airstream. Rodents can get in through ridiculously small gaps so you may not be able to completely rodent-proof your Airstream, but let's not make it too easy for them. Seal any gaps in the belly pan with new rivets or butyl tape. Optionally, a bit of copper wool (available in grocery stores) makes it hard for them to chew their way back in, so you can stuff some of that in a gap before sealing it with butyl tape.

Insects are easier. Wasps and bees like to make nests inside exterior compartments and vents. Obviously you don't want to get stung, so make sure the nest is killed with a good insect spray before you remove it.

Winterizing

If you live in the north, it's a sad day when you've got to put your Airstream to bed for the winter season. When campgrounds in your area start to close, or you see frost in the morning, or the forecast starts to dip close to freezing, it's time to get the Airstream ready for colder temperatures and a period of non-use.

Getting the Airstream properly set for a "long winter's rest" is critical because a lot of damage can occur during the winter. Cold temperatures can cause freeze damage, rodents can move in looking for food and a warm place to stay, vandals and thieves may prey on unattended trailers, and snow/melt cycles can introduce damaging moisture.

But you can prevent all of that with a little pre-winter prep. The interior winterization process is described in detail below. In addition to that procedure, read the discussion above regarding "Choosing a storage location" to make sure your Airstream is parked somewhere safe.

Fall is a good time to check for possible rainwater leaks. During or shortly after a rain, look around for any signs of water intrusion, using the techniques described in the Leak Prevention, Detection and Repair section.

It's also a good idea to check on your Airstream a few times during the winter, to make sure everything is fine. If heavy wet snow has accumulated, consider clearing it off with a soft brush to take some weight off the roof. But don't get on the roof when it's wet or snowy—it's too easy to slip off.

Winterizing procedure

You should winterize the Airstream when it might be exposed to freezing temperatures for more than a couple of hours (except for when you are keeping it warm by running the furnace). You should winterize even if your indoor wintertime storage facility promises "heated" storage, because a big storm can knock out power, leaving you with an expensive repair bill.

Of all the maintenance procedures to do on an Airstream, winterizing is the one that is always made to appear much harder than it is. It's actually quite simple, and with practice you can do it yourself in less than an hour.

The basic idea is to remove everything from the trailer that could cause a problem over the winter, such as water (which can freeze and burst the plumbing) and food or other interesting-smelling items (which might attract rodents or insects).

Removing interesting smells is easy. Take out everything edible, take out your clothing, and generally remove all the stuff that a rodent might want to make a nest from, or which an insect might find tasty to eat. Clean the refrigerator thoroughly, including the door seal, turn it off, and leave both the refrigerator and freezer doors partially open.

Also remove any items from the trailer that might be damaged by freezing, or which might damage the trailer if the container broke.

Removing the water is just a little trickier. If the trailer is stored in a climate where temperatures drop below freezing, you've got to get every drop of water out of the plumbing. There are two schools of thought here. The first school says to use compressed air to "blow out" the water lines. I'm suspicious that RV service centers like this approach because not many people have air compressors at home, so they think they have to take it to the dealer for winterizing. You also need to install a "blow out plug" on the plumbing or buy one that screws onto the city water fill.

The problem with using only the compressed-air technique is that, if you don't do it exactly right, tiny droplets of water can remain in the lines, the faucets, and the water pump. It doesn't take much leftover moisture to gradually gather over the winter, settle in a low spot of the plumbing, and freeze. A little water left inside the pump will result in a non-functional or leaky pump by spring.

The second school of thought says to just pump special non-toxic RV antifreeze through the water system, thereby displacing the water with something that won't freeze. RV antifreeze is a reddish solution that is safe for humans, not like the toxic antifreeze used in cars, and can be found in hardware stores. You don't need any special tools to use this technique.

Airstream Owner's Manuals describe and recommend <u>both</u> techniques. That's a "belt and suspenders" approach for sure, but not a bad idea.

The first step is to level the trailer and empty the fresh water tank. You can do this by opening all the faucets and letting the water go down the drain (with the water pump on, of course). Don't let the water pump run dry, as it could damage the pump. Alternatively, the fresh water tank can be drained by opening its drain valve. On late model Airstream trailers the drain valve is located between the two streetside (left) wheels on all dual axle trailers. Single axle trailers which house the fresh water tank on the interior will have not have this type of drain valve.

The next step is to turn off the water heater (both gas and electric, if you have a dual-heating type) and drain the water heater by removing the white nylon drain plug. A socket (typically 15/16") and a ratchet wrench with a short extension will make removing and reinstalling the drain plug easy. This is a good time to replace the plug, since it won't last forever. Buy a new plug at an RV supply or hardware store so you can install it when you de-winterize in the spring. Look for one with a 1/2" thread.

The water heater contains 6 to 10 gallons of water, which will all glug-glug out onto the ground when you take out the plug. You can speed up the draining by opening the latch on the Pressure/Temperature valve above (this lets air in). See instructions in the "Water heater" section for the location and function of the P/T valve.

Once the tank is empty, you can bypass the water heater by following the instructions in your Owner's Manual. Bypassing the heater means it will stay empty until you reverse the bypass in the spring. It's usually a matter of two or three simple valves.

If you've got a water filter in your fresh water system, remove it and/or bypass it. This is because you probably won't be able to remove all of the water from the filter if using compressed air to winterize, and if you are using RV antifreeze your water may taste funny next summer even after the filter has been flushed.

From here, the steps involved depend on whether you are going to blow out the plumbing with compressed air or just displace any remaining water with RV antifreeze. Whichever path you choose, be sure that all water has been removed or displaced from all of the faucets, the toilet (see notes below for macerating toilets), showerhead, water pump, water purifier (if equipped), external shower (if equipped) and city water inlet.

Pumping RV antifreeze through the lines to displace the water is best done with a winterization kit installed, which allows you to suck Anti-freeze from a jug directly into the fresh water line near the water pump, kind of like an IV transfusion. This winterization kit can be installed if your trailer doesn't have one. Doing it this way eliminates the need to pour Anti-freeze into the fresh water tank, and thereby makes de-winterizing easier next spring. The basic idea is to run each water outlet until you see foamy pink fluid coming out of every one.

If you are going the "blow out" route only, you'll need to open the "low point" drain as well, to ensure water trapped there is blown out. There will be one or two of these drains on the <u>bottom</u> of the fresh water tank. In this case, Airstream also recommends disconnecting the lines to the water pump and purging it.

Finally, be sure that the gray and black holding tanks have been dumped, and pour enough RV antifreeze into the sink and shower drains to fill the traps. Some RV antifreeze in the toilet bowl will help keep the toilet seal from drying out, too.

Winterizing the Dometic macerating toilet

The following only applies if you have an electric macerating toilet. For storage of more than two weeks, Dometic recommends the following procedure:

1. Flush the toilet in "Normal" mode with 4 ounces of liquid biodegradable laundry detergent (without bleach).
2. Flush the toilet at least five more times.
3. Turn off the water supply to the toilet (typically, this is just a matter of shutting off the main water pump, but if there's a shutoff valve on the toilet's water supply line, that will work better).
4. Flush the toilet without water, three times. This step is to eliminate water remaining in the macerator pump.
5. Turn off power to the toilet.

Over-winter battery storage

During long-term storage of your Airstream, the house batteries need to be kept charged.

Unless the Airstream is plugged in at least weekly, the batteries will slowly lose charge, *even with the USE/STORE switch in the STORE position.* (That's because some electrical consumers like the propane detector continue to operate, and because lead-acid batteries self-discharge naturally.)

A fully charged battery won't freeze, but a discharged one can. If it freezes, the case can burst and the battery acid will leak, causing big problems. Even if it doesn't freeze, letting a battery run down during storage will shorten its overall life.

The catch with plugging the trailer into power is that Airstream does not recommend leaving a trailer plugged in while it is in storage. Over time, the water level on a battery can drop and cause premature failure of the battery. You'd need to check on it regularly. If you have your Airstream parked next to your house this is not such a big problem.

Solar panels are a good option for many people but the catch is that you'll have to go clean the snow off the panels and monitor the batteries to make sure they are staying charged. (See "Solar panels" in the Electrical section for details.)

If power is available at the storage location, you can set the USE/STORE switch to STORE, electrically disconnect the batteries (remove the power cables), and connect a battery minder device. These are easily found in auto parts stores, and will safely maintain the charge level in the batteries.

For most people, the best plan is usually to completely remove the batteries from the Airstream during winter storage. Removing the batteries gives you the opportunity to inspect the batteries following the procedure outlined in the Electrical section of this book. Then you can store the batteries where they won't freeze and where you can keep them charged.

As part of this annual service, you may wish to have your battery load-tested (which any battery supplier can do, such as an auto parts store). This will tell you if the battery is good for another season of use.

Final winterizing steps

Once you're done with the major part of winterizing, take a moment to walk around the trailer and run through your Departure Checklist. That will help you verify that the propane is turned off, the vents and windows are closed, the doors are locked, etc.

Here are a few other optional, but recommended, steps:

1. If the tires will be exposed to the sun, you can extend their life by covering them. Inexpensive fabric or vinyl tire covers are available at RV stores.

2. Apply dielectric grease to the 7-way cord connections to prevent corrosion. You can buy this at hardware stores. Just smear a thin

coating onto the blades of the connector after cleaning the 7-way cord following the instructions in this book. Dielectric grease is also good for protecting battery terminals and battery cable ends.

3. Do a roof inspection (see "Roof Inspection" procedure in this book) and correct any issues you may find that could allow a leak of rain or snowmelt over the winter.

4. Lubricate all door hinges, locks, stabilizer jacks, window seals, and entry step (see "Lubrication"). This only takes a few minutes.

5. If you have the aluminum-framed Airstream windows (not Hehr), consider leaving threads of dental floss hanging out the bottom of the window seals. Sliding the dental floss around will make it easier to get the window open, if it sticks next spring.

6. If you are concerned about security, you can make things harder for a thief by lowering the hitch down a bit (below a point where it would be easy to put on a truck's tow ball) and then removing the power hitch fuse. On most late-model Airstreams it's an in-line fuse near the bottom of the power hitch jack.

You don't need to remove or empty the propane bottles, because propane won't freeze, but make sure the propane valves are closed. If everything looks good, give your Airstream a pat and promise to come back for a Storage inspection later in the winter.

Routine checks while in storage

The other thing you can do this winter is check over your Airstream periodically. This time of year people put away their trailer for the winter not realizing there's a slight leak, and in the spring they find a smelly, moldy, and water-damaged mess.

A slowly-melting blanket of snow atop the roof will severely challenge the waterproofness of everything on the roof, even spots that didn't leak in the last gentle rain. So it's a good idea to run through the rainwater leak detection procedures outlined in the Leak Prevention, Detection, and Repair section. Also see the "Storage inspection" procedure outlined in this book for further suggestions on how to check your Airstream while you aren't using it.

I sometimes recommend to people that they periodically go spend an afternoon in the trailer during storage, assuming the battery hasn't been removed. Plug it in, fire up the furnace, turn on the lights, put on some music and bring some snacks. Make the place feel alive again. You can watch a football game on the TV, read a book, plan your next trip, or just hang out for a while. With nowhere to go, you'll have time to think about what you'd like to do next and what you can do to improve the Airstream. Trust me, spending a little time with your Airstream will make you feel better, like a mini-vacation, and may well extend its life too.

Springtime de-winterizing

De-winterizing is easy and actually kind of fun, because you know you're getting ready for new adventures. The process is basically the reverse of winterizing (putting fresh water into the holding tank, un-bypassing the water heater, displacing the RV antifreeze with fresh water, putting your personal items back, etc.).

Before reinstalling the white nylon drain plug for the water heater, inspect it for damage or cracks. If the plug is damaged or more than a couple of seasons old, get a replacement at an RV supply or hardware store, as these plugs are soft and can break. Be sure to wrap plumber's tape around the threads of the white drain plug 2-3 times, to help prevent leaks. Don't over-tighten the plug as you reinstall it, as you can break the head off if you use excessive force. It just needs to be tight enough to avoid leaks.

If you disconnected or removed the batteries, the propane leak detector may alarm for a while when they are reconnected. This is normal. Check the Airstream Owner's Manual for details.

De-winterizing is a good time to sanitize the water system. Not only will you start the season with a fresh system, the sanitizing process can help remove some of the lingering taste of RV antifreeze.

After you've done that, check the air pressure on all the tires (including the spare). Fill up the propane tanks if needed and give all the major systems a test: furnace, refrigerator, water heater, stove, oven, lights, water pump, air conditioner or heat pump, and fans. Once the water heater is up to temperature, check the drain plug to ensure it's not leaking.

Check the interior of the Airstream, including inside cabinets and closets, for signs of leaks that might have occurred over the winter. A flashlight is helpful here, to see water stains in dark corners. See "Leak detection" in the Leak Prevention, Detection, and Repair section.

Check that none of the windows are sticking shut. If you have a problem getting a window open because the gasket is sticky, try a plastic card (like a credit card) from the outside to help unstick the gasket. Remember to clean and lubricate the window gaskets afterward, as described in the Interior Cleaning and Appearance section.

Press the Test button on the smoke and/or Carbon Monoxide detectors. They probably could use fresh 9-volt batteries, so have a few handy to pop in. Also, if your Airstream has a built-in water filter, it's probably time to replace the filter cartridge. See "Expiration Dates" below for more things to check.

Whether you removed the house batteries or not, you should check the water level in them and add some distilled water if needed. (See "Topping Up Battery Water" in the Electrical section for details.)

Lube the hitch as recommended by the manufacturer. Once hitched up, check all the trailer lights and verify proper braking. As you go, listen for any strange noises from the hitch and trailer that might indicate a need for repair or adjustment.

Expiration dates

When you hear the term "expiration date," most people think about that quart of milk in the fridge. What few realize is there are many things in your Airstream that should be replaced due to age. Here are some of the often forgotten but important things that need to be checked to make sure they will work reliably.

Smoke Alarm. This is probably the most important, but also the most overlooked piece of safety equipment in your Airstream. Not only should the battery be changed at least every six months, but the detector itself also has an expiration date. This is usually ten years from the date of manufacture, and is generally printed on the back. Check the detector every time you load up to go camping, and not by accidentally burning dinner. Push the "test" button on the outside of the detector. Replace it when it gets too old, or fails to sound off when tested.

Carbon Monoxide Detector. This one has an expiration date as well. In addition to testing and battery replacement, the same as the smoke alarm, you may have to hard wire in the replacement, as some CO detectors are wired into the 12 volt electrical system, with the batteries providing only emergency backup power.

Water Filter. This is supposed to be changed at least every year. The best time is when you are getting ready for the camping season. That way, you can have clean water all summer long, without having to find a new filter while you are on the road. It's important to change this, as an old water filter can actually harbor bacteria, having the opposite effect of what we expect.

First Aid kit. This one gets overlooked if no one has had to use it for some time. Many of the items in the kit have expiration dates, from the aspirin to the antibiotic ointment. Many of these things can become harmful if they sit around too long. While an old bandage won't do much except fall off if it's too old, virtually everything used to treat an injury needs to be fresh.

LP Tanks. These will need to be recertified within 12 years of the date they were manufactured. Many LP tanks are older than our Airstreams, some by a year or two. A visual certification usually will suffice for an aluminum tank, but steel tanks require a more involved test. (Most newer Airstreams come with steel tanks.)

The production date is located on the collar at the top of the tank, and is usually a numerical month and year stamp. Take a look, and avoid an unpleasant surprise halfway through your trip, when the LP guy won't fill your tank because it's too old. Tanks permanently mounted on motor homes have different rules as to whether they get replaced, and when.

Tires. As mentioned in "When to replace the tires" in the "Running Gear and A-frame" section, the tires can get too old for safe use, even when the tread is still good. See that section for instructions on how to check the date of manufacture for the tires.

Batteries. This is more of a recommendation than a rule, but you should take a close look at the batteries in your Airstream after three years of use (assuming they are "wet cell" or "flooded" type batteries—replacement AGM-type batteries will usually last longer). The batteries currently installed at the factory have a date sticker on top, with either numerical or abbreviated month and two digit year on the sticker. As in all the others, this date could be several months older than your Airstream, especially if you bought it new.

Fire Extinguisher. Most fire extinguishers used in our Airstreams don't have a date on them. Most fire extinguisher service companies recommend annual inspection and replacement after ten years. In RV use, the constant shaking of travel can cause the powder in the extinguisher to pack down, so it might be a good idea to shorten that ten year recommendation to five years. Even though the extinguisher might work, it's too late for a "re-do" if you pull the trigger and nothing happens.

If yours needs replacement, keep in mind that the National Fire Protection Association recommends B:C rated fire extinguishers as a minimum, and one should be mounted within 24 inches of the primary exit. The "B" rating is for flammable liquids, and the "C" rating mean the extinguishing agent won't conduct electricity back to the user.

Propane Leak Detector. This device is mounted near the floor and "sniffs" the air for propane leaks. Replace as needed or as suggested by the manufacturer. Typically, this is every five to seven years. Dust, pet dander, and dirt can shorten the life of this detector. For more information, read the "Propane Leak Detector" discussion in the Propane System section.

Breakaway Switch. The breakaway switch will eventually degrade with time and exposure to weather. This should be tested annually and replaced approximately every five years to ensure that it will work if there's an emergency.

Electrical

Electrical overview

Your Airstream has two electrical systems, one for 120 volt AC power (household power) and one for 12 volt DC power.

The 120 volt AC system is only functional when the trailer is plugged in, and it powers the air conditioner, microwave, television, household power outlets, and refrigerator (when running in electric mode). It also goes to the power converter, which turns some of that 120 volt AC power into 12 volt DC power. This is used to recharge the battery.

Your Airstream may have a 30-amp power cord and plug, or a larger and heavier 50-amp cord (on models with dual air conditioners). If you have a 50-amp cord and dual air conditioners, you can use an adapter to plug into 30-amp power when that's the only power available, but you won't be able to run both air conditioners at the same time. Doing so would draw more than 30 amps, which should trip the circuit breaker in the campground's power pedestal. It might also create a dangerous situation elsewhere in the wiring, so even if the circuit breaker doesn't trip you should be careful not to overload.

Once in a while you may need to plug the Airstream into a regular household outlet, which generally provides just 15 amps. This is fine for keeping the Airstream charged and powering low-wattage AC appliances, like portable fans and laptop computers. But it's a very bad idea to run the air conditioner on 15-amp power. It might seem to work, but long term it's likely that the voltage will drop and you run the risk of damaging the air conditioner's compressor or other electrical components.

At rallies where you are sharing power outlets with other Airstreams, it's common to have as little as 3.75 amps per trailer (one 15-amp circuit divided by four trailers). That's still enough for your 12 volt DC items (lights, water pump, vent fans) and keeping the batteries charged—but nothing else.

The 12 volt DC system is driven by the batteries, and it is responsible for powering everything else in the Airstream, including lights, water pump, furnace, "cigarette lighter" 12 volt outlets, fans, refrigerator (when running in gas mode), propane leak detector, stereo/DVD player, breakaway switch, etc. This system also requires very little maintenance, mostly in the area of the batteries.

Solar panels

If you have solar panels, keep in mind that they only charge the batteries. They don't provide power directly to anything else. The only regular maintenance a solar panel needs is cleaning (because dust, leaves, etc., will interfere with its ability to make power) and an occasional inspection for physical damage.

If you are considering adding solar panels, keep in mind that the solar panels should be sized to approximately match the capacity of the batteries in the Airstream. If the panels produce a lot more power in a typical day than the batteries can store, you'll have wasted money on expensive panels. If the panels are too small, they might not produce enough power to keep the batteries charged, which can lead to short battery life if the trailer is not plugged in regularly (such as during long-term storage).

RV solar specialists are in many parts of the country (some are even mobile and will come to you), and they can help determine the optimal size of your battery bank and provide solar panels to match.

Preventative maintenance

There's not much maintenance of the electrical system. Primarily, preventing problems is a matter of being observant at the campground. Campground power outlets are usually OK but sometimes you'll encounter a scary one. Cracked outlet covers or circuit breakers, burn marks, visible wires, wasp nests, a loose outlet, and wobbly power pedestals are a few signs of a poorly maintained campground power system, and you should be cautious when using it.

The best protection is to test an outlet before you plug into it. A simple 3-light tester (usually supplied with new Airstreams) will confirm that the wiring is correct. To test a 30-amp plug, you'll need an adapter.

A more sophisticated tester will verify the voltage as well. This is crucial, because incorrect wiring might cause a very unsafe condition. Low or high voltage can burn out your air conditioner or other appliances. A smart power protection box like those sold by Progressive Dynamics will check the power for you and cut it off if there's a spike, brown-out, or other unsafe condition. These are a good investment for frequent travelers.

When you plug in to campground power, make sure the connection is tight. Loose connections can cause the power cord prongs to melt. If you find any problems with the power, tell the campground manager and request another site.

Every time you plug in, take a look at your power cord, as well as the power connector on the Airstream. Blackened or dark brown prongs mean that it has been overloaded or connected loosely at some time. The dark corrosion will inhibit good electrical flow and cause overheating, which can result in the plug melting later. If the prongs are still in good condition (not melted or damaged), you can clean them up using the techniques described in "Maintaining the 7-way plug" below.

If the prongs aren't good, you can replace the entire head of the cord with one from a hardware or RV parts store. Be sure to rewire the new plug carefully. If you swap the wires by accident, you will have reversed the polarity of the power coming into your Airstream. This can lead to a condition called "hot skin" where the body of the Airstream is carrying current. If you've ever touched the Airstream on a damp day and felt a tingle of electricity, that's "hot skin" and you should immediately unplug the trailer and get the problem fixed. This is a very dangerous condition which can kill you.

Fuses, circuit breakers, and Ground Fault Interrupters (GFI)

Fuses are used on the 12 volt DC wiring. They are little plastic squares in various colors. A wire inside the fuse melts when the circuit is overloaded.

On most Airstream trailers, the fuses and circuit breakers are behind a brown or black metal panel located either below the refrigerator, below the front sofa or below the dinette. The location on yours might be different, but the black panels look about the same. There's a tiny square plastic knob at the upper part of this panel. Turn it 90 degrees and then you should be able to pull the access panel open from the top, revealing the circuit breakers and fuses.

The Owner's Manual includes a diagram of all the fuses, but there is probably also a list printed on a label inside the door. If you've lost power in part of the electrical system, this is the first place to check. There are more diagnostic tips later in this section.

To check a fuse, pull it out and then hold it up to the light. (An inexpensive plastic fuse puller, available at hardware or automotive stores, is helpful.) You will see a curved wire inside the colored plastic. If the wire is broken or you see a burn mark, the fuse has blown and you'll need to replace it with the same color fuse. Some Airstreams have LED lights above each fuse that indicate when a fuse has blown.

The amperage rating will also be printed on the flat edge of the fuse (usually a number between 5 and 30). Never replace a fuse with one that has a higher rating. If the fuse blows again, you need to find the electrical problem causing it before you replace the fuse again.

Circuit breakers are used on the 120 volt AC wiring. They are large black switches that snap open when the circuit is overloaded. To reset a breaker you push the switch all the way to the open position, then snap it back to the closed position. If it snaps again immediately, you've either got a wiring problem, a problem with an appliance connected to that circuit, or the breaker itself has failed (and must be replaced by an electrician). Either way, don't reset it again without resolving the problem first.

There's no maintenance needed here other than the occasional fuse replacement or circuit breaker reset. Don't go poking around here unless you are qualified to work on AC power, and never attempt service (other than resetting a breaker) while the Airstream is connected to AC shore power or a generator.

It's not common to blow fuses or circuit breakers. Overloading a circuit is the primary reason, and you can avoid this by simply thinking about the electrical loads you are placing on the system. For example, if you find a breaker trips when you run the air conditioner and microwave at the same time, don't do that. Airstreams with 30-amp power plugs can briefly pull more than 30 amps with the air and microwave on (or another hungry appliance like a hair dryer, toaster, coffee maker, or anything with a heating element in it) at the same time.

There are a few other appliance-specific fuses in other places. For example, every Fan-Tastic Vent has a glass fuse in it, which is easily accessed through a black knob on the face of the vent. Some macerating toilets have a separate fuse, as do some refrigerator control panels. The power hitch jack has an "in-line" glass fuse in the wire that leads to it (it's inside a plastic waterproof cover, near the base of the jack). If your Airstream has a factory-installed inverter, it should have a special high-current in-line fuse next to it.

Your Airstream may also have some very large fuses (or fusible links) toward the front of the trailer, either in a forward closet, under the front sofa, or inside a compartment. If you go hunting around you'll find this area, filled with a rats nest of wiring. Sometimes the wires are hidden under a false floor or access panel. Take a look with a flashlight or check the electrical schematics in the Owner's Manual to see if there's a main fuse here, just for future reference.

Inside the Airstream, power outlets near wet locations like kitchen and bath (or the outside outlet) may be labeled "GFI" or "GFCI", and have little RESET buttons. These are designed to cut off the electricity when there's a dangerous condition. You can test them by pressing the TEST button, which should cause them to trip off.

Sometimes GFIs trip off when they don't need to, or when they are failing. If you have no power at a single outlet, check to see if it is a GFI type. You can reset the GFI at any individual outlet by pressing the RESET button on the face of the outlet. If it trips off repeatedly, it might need to be replaced, which is an easy job for an electrician.

Airstreams from the early 1960s and through the 1970s originally came with lights to indicate incorrect power polarity (this light may have been removed later by an owner). If your trailer has one of these and you are finding that a campground GFCI outlet is tripping off repeatedly, try removing or disconnecting this light. It was designed before GFCI outlets, and isn't compatible. Today a safer system is to install a GFCI main breaker in the trailer's power panel.

Troubleshooting power problems

If you've got a "no power" problem, it's important to work logically and methodically to isolate the issue. First, identify whether you've got a problem with the 120-volt AC power system, the 12-volt DC power system, or both.

No AC power

If AC appliances like the microwave, television, air conditioner, or something you've plugged in don't work, that's an AC power problem. In this case it's likely that the batteries aren't charging either, because the charger runs off AC power. (If you have solar panels the batteries will still receive power from them.)

If the problem is only happening with one appliance, or only one AC outlet, and everything else works, you've already got a hint at the problem's location. Check the GFI circuit at the outlet as described above, or try a different appliance in that plug.

If the problem affects all AC appliances and outlets, then move outside to the campground power connection to verify that there really is power at the plug. Are the circuit breakers on the campground power box turned ON? Try resetting the breakers by flipping them OFF and then ON again. They should snap into the ON position.

Next, verify power is available at the outlet. If you have a power cord with a built-in light, you'll know right away if the Airstream is getting power. You can also use an electrical voltmeter or a simple plug-in tester for this.

If the power pedestal has more than one outlet, try a different outlet.

If there is power at the outlet, and your tester says it's good, move on to your power cord. If you have a voltmeter you can verify that power is available at the other end. Sometimes extension cords fail invisibly, but often you can see problems with a cord. Look for burned-looking prongs on the cord or the Airstream, looseness in the power cord head, cuts in the cord itself or any other signs of damage.

Don't take chances with a questionable extension cord! Replace it or fix it. Replacement heads are available at RV supply stores, and you can install a new head in about ten minutes if you have a wire stripper, screwdriver, knife, and a steady hand. Make sure you attach each wire tightly to the correct screw on the new plug, and check that no strands of wire are loose to cause a short.

If power is getting to the Airstream but not to your AC appliances, the next stop is the circuit breaker panel. Read the section above on "Fuses, circuit breakers, and Ground Fault Interrupters (GFI)" for details on where to find the power converter and check the circuit breakers.

If everything checks out OK and you still don't have AC power anywhere, it's probably a wiring problem. Problems of this nature get beyond the scope of this book, so consider hiring professional help to resolve it.

No DC power

A 12 volt DC power problem will affect things that are connected to the batteries, such as lights, water pump, 12 volt outlets, and the refrigerator. Most often, people notice a DC power problem when the lights go dim or the batteries won't hold a charge.

First, is the problem confined to a single appliance, such as a fan or light that won't go on? If it's really just one thing, then that appliance most likely has the problem. Check the fuses first, as described above in "Fuses, circuit breakers, and Ground Fault Interrupters (GFI)".

If more than one appliance is affected, check the USE/STORE switch, which is usually located somewhere near the entry door. It should be in the USE position, which means you are using the trailer. If it's in the STORE position, 12 volt DC power will be cut off to most of the Airstream. On Sport models this may be a Battery Disconnect Switch which should be ON.

If the trailer is plugged in, DC power should be coming from the power converter, through the fuse panel and the battery, to supply the appliances. So the next stop is the fuse panel. Read the section above on "Fuses, circuit breakers, and Ground Fault Interrupters (GFI)" for details on where to find the power converter and check the fuses.

In addition to the fuses on the Airstream panel, many late-model Airstream trailers use a Parallax power converter that has two 30 amp DC fuses on the front. <u>Disconnect the Airstream from shore power,</u> then check and replace those two fuses before condemning the power converter.

Intermittent or weird DC power problems can sometimes be caused by poor electrical grounds. Corroded or loose ground connections are easy to fix. See the Exterior section of "The Storage inspection" procedure for locations of the ground wires and how to clean them.

If the trailer is running on battery power and you still have DC power problems after making the checks above, you need to check that the batteries are OK. See the discussion "Routine battery inspection" below for details on checking the battery connections and water level. Then test the battery power at the battery posts with an electrical voltmeter. A fully charged wet cell battery should ideally produce about 12.6 volts (AGM type batteries may have higher voltage). If you suspect a bad battery, take it to an automotive shop and have it tested.

Replacing light bulbs

Airstream has used so many different types of light bulbs and fixtures over the years that it's impossible to cover all the specific replacement procedures. See your Owner's Manual for a list of the bulbs used in your trailer.

However, we can cover a few of the common recent bulbs and fixtures. The incandescent light bulb #1141 (or #1156, which is similar) has been used in Airstreams for decades. It's widely available through hardware stores, auto parts stores, RV dealers, and online. It's cheap and goes in most of the fixtures that take a round base bulb. If you have some of these, get a couple of extras to carry around in your spare parts kit.

The white plastic double-light fixtures with a central switch that are found mounted on the ceiling of many Airstreams take these. To access the bulb, you squeeze the plastic lens of the light from the sides until it can be pulled away from the fixture. Rotate the bulb a quarter turn and it will come out.

Another common bulb is the 10-watt or 20-watt halogen bulb with G4 (two-pin) base, which is found in recessed ceiling fixtures and swivel-base reading lamps. A new halogen bulb should not be touched by bare hands. The oils on your fingers will cause hot spots on the bulb and shorten its life. Instead, handle the bulb with a cloth, tissue, or gloves.

In the swivel base reading lamp you simply twist the lens ring until the lens comes off and pull out the old bulb.

The round ceiling fixture found in International CCD, Safari SE, Flying Cloud, Interstate motorhomes and class A motorhomes is a little different. A small screwdriver is helpful to pry off the lens trim ring. Be careful not to scratch the fixture. The lens should snap out of the socket.

Bulbs are generally marked on the base with their type. Note that there are many equivalent model numbers, so a quick online search will tell you which bulbs can be used to replace it. All bulbs used in Airstreams are 12 volt DC.

Exterior lights

You can easily tell whether your Airstream has incandescent or LED exterior clearance lights. Incandescents have one or two bulbs, where LEDs have many small elements that you can see through the red or yellow colored lens.

Incandescents are generally replaced by removing one screw on the lens or by prying the lens off with a small screwdriver at a little indentation along the edge of the lens.

LED clearance lights rarely fail, but when they do you must replace the entire fixture. The same is true of LED brake/tail lights and turn signals.

Note that if your trailer has LED exterior lights, some European tow vehicles will not recognize that the trailer is plugged in, and may even disable the brake controller. This is because the vehicle is looking for a certain amount of electrical current draw from the lights, and the low draw of LEDs doesn't register. A work-around is to wire in some incandescent lights in the lighting circuit (usually hidden away under a cabinet or in a closet) to give the car what it expects to find.

LED versus incandescent

Airstream has gradually transitioned from traditional incandescent bulbs to LEDs over the last decade or so. Some trailers came with LED taillights only at first, but later models have LED lighting throughout, including the exterior clearance lights and interior light fixtures.

Those who still have incandescent bulbs can usually upgrade to LED easily. Drop-in replacements are available from online LED specialty stores for the common light types used in Airstreams. One such vendor is LED4RV.com.

LEDs make sense for their extremely low power consumption and low heat output. If you frequently camp off-grid, relying on battery, solar, or generator for power, using LEDs for interior lighting is the single best way to cut the power requirements of your Airstream. A typical #1141 bulb will consume about 0.8 DC amps, whereas the typical LED replacement bulb (outputting the same amount of light) will consume about 0.1 DC amps. This is a huge savings on the power budget.

However, there are some downsides to going LED. First, they're very expensive. A good drop-in replacement for a #1141 bulb will cost about $12-15 at retail at present. Most of the fixtures that take #1141 bulbs require two. This adds up quickly if you are upgrading many lights.

Second, LED lights are more susceptible to low voltage. Good LED units have integrated power regulation, so that they aren't as affected by the normal spikes and declines of DC (battery) power. Even those may show some flickering when you run the water pump. If this will drive you crazy, buy a couple of LEDs as a test before you swap out all of them.

Third, most of the LED replacements for bulbs aren't dimmable. If you have a dimmer you may have to disable it or search for a specifically dimmable LED. It probably won't have the range of dimming that your incandescent bulbs had.

The fourth common complaint about LEDs is color temperature. "Cool white" LEDs often look bluish, or blue-green, more like fluorescent lights. For this reason, many people choose "Warm white" LEDs. Even those will be "whiter" appearing than the incandescents they replace. Again, try them out and see if you like them.

If you have an Airstream that came with LEDs that are too "cool" in color, it is possible to purchase orange-colored gels designed specifically for lights. These gels are thin sheets of plastic that can be inserted into the light fixture to "warm" the color temperature.

Maintaining the 7-way trailer plug

The 7-way cord contains all the wires needed for the trailer's lights (clearance, brake, turn), brakes, and power to keep the battery charged while towing. All Airstreams since 1989 have used the same wire arrangement, shown in the diagram. Earlier trailers may have different wiring, but typically they have long since been rewired to fit modern tow vehicles.

The only maintenance for the 7-way plug on the trailer is to periodically clean off corrosion on the seven spade connectors. It's difficult to do without the right tool, so we recommend a kit available in the Airstream Life Store which includes a special flat burnishing tool and premium electrical contact cleaner.

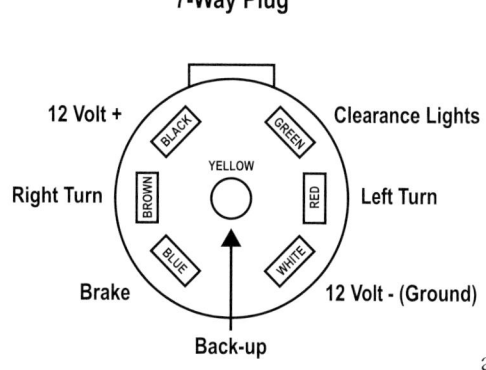

7-Way Connector - Trailer End
Airstreams from 1989 through present

First, apply a small droplet (a little goes a long way) of the contact cleaner on each metal spade connector. With the file, gently scrub the contacts until all green or white corrosion is gone or the metal spade connectors have turned from dull green-brown to a brighter yellow. You'll notice some of the brownish corrosion on your file. You can clean that up with a rag.

You can also use the same tools to clean the connectors in the tow vehicle's 7-way outlet, if they need a little help. Plan to do this simple cleaning job at least once a year as preventative maintenance. With the right tools it takes just a few minutes.

If your clever modern tow vehicle complained that some of the trailer lights or brakes weren't working, this procedure may resolve the most common cause of the problem. You can plug in the trailer to confirm that the problem has been resolved.

Note that LED testers don't work on some European vehicles. Their computers expect to detect incandescent lights, and the LED tester doesn't draw enough current, so the computer thinks there's nothing attached. In this case you may see all the LEDs on the tester flashing rapidly, or nothing at all.

If the 7-way plug has become detached or worn out, you can get a replacement plug end through RV, automotive and hardware stores. You'll need a knife, a wire cutter-stripper tool and a screwdriver to cut off the old end, strip the wires, and reattach them to the new plug end. Be careful and make sure you attach each wire tightly to the correct screw on the new plug, and check that no strands of wire are loose to cause a short.

Battery basics

While largely taken for granted, batteries are critical when we take Airstreams off the beaten path of RV parks. Airstreams use batteries similar to the one in your car or tow vehicle, with an important difference: Starting a vehicle can take anywhere from 100 amps to several hundred amps, but the duration of such output is very short. The design used in vehicle batteries is tailored to that requirement.

In our Airstreams, we never require the batteries to output more than ten or twenty amps, but we expect them to do so for many hours before requiring a recharge. As a result, a different battery design is used, which is often marketed as a "deep cycle" battery.

Lead-acid batteries are available as either "wet cell" (liquid electrolyte), or Absorbed Glass Mat (AGM), which is gel electrolyte in a fiberglass mat. Most Airstreams have wet cell batteries, although many Airstreamers switched to AGM types for replacement batteries. The AGM battery requires no checking of the water level and typically lasts longer. Some AGM batteries can be mounted in any location or position.

Decades ago, batteries had a limited role in Airstreams. They powered a few 12 volt bulbs and a fan or two. Over the years this role has expanded to include powering water pumps, furnaces, stereos, TVs, propane detectors, and the electronic circuit boards that control air conditioners, refrigerators, and water heaters. For this reason, newer Airstreams come with one or two Group 24 or Group 27 (size) lead-acid "wet cell" batteries.

The batteries are housed either in a box suspended between the A-frame rails at the front of the trailer or in a special compartment built into the exterior body of the Airstream. If your Airstream has been modified (for example, enlarging the battery bank for solar power) they may have been relocated under the front couch or another location, and you may have another type of battery.

Battery maintenance

The original equipment batteries are basically the same as car batteries, which means that they have a lifespan of 3-5 years and replacements can be purchased at auto parts stores.

A "maintenance-free" battery is permanently sealed and never needs water. Absorbed Glass Matt (AGM) batteries also are permanently sealed, and can last seven years or so if they are treated well.

However, there really is no such thing as a completely maintenance-free battery. They need to be kept charged. When discharged, the internal plates of a lead-acid battery become covered with "sulfation" over time, which permanently reduces the ability of the battery to hold a charge. The longer the battery is left discharged, the worse the sulfation gets. Battery manufacturers say that sulfation is strictly the result of a battery not being charged or maintained, and they won't cover it under warranty. So it's up to you, the owner, to make sure that the battery stays charged.

If a new deep-cycle battery is routinely discharged to 10% or less remaining and then properly recharged (i.e., initially a high current bulk charge, followed by lower topping-off current charge), it will have an average life of about 300-350 cycles. This amounts to a few years of typical usage for most people.

On the other hand, if that same battery is routinely discharged to around 40% to 50% remaining and then recharged, that battery will have a life span of around 3,000 cycles. This difference in life span applies equally to wet cell and AGM technologies. So it's worth the trouble to treat your batteries kindly, and avoid discharging them below 50% of their rated capacity (learn more about battery capacity below).

Freezing weather is another reason to keep your batteries fully charged at all times. A discharged battery will freeze around 29 degrees. Once frozen, it's ruined. But a fully charged battery won't freeze until it reaches near-Arctic temperatures.

By the way, the old tale that says a battery sitting on concrete will discharge is false. All lead-acid batteries will self-discharge over time. So the best way to maintain the battery during long-term storage is to remove it from the Airstream and store it, connected to a device like a Battery Tender®, which is specifically designed to keep automotive batteries topped up. Alternatively, if you are able to plug the Airstream in between short trips, the Airstream's charger will do this job.

Routine battery inspection

Battery inspection is quick and easy. First, be mindful of safety: absolutely no smoking or open flames! Batteries normally emit hydrogen gas when charged, and hydrogen is explosive. Don't wear jewelry while you are working on the batteries, either.

You won't be hurt by the 12 volt power output of the battery, but take care not to let a loose cable touch the other or you'll get a dramatic spark and possibly blow a fuse or circuit board in your Airstream.

If you need to remove the cables, first unplug the Airstream from shore power. Then make a note of the cables' original positions so you can reconnect them to the correct posts. The battery should be marked with + and – symbols as well. The red cable goes to the + (positive) side and the black cable goes to the – (negative) side.

Keep the top of the battery clean and check the cable connections for tightness. If there's any corrosion, remove the battery cables with a wrench. Then clean up and neutralize the corrosion with a solution of baking soda and water. Clean with plain water afterward and wipe dry.

Likewise, if the post of the battery or the cable connector are dirty or corroded, scrape or brush until the metal is shiny. You can buy inexpensive battery terminal cleaners at automotive stores. Clean contacts ensure a good electrical connection. After reconnecting and tightening, apply a thin coating of petroleum jelly or dielectric grease to help protect the connections.

A strong "rotten egg" smell can be an indicator of a battery problem. The battery case should not have any cracks or indication of leakage.

Topping up battery water

If you do not have a "maintenance-free" battery, then you must regularly check the water level and top it up with distilled water. Check your battery more frequently in the summer months, since water evaporates more quickly in warm weather.

To do this, pry off the vent caps and check the water level in each cell of the battery. The acid-water level should be just below the bottom of the inspection hole. If you need to top up the water, wear gloves and have baking soda on hand to neutralize spills. Remember, this is sulphuric acid and you don't want to get it on anything.

Use only distilled water and do not over fill the water level! This can cause the acid-water mixture to leak. Put the vent caps back onto the battery, make sure they are on tight, and clean up as needed with a baking soda and water mixture.

Understanding battery capacity

The capacity of a battery is very dependent on the rate of discharge. The more load you put on it, the less overall power it will yield. Most batteries are rated at a capacity that will allow a given current to be delivered for a period of 20 hours before exhaustion (known as the C/20 capacity).

For instance, let's say the battery is rated at 75 amp-hours at the C/20 discharge rate. This means that this battery will deliver a constant 3.75

amps for 20 hours, which is the equivalent of leaving on a couple of 12v incandescent bulbs. You can see that it is fairly easy to overextend the capacity of your batteries if conservation and monitoring is not employed.

The furnace in an Airstream can pull 7.5 to over 10 amps while running. Fan-Tastic Vents require from 1-4 amps depending on fan speed. Each incandescent bulb used in older Airstreams pulls one amp or more (dependent on type of bulb) and the fluorescent lights used in many Airstreams pull about 1.5 amps per fixture. LED lights are far more efficient, so they consume only a fraction of an amp.

The C/20 capacity rating is the maximum capacity, not the typical. If you discharge the battery at a lower rate, the battery will deliver more total amp-hours. Conversely, a higher discharge rate results in fewer total amp-hours delivered. So you can see that there is no exact capacity rating for a battery—it depends on how you use it.

Monitoring your battery capacity

Airstream has included a voltmeter as part of their trailer monitoring system for many years, but it's not highly accurate. For battery voltage to be an accurate indicator of battery condition, the system must measure the stable internal temperature of the battery after the battery has rested with no discharge or recharge activity for at least an hour before measurement. This doesn't happen during camping, since you are always charging or discharging the battery. Even if those conditions are met, the reading is at best +/- 10%.

Because they are measuring voltage, monitors of this type will show Yellow when there's a heavy power demand even if the batteries are full, and they will sometimes show Green when the batteries are actually quite discharged but have recently been charged just a little. Imagine a car's fuel gauge that goes to Yellow every time you press the accelerator.

You can observe this phenomenon yourself. Use your batteries for a day or two, until the monitor shows Yellow constantly. Then plug in for 30 minutes, unplug, and watch as the monitor reports Green or "100%". This is what fools people, but don't fall for it. The monitor is seeing what is sometimes called a "surface charge." The voltage pops up for a short time after charging, but it won't last.

In short, battery voltage is better than no indicator, but only marginally so. The battery monitor can easily mislead you into thinking that the battery is more charged than it is, so you might not charge it fully, which leads to more sulfation and an overall shorter battery life.

For this reason, installing an amp-hour meter like the Tri-Metric series by Bogart Engineering is a popular upgrade. Devices like this measure every milliamp that goes in or out of the batteries, and thus are able to display a near-exact report on their state of charge. It's an essential upgrade if you plan to rely on solar power and your batteries for extended camping trips.

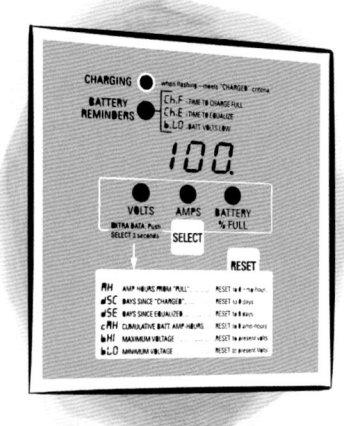

If you discover, after installing an accurate amp-hour meter, that your batteries are not getting a full charge, or you've upgraded to Absorbed Glass Matt (AGM) or another type of battery chemistry, you may need to upgrade the converter/charger. Until 2015, the converter/charger that was built into new Airstreams had output voltage preset for charging "wet cell" batteries and temperature compensation was not available. Some post-2015 models can be upgraded to have temperature compensation for optimal charging in cold or hot conditions, and aftermarket replacement converter/chargers are also available with voltage settings specifically for other types of batteries.

Extending battery capacity with equalization cycles

A maintenance process that is seldom used, but critical to long battery life and consistent capacity, is "equalization" (also known as "desulfation"). During normal use, sulfuric acid migrates deep into the batteries' lead plates. During recharge, the sulfuric acid is driven out of the plates. Unfortunately, this process results in some sulfuric acid converting into crystals that lodge in the lead plates.

Over time, these crystals accumulate and can significantly reduce the overall capacity of the battery. Curing the sulfation problem involves charging the battery fully and then raising the charge voltage to about 15.5V for a period of time. The period of time required is relatively dependent on how it has been since the last equalization.

During the process, the battery will become warm to the touch, but should not be allowed to become hot to the palm of the hand. The batteries must be monitored during the process for overheating. Equalization causes the sulfuric acid crystals to break down and migrate out of the lead plates, returning capacity to the lead plates. In wet cell batteries, equalization causes the electrolyte to bubble (releasing hydrogen gas) which is normal and occurs during charging as well. For this reason it is important to allow for venting of the hydrogen gas away from the batteries during the process.

Without a tool to measure the battery's ability to deliver under a load, there is no way to know when a battery is fully equalized, but doing a routine equalization cycle every 30 days for about one hour will keep most batteries in excellent shape. Unfortunately, no Airstream factory-installed converter/charger offers equalization.

Some aftermarket power converter/chargers have automatic equalization cycles. There are also aftermarket equalization chargers that can be attached temporarily to your batteries, and some solar panel controllers like the Blue Sky SolarBoost 2000e offer an equalization capability.

Charging batteries

If you've had the experience of plugging in your Airstream and discovering that it takes a lot longer to get a full charge than the battery meter claims, read on. Batteries charge slowly, and as they get more charged, they resist, and so the rate of charge declines.

For example, let's say your batteries will accept a charging rate of 15 amps (DC) when they are really heavily discharged, and 2 amps when they are 25% discharged, and 0.5 amps when they are 10% discharged (these numbers are only for illustration). If you've got an 80 amp-hour battery bank, getting from 90% to 100% charge (8 amp-hours) would take 16 hours of charging, even though the voltage-based battery meter might have told you they were charged up long before.

It doesn't matter whether you are plugged in or using a really big generator; you could plug those batteries into a nuclear power station and they still won't charge any faster. A "smart" three-stage charger may slightly improve the rate of charge compared to the typical 2-stage factory-installed charger, but only to a limited extent.

The illusion of a full charge leads to shortened battery life because, as discussed above, partially discharged batteries will sulfate much more quickly than batteries that are kept charged. So for the longest possible battery life, be sure yours are fully charged <u>before</u> putting the Airstream away after a trip. This could take a full day if the batteries are deeply discharged. Again, this is a reason to consider upgrading the battery monitor to an amp-hour metering type, so you'll know for sure when the batteries are fully charged.

Generator or solar for recharging?

If you want a generator solely to recharge your batteries while camping off-grid, you'll find that it doesn't matter whether you have a 1000-watt generator or a 2000-watt generator. A 1000-watt (rated) generator can typically produce 75 DC amps at its normal maximum output rate, and that is far more than the batteries will accept at any given time. The rest of the power is wasted, unless you are running the microwave or some other AC appliance while the generator is running.

So the best use of the generator is when power demand is high. It's much easier to <u>avoid</u> using battery power by being plugged into the generator, than to try to recharge battery power later. Use the generator in the morning and evening when you are cooking and using lights and water pump, and the power needed will be supplied by the generator rather than coming from the batteries.

Solar's advantage is in recharging. Rather than pumping out large amounts of power in short time periods, solar provides a steady all-day charge will and have a much better chance of getting your batteries up to 100%. It's like the turtle and the hare. With batteries, slow and steady wins the race.

If you have both a generator and solar panels, use the generator when the batteries are heavily discharged (for an hour or so in the morning, for example) to get the bulk charge done quickly, and then let solar finish the job over the course of the day.

If you only have solar, keep in mind that during the morning and mid-day, moderately or heavily discharged batteries will probably accept every amp the panels can generate. Then the charging rate naturally slows down. If the sun is still shining at that point you have surplus power, and so that's the time of day to plug in all of your rechargeable accessories like phones, cameras, laptops, etc. This strategy takes maximum advantage of the power being generated.

TV antenna

If you have a fixed (not moveable) TV antenna, there's no maintenance required for it, but the Winegard TV antenna that elevates with a crank might need a little lube once in a while. The elevating gear and the rotating gear, both of which are located on the roof at the base of the antenna, can be lubricated if the antenna becomes difficult to move.

Silicone spray is recommended for this. With the antenna fully down, spray downward into the top of the elevating gear. With the antenna fully up, remove the setscrew or plastic plug on the gear housing (rotating base of the antenna), and spray into the hole as well as under the base. Operate the antenna a few times until it moves smoothly again. Winegard recommends doing this twice a year.

If the crank-up Winegard TV antenna rocks in the wind when it is up, the gearbox may have loose or worn gears. The internal gearbox assembly can be tightened with a special Winegard tool, similar to a 15/16" deep-well socket.

But before trying this, ensure that the antenna is mounted and secured properly. The base should be securely attached to a solid portion of the roof. (See "Getting on the roof" in the Exterior Cleaning and Maintenance section.)

While you're checking the antenna base, verify that it is sealed to prevent water intrusion, and that the sealant is not dried out or cracking.

Winegard also offers a gear replacement kit for old-style gears. You can tell if you have the older gears by inspecting the cranking rod from inside the Airstream. Remove the crank handle and spring by loosening the set-screw, and take a look at the shaft that extends down below the ceiling. If the rod is round, it's the older style; if it's a hexagon shape, it's the newer style.

Propane System

Liquid propane ("LP" or just "propane") is the lifeblood of many of your Airstream's appliances. While it should be treated with respect, when the propane system is maintained it is safe and convenient.

The "propane system" includes the tanks that store the LP at the front of your trailer, the regulator that maintains its pressure, and the plumbing that distributes it to the appliances. The appliances that use propane (refrigerator, stove, oven, furnace, and water heater) and the propane leak detector are discussed in separate sections.

Propane won't freeze or go bad in storage. So you don't have to do anything special during winterizing or long-term storage. Usually the only thing that happens is that air gradually gets in the gas lines, so the next time you use the trailer you have to try a few times before the gas appliances will light. A good technique is to light the stove before trying any of the other gas appliances (refrigerator, water heater, furnace, oven). That way you know the air is out of the lines.

There are many safety features built into modern propane systems. All new tanks are equipped with Overfill Protection Device (OPD) valves which help prevent overfilling and prevent the flow of gas when there's nothing attached to the tank. The green Acme nut that screws to the propane tanks also includes some features designed to cut off most of the gas flow if there's a sudden leak or a fire.

This means that if you notice a sudden loss of pressure (say, at the stove) it may be that the OPD excess flow valve has kicked in because there's a big leak somewhere. This excess flow valve can also cut in if you open the tank valve too quickly, so if that happens, try closing the tank valve again and reopening more slowly. The other possible causes of sudden pressure loss can be a minor clog in one of the gas lines or a fault in the propane regulator, so later in this section we'll discuss how to check for correct pressure.

Propane tank inspection

A lot of propane system maintenance is just being observant. While you are in the area of the propane tanks, your nose might tell you that there's a leak of propane occurring. You might notice a loose gas line during a routine inspection, or notice that one of the tanks has gotten rusty when you are getting a refill.

To keep you safe, there are a lot of safety regulations covering the use of propane. Mostly you'll encounter those when refilling the tanks. They can only be refilled by people who have been certified, and those people are required to inspect the tanks (cylinders) before they fill them. They're looking for:

1. Evidence of damage to the cylinder's exterior including dents, bulges, cuts, cracks, welds, rust, pitting, or signs of heat.

2. Presence and condition of the cylinder foot ring, cylinder collar, and valve cover.

3. Leaks, a defective valve, discoloration of the valve, or an out-of-date valve. All cylinders today have OPD valves (Overfill Protection Device) which have three lobes on the handwheel. Without this kind of valve, the cylinder can't legally be refilled.

4. The date the cylinder was manufactured or last recertified. This is stamped into the metal of the cylinder collar. Cylinders can be recertified after 12 years of use, for five-year periods of time.

In reality, many LP personnel give the cylinder only a quick glance, so you can improve safety by taking a good look at your gas cylinder every time you remove it. Since you know your tank is the right type (meaning that it has the foot ring, collar, OPD valve, etc.) your inspection can focus on finding damage or leaks.

Checking for propane leaks

Checking for propane leaks periodically is a good idea even when you don't smell gas, just as a preventative measure. It's fairly common for leaks to develop in the black "pigtail" hoses with large green knobs that connect the tanks to the regulator, especially around the fittings at either end, and because it is outside you may not notice until the leak has become fairly large.

If you ever suspect a leak in the propane system, get out of the trailer and shut off the gas at the tanks before you do anything else. Don't use anything that might cause a spark, including the vent fans or light switches! You probably don't need to be told that smoking would definitely be harmful to your health.

If you have a late model Airstream it was factory-equipped with a propane leak detector, but your nose may be the first to alert you to a problem inside the trailer. Regardless of whether the alarm goes off, if you smell gas inside or outside the Airstream shut off the gas at the cylinders and wait outside at a safe distance until it dissipates.

Sometimes a very slow gas leak inside the trailer will smell like kitchen garbage, rather than the typical "rotten egg" smell that is added to propane. We've noticed that some aftermarket catalytic heaters seem to have this problem, so if you have added an appliance to the propane system, make sure it has a separate gas shut-off valve for times when you aren't using it.

One common "leak" is caused when a stove knob is accidentally bumped on. It's embarrassing, but at least it's easy to fix.

The easiest method to confirm a leak is to use the automatic changeover regulator that is standard equipment on Airstreams. Make sure all gas-using appliances are off, including the refrigerator, stove, oven, furnace, and water heater. Then, turn on the gas at the tank valve and observe the indicator on the automatic changeover regulator turn green. If you hear hissing or smell gas, obviously the leak is right nearby, but even if you don't, shut off both tank valves and watch the indicator.

The indicator should stay green for at least five minutes. This tells you the system is holding pressure. If it turns red, you've confirmed there's a leak somewhere. This test doesn't tell you the location of the leak but at least now you know you weren't imagining things. This is also a quick test you can do anytime, even as a routine part of your Pre-departure checklist.

Note that a very slow leak may not be detected by this test. A more accurate version of this test is done with a manometer, which is an instrument that measures pressure. If you have a manometer available, the correct pressure in the system (after the regulator) is 11 water column inches. If it slowly declines, there's a leak. (If it's consistently the wrong pressure, your regulator may need adjusting. See "Propane regulator inspection and adjustment" later in this section.)

You can buy a propane "sniffer" or commercially-made leak detection liquid, but for most people the chief leak detection tool is a spray bottle of soapy water made with liquid dishwashing soap. Set the spray bottle so that the tip of the sprayer shoots a sharp stream, not a mist. If you don't have a spray bottle you can use a sponge dipped in a bowl of soapy water.

If you suspect a leak, go hunting after the gas has dissipated. You may have to briefly open one of the propane tanks to repressurize the system in order to find the leak.

Leaks most often occur at connection points (gas fittings), tank valves, appliance valves, and hoses. (This is one reason why the gas lines run beneath the belly pan of the Airstream. This keeps the propane outside until the last possible moment.) Some Airstreams have valves on the lines under the belly pan, which greatly helps finding a leak, since you can shut off parts of the system and isolate where the gas is escaping. If you have such valves, close them all and then check again to see if pressure is holding. If it does, open them one at a time to see when the leak restarts.

Spray the soapy water on every fitting or valve that you want to check. Once you find a spot where the soapy water makes bubbles, you've found a leak. Do them one piece at a time, checking each one carefully on all sides for bubbles. Often the bubble will appear only on one side of a fitting or connection. Also, while you're under the trailer, check the copper gas lines themselves for signs of damage from road debris.

Generally the bigger the bubbles, the bigger the leak. But any leak is a problem to resolve before you use the propane system again.

Valves, appliance controls, and flared fittings that leak must be replaced. Don't attempt to replace parts unless you have been trained to work on gas plumbing and have the correct tools. When loosening or tightening connections on copper gas lines, always use two wrenches—one to turn the fitting, and the other to hold the opposite part so that you don't twist or kink the soft copper gas line. Always retest every propane connection you tighten or re-connect, using your soapy water solution.

If you can't find or stop the leak, or if it is in an appliance like the refrigerator, or if a gas line is damaged, close the tank valves and take the Airstream to a service center. Gas leaks are nothing to be casual about.

Replacing propane "pigtail" hoses

You should expect to replace those "pigtail" hoses every couple of years. It's not a bad idea to have a spare hose on hand for long trips, since the hoses sometimes spring a leak without any warning and it can be difficult to find the exact type and length you need while traveling.

Measure the length and note the style of fittings on both ends of the hoses your trailer uses before you go shopping. If your trailer has a Marshall Excelsior or Cavagna regulator, as most late model Airstreams do, you'll need a 1/4" (Inner Diameter) hose with an Acme Type 1 (green) fitting on one end and a 1/4" Male Inverted Flare fitting at the other end, running 12 to 15 inches long.

When replacing a hose, you'll need an adjustable wrench and some plumber's (PTFE) tape that is specified to be compatible with propane, to wrap around the fitting threads on the new hose, so carry those in your tool bag.

Filling the propane tanks

The stuff you are buying to fill the propane tanks (or "gas cylinders") is actually Liquid Propane, or LP. This is a compressed form of propane that expands about 270 times when it is released. That's why you can buy just seven gallons of LP in a 30 pound tank and it lasts for a long time. As it is used it can expand to yield as much as 1,890 gallons of gaseous propane. If released, this would in turn mix with air to make about 70,000 gallons of explosive atmosphere. That's enough to fill a house and send it to Kansas.

So you don't want to let this stuff loose accidentally. There are three important rules to observe:

1. If you need to transport the gas cylinders, always transport the tanks upright. The OPD relief valve must be in contact with the

"vapor space" at the top of the liquid propane. If not, the OPD valve might open, which would release the gas. An old milk crate may help hold them upright in the truck.

The only exception is for gas cylinders which are specifically designed for horizontal use, and those will be marked accordingly. They were used in Airstream motorhomes, Limited trailers, and "squarestreams."

2. Don't leave propane cylinders inside a car, truck, or house. The OPD valve is designed to open when pressure inside the tank gets too high. Heating up inside a car could cause this happen.

3. The third rule should be observed by the certified propane technician who fills your tanks: never fill above 80% of rated capacity. The 80% rule allows for some expansion. Normally the OPD valve does its job and prevents the propane tech from overfilling, automatically.

When you replace the propane tanks on your trailer, take a moment to quickly check a few things. Make sure each tank is sitting flat, and that the base is not pinching the wires for the breakaway switch. Notice if the long threaded rod of the tank hold-down is secure. Give the tanks a push to make sure. Finally, make sure the valves and hoses are all seated together nicely and nothing is hissing.

Propane regulator inspection and adjustment

The propane regulator is a mechanical device that simply ensures that the propane gas to your appliances is delivered at the pressure they need. Your appliances are looking for about 11 inches of Water Column (W.C.) pressure, in other words a very low pressure. If the pressure is too low or too high, the appliances may not work well, especially the refrigerator.

Fortunately, the regulator is a pretty reliable device that doesn't need any routine maintenance. There are a few things you can check on it to just make sure all is well.

Most late model Airstreams have an automatic changeover regulator installed. The Marshall regulator pictured on the next page is typical of pre-2012 models. It has a black switch ("changeover lever") and a red/green

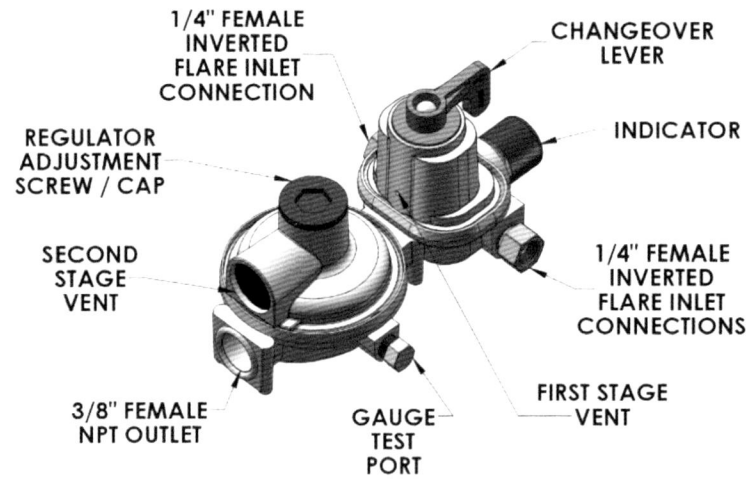

indicator that tells you when one tank has gone empty. Later models use a Cavagna regulator with a much larger round indicator (illustrated below), but it functions identically.

Look closely at the bottom of the regulator (near where the main black hose goes in). You should see a screened vent. This vent always faces down to reduce the possibility of getting clogged. If it's not clean, try using a brush on it.

This bottom part you've been studying is the second stage of the regulator. The first stage is the upper part, and on the bottom of the first stage there's another vent. This one is just a tiny hole, about the size of a pencil tip. It should be clear of debris too.

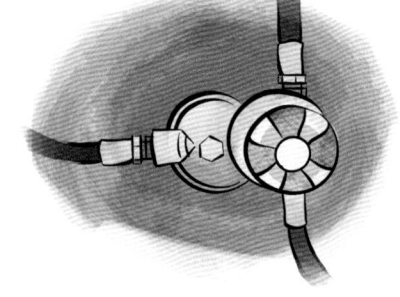

To get a rough idea whether the regulator is putting out the right pressure, try this test: Turn on all of the gas appliances (furnace, stove, oven, refrigerator and water heater). If they all work and the stove has a good adjustable flame, the regulator is probably putting out the right pressure. If not, the regulator may need adjustment or replacement.

Low propane pressure can stem from a loss of tension in the regulator springs over time, or the regulator may simply have been poorly adjusted from the factory.

Humming regulator

It's normal for a regulator to make a humming noise when it is working. This is the internal diaphragm doing its job. However, sometimes the regulator can produce a loud or annoying buzzing, humming, "chirping" or "singing" sound, especially during times of high gas demand.

The pigtail hoses connecting the regulator to the propane tanks contain a check valve which can sometimes cause this issue. Before you swap out the regulator, try a new set of pigtails.

Adjusting the regulator

Further testing and adjusting of the regulator is a task best done by someone with the proper equipment and training. Most people should stop here, rather than mess with the propane system further. But if you are a hard-core DIY type, you can obtain or build a U-tube manometer (which accurately measures pressure in Water Column Inches).

Depending on the models you have, there may be a pressure test port on the regulator itself, or on the refrigerator or water heater. After shutting off the gas at both tanks, remove the small threaded plugs for the test port and screw the manometer in its place. On recent Dometic refrigerators, you must first remove a shield plate for access to the test port.

To properly test the regulator, you should be using about half the maximum propane load. You can either light several stove burners or the water heater in addition to running the refrigerator while testing. Set the refrigerator to gas operation and read the manometer.

The pressure should be between 11 and 12 inches of water. With all other propane load off, the reading should not exceed 12 inches of water.

If the reading is out of bounds, remove the plastic shield from the propane regulator and unscrew the gray or black plug from the side of the regulator with a wrench. Remove the spring inside if present. The spring does not affect the pressure setting; it is intended to prevent regulator creep due to vibration.

You now can access an internal threaded plug. Use an Allen wrench to turn the internal plug clockwise to increase the pressure or counterclockwise to decrease the pressure. The threads are very fine; it will take multiple turns to make a difference. When the manometer reading is 11" to 12", replace the spring, the outer black plug, and the plastic shield.

Propane leak detector

Every modern Airstream has a propane detector built in. This device is mounted low in the Airstream (usually in the kitchen), and it is always on even when the Battery Disconnect switch is set to "STORE." That's for safety.

In 2012 Airstream began installing Atwood propane detectors that have an audible "end of life" alarm feature. After seven years a chirp will sound every 30 seconds and a yellow light will flash. This signifies that the detector is no longer reliable and must be replaced. An "end of life" label may be affixed to the top of the detector to let you know the month and year to expect this alarm.

You can silence the alarm once, for 12 hours. After that, it can no longer be silenced and it won't sense gas leaks. It's time to buy a new propane detector.

Resecuring gas lines

Occasionally one of the clamps that hold the propane lines to the underside of the Airstream's belly pan will come loose. You may have spotted one during one of your inspections.

To fix it, simply remove the existing rivet (if it is still there) and re-attach the clamp with a new POP rivet. (See "Replacing a POP rivet" in the Aluminum Body Repair section.) If the clamp is missing, you can find replacements at most hardware stores.

If the rivet hole has become enlarged so much that a regular POP rivet won't hold, see the discussion of "Belly pan repairs" for tips.

This minor repair is one of the many good reasons to carry a rivet tool and a few sizes of rivets with you on extended trips. See the Resources section for places to get various sizes of rivets and rivet tools.

Climate Control

The climate control systems in an Airstream are generally low maintenance. The climate control systems include the roof vents (powered Fan-Tastic Vents or manual crank-up vents if they were installed by the factory), the air conditioner(s), the furnace, and the thermostat. Vent fan maintenance is discussed in the Windows, Doors, Locks, and Vents.

Your Airstream is well insulated by travel trailer standards. There's insulation inside the exterior walls and ceiling and under the floor. Airstream also installs thermal breaks in some places to cut down on heat transfer between aluminum parts of the body. A small amount of heat from the furnace is directed to the underbody holding tanks to keep them from freezing. In some Airstreams a 12 volt heating pad provides this function instead.

Still, you can't expect a travel trailer to perform as well as a modern building in extreme temperatures. Airstreams are fine in sub-freezing temperatures, but at some point the capacity of the furnace is going to be overcome. A night in the 20s (Fahrenheit) is no problem as long as you have plenty of propane and electricity for the furnace.

Similarly, the air conditioner will produce air about 18-22 degrees colder than the incoming air, which is good enough for most people on mildly hot days, but unless your Airstream has dual air conditioners it will probably be a little uncomfortable on a 100 degree day in full sun. That's why your maintenance efforts will be aimed at keeping these systems running as efficiently as possible.

The thermostat used on most late model Airstreams is a fairly smart digital model, which controls both heat and cooling. For example, if your Airstream has a heat pump, this thermostat can automatically switch from heat pump to furnace at the appropriate time (when outside temperatures dip below freezing).

On some models the thermostat also works with the Dometic air conditioner to govern defrost cycles so that the air conditioner doesn't freeze up in very humid weather. Some thermostats can even switch from cooling mode to heating mode by themselves if you program them correctly. It pays to take some time to learn how the thermostat works in your Airstream, and the instructions should be in the Owner's Manual package.

One common problem with the Dometic "Comfort Control Center II" digital thermostat is the famous "E7" error code. This code simply means that the thermostat was set to run the air conditioning (or heat pump) but couldn't. Usually it is because there was no AC power to the trailer. To fix this, just plug in the trailer and switch the thermostat off and on to reset it.

Air conditioner

Most Airstreams have Dometic air conditioners. These may be straight A/C units or they might have heat pump capability, which means they can also produce some heat on days that are above freezing. Late model Airstreams often have dual air conditioners, which requires 50-amp power instead of the usual 30-amp power.

Maintenance of the air conditioner is simple, because it's a generally trouble-free device and because the refrigerant is sealed and can't be recharged.

The best thing you can do for the long life of your air conditioner is to feed it the proper electrical voltage. Low voltage will damage the compressor and doom your air conditioner. Don't expect your air conditioner to start with less than 103.5 volts, and running it on a day when the campground voltage is less than 108 volts is risky. It only takes a short "brown out" to drop the voltage below a safe level and cause damage, and it can happen while you aren't looking. This is one reason why you should have an AC voltage monitor somewhere in your Airstream, or (better yet) an electrical protection device that cuts off the power when the voltage is too low.

Even newer campgrounds can have voltage problems. If it's a hot, humid day and everyone is running their air conditioning full blast, be wary and check the voltage. Likewise, don't run your air conditioner on a household extension cord or a household 15-amp outlet.

Air conditioner filter cleaning and replacement

To maximize the efficiency of the air conditioner, clean dust off the filters regularly. Dust builds up quickly and can severely reduce the amount of cool air you get. Also, dirty filters cut down the amount of air that can circulate and will encourage frost to form on the cooling coil, which means the air conditioner is more likely to ice up.

Depending on the model of air conditioner you may have two knobs and then two screws to drop the shroud (older style), a pair of surface-mounted plastic vents with tabs to release, or a pair of small filters that can be slid out from the front.

Airstreams with ducted air (25-foot and longer trailers starting with model year 2015) have filters located above the return air grills in the ceiling. Replacement filters are available from Airstream dealers, part #382236.

To remove the return air grill on a trailer with ducted air conditioning, just pry it out with a non-marring tool at the short edges of the screen. The filter lies atop the grill.

Most filters are washable, so you only need to replace them when they can't be cleaned or when they get torn.

While you've got the filters out, look inside for excessive dust, bugs, cobwebs, etc. You can vacuum this out with a brush attachment.

Top side inspection of the air conditioning

During a roof inspection or trailer washing, you can take a look at the air conditioner from the top and see if the fins are badly bent or clogged with anything. First, remove the shroud (just a few screws) in order to get a good look at the condenser fins and compressor coils.

You can spray the fins with a water hose or compressed air, from the inside out, to clean them up, and bend the fins straight again. There's a tool called a "fin comb" that can be used to straighten them out.

Take note of the shroud's condition. Is it beginning to crack? They don't last forever, so after ten years or so it's not uncommon to need to replace it. Check for mold, wasp nests, etc., and clean everything.

If you suspect problems with the air conditioner, it's probably best to take it to an RV technician. The tech will compare the incoming air temperature to the outgoing air temperature (the "temperature delta") to see how well the unit is cooling. Other checks include a more thorough inspection of the components, checking the amperage draw, inspecting the condensate drain, the condition of the roof pan and mounting bolts, and perhaps oiling the fan motor.

Air conditioner tips

The quality of cooling you get depends a lot on the circumstances. To get the best cooling inside your Airstream, do what you can to park in shade, and:

1. Close curtains, shades, and blinds.
2. Insulate your windows, vent fans and skylights. The "bubble wrap" type of insulation with silver coating works well and can be cut to fit.
3. If you can't park in shade, try to park on gravel or grass.
4. Put out your patio awning and window awnings if you have them.
5. Cook outdoors or use the microwave oven to avoid adding heat to the trailer.
6. Limit use of incandescent lights. Each one of them is like a little 10 watt heater.
7. Don't use an extension cord rated for less than 30 amps (50 amps for Airstreams with two air conditioners), and never use a household (15 amp) outlet.
8. Keep filters, condenser fins, and all other parts clean.

If you find that your air conditioner is dripping water inside the trailer, it's probably the result of a plugged condensate drain. Normally on an Airstream condensate water runs through a tube and out by the wheel well, or the water drips down from the roof (depending on the installation). When the water can't go the right way, it fills up inside the unit and eventually drips out onto the floor. This usually can be cured by blowing out the drain tube with compressed air.

Furnace

Like most of the other appliances, maintaining your furnace is mostly a matter of periodic inspection and cleaning. Basic cleaning requires almost no tools at all, but advanced cleaning requires a basic set of SAE (e.g., not metric) wrenches, assorted screwdrivers and pliers, a 12 volt test light, and a bottle of liquid leak detector (soapy water).

Before you start working on the furnace, make sure the thermostat is off so you don't get a nasty surprise part way through when the furnace comes on. Also, for safety, turn the gas valves at the propane tanks off.

On newer model Airstreams with the Atwood HydroFlame-type furnace, access is easily gained from the outside. Use a flathead screwdriver on the two screws holding the access hatch closed on the outside of your Airstream. Remove those screws and the cover will swing down out of the way, allowing you to also swing the inner cover down and out of the way. On most models, the inner cover is a type of heavy plastic.

Now you can access the innards of the furnace. You can start your maintenance by using compressed air to blow out the area around the inlet-outlet grate before removing it. That way, bugs and dirt will get blown out before they have a chance to get in to the furnace. After blowing the dirt and debris away from the furnace, you can pull out the grate/tube and continue cleaning.

Once this is done, nearly anything else you would do to the furnace will require removing it completely from the trailer. If you are mechanically inclined, read on.

In order to remove the furnace for further cleaning and maintenance, you will need to disconnect the LP line and electrical wires and unscrew the mounting screws around the perimeter of the furnace. While not exactly something for a rookie, it isn't too bad. You will probably have to disconnect the LP line both at the furnace and the connection under the trailer, so the line will drop out of the way enough to allow the furnace to clear it when you slide the furnace out.

People who have the older Suburban NT-type furnace will find that getting the furnace out for maintenance is a little more involved, as it has to be removed from inside the trailer. In many cases this involves removal of some furniture or cabinetry. Like the externally-accessed Atwood HydroFlame furnace, the Suburban NT will come out by itself, leaving the outer case in place. The inner cover will need to be removed, and the LP line.

On the Suburban furnace, there is a plug with three wires that goes through the outer case and into the control board. That will need to be unplugged so the furnace will slide out of its case. There is usually also a single Phillips screw holding the exhaust tube to the furnace. This screw is found on the outside of the trailer in the middle of the (usually) upper vent. After getting all the screws, wires, and lines off, you should be able to slide the furnace out of its case for cleaning. After you get it out, you can blow all the rust, dust, and bug nests out of it.

It will help (though depending on model may not be completely necessary) to remove the control board before removing the furnace. When you start pulling out on the furnace, watch closely to make sure you have everything disconnected.

Once the furnace is out, you can access the heat exchanger to blow all the accumulated dirt, rust, mud dauber nests, and spider webs out of it. There are several little screws holding the unit together.

On both Suburban and Atwood models, pay close attention to how everything comes apart, so you can put it back together. A digital camera or cell phone that takes pictures can be your friend. Take reference photos of everything you disassemble.

Check the fans for damage such as cracked or bent blades or wasp nests built within them. Check to see that the motor rotates freely, with no roughness and little to no noise as it spins.

Check the heat exchanger for any holes, usually from rust, before you put it back in. Any holes are a "fail" as far as further use. A hole in the heat exchanger will cause carbon monoxide to leak into the air you breathe inside your Airstream. Carbon monoxide can kill anyone in the trailer in short order, so holes mandate replacement of your furnace.

Providing your furnace passes muster, you can put it back in the opposite way you took it out, referencing the photos you probably forgot to take when removing it. When you slide the furnace back in, verify that you aren't pinching any wires and that everything lines up properly. Reinstall the wires, control board, and gas line.

Once everything is reconnected, turn on the propane at the tanks and liberally spray down the connections to the furnace with your leak detecting solution to make sure you have no leaks. Checking for gas leaks is extremely important. Just because NASA uses Airstreams, you don't really want to try to launch yours into orbit from a gas leak.

Close the access doors, then turn on the furnace and verify that it works like it should. Keep in mind that there may be air in the gas lines that has to work its way out before the furnace will light.

One more important step: since you've taken the time to check and clean your furnace, take a few minutes more to replace the battery in your Airstream's carbon monoxide detector (or install one, if your trailer didn't come with it).

Catalytic heaters

Airstreams don't come with catalytic heaters from the factory. If yours has a catalytic heater installed, it was installed by an owner previously. The reason is that catalytic heaters are indoor "unvented" heaters and thus not compliant with safety codes for the RV industry.

A catalytic heater doesn't burn propane; it catalyzes it, meaning that the propane undergoes a chemical reaction with oxygen and a catalyst pad built into the heater, which turns the propane directly into heat, carbon dioxide and water vapor. People often get confused about this, thinking that carbon dioxide (CO_2) is the same as the deadly carbon monoxide (CO). A normally functioning catalytic heater does not produce carbon monoxide.

People install catalytic heaters because they are silent, nearly 100% efficient, and don't need electricity. You can see how this is great for boondockers who are watching their power budget. Not only does a "cat" heater eliminate the 7.5 to 10.0 DC amps that a typical furnace will draw, but it uses much less propane than the furnace.

There are two drawbacks to using a catalytic heater. It consumes oxygen, and it produces water vapor. Common practice is to leave a window cracked about an inch near the heater and a roof vent cracked open at the farthest end of the trailer. Cold dry air from outside will spill in through the window to the floor and be warmed by the heater. Warm moist air will rise to the ceiling and eventually out the roof vent. This solves both problems and helps ensure even heat throughout the trailer.

Since RV catalytic heaters don't generally have thermostats (just Low-Med-High settings), you can control the indoor temperature by opening the window and roof vent more or less, as long as you don't close them so much that the heater is getting less fresh air than recommended by the manufacturer.

Catalytic heaters get a lot of grief over perceived safety issues. If you want the benefits of lower power and propane use (and blessed silence), take a few steps to ensure your safety.

First, always follow the manufacturer's recommendations regarding venting of interior air and heater maintenance. This includes keeping the heater clear under a cover when it is not in use. Dust contamination can damage the catalyst pad, which will make the heater function poorly or not at all. Similarly, catalyst pads can be ruined by bad propane. If yours doesn't light well or seems to be performing poorly, have the heater serviced or replaced.

Second—and this is a recommendation for <u>everyone</u> no matter what form of heat you use—always have a functioning Carbon Monoxide detector and Propane Leak Detector. See "Expiration Dates" in the Storage and Seasonal section.

Third, use your catalytic heater during the day to save propane and power, and switch to the furnace at night if you aren't comfortable sleeping with the catalytic on.

Fourth, when installing a cat heater, be sure to include a shut-off on the gas line. That way you can be sure there's no leakage of propane into the living space when the heater is not in use. Also, try to mount the heater near the center of the trailer, for even heating.

Finally, choose a catalytic heater that mounts on the wall and is specifically designed for indoor use. This way the propane is stored safely outside and the heater can't be tipped over like a portable one could.

Gas Appliances

The gas appliances in an Airstream are generally pretty reliable. From a maintenance point of view, they don't need much attention from you—except for the water heater, which is discussed later in this section. As with most other parts of the Airstream, maintenance is mostly about keeping things clean.

Propane appliances need good ventilation. For the refrigerator and furnace, we'll review how to check the exhaust vents to make sure they aren't plugged up. For the water heater, there's also a burner tube to check. Details are provided later in this section.

The gas appliances have the advantage of being mature products, meaning that they are the result of decades of gradual improvement and are based on the same basic design as all other RV appliances. So when something goes wrong it's easy to find a repair shop that understands them and can help. For appliance-specific problems, you don't need to work exclusively with Airstream repair centers.

It's a good idea to gather some information before speaking to a technician. Primarily this comes down to verifying the supply of power and propane.

If a 12-volt appliance such as refrigerator, gas water heater, or stereo won't turn on at all, verify that you have good 12-volt DC power in the Airstream. The refrigerator and water heater in particular need 12-volt power even when running on gas to operate their internal circuit boards. A bad battery, faulty power converter, loose connection, bad ground connection, or blown fuse could be at fault. See "Troubleshooting power problems" in the Electrical section for more details.

Likewise, propane appliances need a certain amount of gas pressure to operate correctly. Check the Propane System section of this book, especially the discussion of using a manometer, to see if this is a diagnosis you are comfortable making.

In any case, you can safely and easily check for gas leaks using liquid leak detector at all connections. Make sure the propane valves at the tanks are open, and spritz on a little of your soapy water solution to look for bubbles. Any gas leaks need to be corrected immediately (see "Checking for propane leaks" in the Propane System section.)

Refrigerator

Except for some Interstate and all Atlas motorhomes and Nest trailers, late model Airstreams generally have a special refrigerator that can run on either propane gas or electricity, called an "absorption refrigerator." Unlike your home refrigerator, these RV refrigerators have no compressor, are completely silent, and require very little maintenance. The major downside of this design is that it is slower to cool down, which is why you want to turn the refrigerator on at least a day before you leave on a trip.

The basic principle of operation is that a heat source (either a little propane flame or a small electric heater) provides energy to drive evaporation of refrigerant, which then absorbs heat from the refrigerator compartment. In other words, it manages to make cold from heat!

Since the cooling unit is permanently sealed there's no maintenance of that part, except for occasionally vacuuming dust off the coils.

Heat from the refrigerator is exhausted either through a vent in the roof or a louvered door on the side of the Airstream. This vent must be open and clean for efficient operation. During the Storage inspection you may have looked inside the refrigerator compartment briefly, but a thorough check means looking with a flashlight as far up the vent as you can for obstructions like wasp or mouse nests. If you go on the roof, you can also inspect the refrigerator vent from the top. (See "Getting on the roof" in the Exterior Cleaning and Appearance section.)

If the refrigerator cools on electricity but not gas, or vice-versa, there's a problem with one of the heating elements. The electric heating element can burn out and the gas burner can be blocked or out of adjustment. Both of these are easily serviced by a qualified RV refrigerator technician. It's also possible that the propane gas pressure is too low, which can be caused by an improperly adjusted propane regulator. See "Troubleshooting" below, and the Propane System section for more details.

Adjusting the door gasket

The vinyl gaskets on the main refrigerator and freezer doors contain a magnetic strip so that they form an air-tight seal to the refrigerator frame. They should be kept clean. Dried food spills or other material can cause the gasket to seal loosely, which will result in rapid frost build-up inside the refrigerator and poor cooling.

Dometic, the manufacturer of original-equipment Airstream refrigerators, recommends checking your door gaskets as the first step in troubleshooting a cooling problem. Check the gasket on the doors to be sure of a positive air seal by closing the door on a dollar bill and then pulling the dollar bill out. If no resistance is felt, the gasket in that place is not sealing properly.

This should be done on all four sides of the door in several places. If a gasket is not sealing properly, you can try bending it slightly to fit better. If that doesn't help, you can lift up the inside of the door gasket and insert a 1/4" ball of fiberglass insulation at all four corners on both doors. This is especially important to the top corners.

Next, warm the gasket material with a hair dryer. Then close the door and the magnetic strip should pull the gasket to the metal frame. Leave the door closed until the material has cooled, then recheck with your dollar bill. If a good seal cannot be achieved, you may have to replace the door gasket.

Defrosting

If you leave the refrigerator running between trips, you won't do it any harm but it will need defrosting occasionally. When the cooling fins inside the refrigerator start to get iced up, it's time to defrost. Just turn the fridge off, leave the door open, and let the ice melt. You'll notice water dripping out of the outside refrigerator access door, which is normal because there's a condensate drain there running down from the refrigerator compartment.

A hair dryer is a quick way to melt the ice, but Dometic doesn't recommend this technique because you could at least theoretically warp a metal or plastic part. If you use a dryer be sure to wave it around the interior so that you don't create a hot spot, and be careful working near the melting ice. Water and electric hair dryers don't mix.

Also resist the temptation to use an ice pick or other sharp tool to break the ice. Let it soften on its own, rather than risk poking a hole in the cooling unit and releasing ammonia. Toss chunks of ice into the sink as they come loose and have a big sponge or towel handy to dry the interior.

While you're waiting for the ice to melt is a good time to do some cleaning of the vinyl door gasket and the interior walls and shelves, with a sponge. Don't use an abrasive cleaner. A mild dilution of dish detergent in warm water will do fine. Some folks like to use a few drops of vanilla in the rinse water to leave a pleasant neutral odor after cleaning.

Operating tips

An absorption (gas) refrigerator must be level when it is running. Without proper leveling, refrigerant within the cooling unit will collect and stagnate, causing a blockage. This will stop the cooling process and can permanently ruin the cooling unit.

A good rule of thumb is that if you are comfortable in the Airstream, then the refrigerator probably is too. That means the floors and walls of the trailer should not be noticeably sloped, or to put it another way, the trailer should be within three degrees of level.

Don't worry about being off-level while towing. When the Airstream is moving, the rolling and pitching movement of the vehicle will pass to either side of level, and that's enough to keep the refrigerant from stagnating in the piping.

Let the refrigerator run the night before a trip. If you pre-cool items that are to go into the refrigerator (using your home refrigerator), it will help. To speed the process of initially cooling the refrigerator, you can put in a bag of ice.

If you plan to turn the refrigerator off between trips, you should take a moment to wipe down any food spills and leave the door ajar. This will allow the interior to dry and discourage nasties from growing inside.

It's a good idea to keep a thermometer in the refrigerator so you can keep an eye on the internal temperature. Many people use a wireless digital thermometer so they can check the temperature without opening the door. Unlike your home refrigerator, the absorption type is slow to cool, so it takes a while to restore the coolness inside after you've opened the door.

If your refrigerator seems to work well most of the time, but not very well on extremely hot days (on both gas and electricity), there are a few things to try.

- Pack the refrigerator and freezer more fully with food, ice, or ice packs. More "thermal mass" inside the refrigerator will help it resist swings in temperature. Also, minimize opening of the door during the hottest part of the day.

- Check the temperature setting on your refrigerator if it has one. Some of the larger Dometic units have a one-to-five cooling scale, and in extreme heat you should use the highest setting (5). If it has an "LAC" or "Low Ambient" button, turn it off. That button is only for cold days. (You can read more about it in the Dometic owner's manual for your refrigerator model.)

- If you've tried all the above and are still having problems on hot days, your refrigerator may not be able to exhaust hot air through the chimney efficiently. If the ambient temperature is very high, the hot air produced by the cooling unit doesn't rise as rapidly, which makes the cooling unit's job harder. Check for obstructions in the chimney and use a large cleaning brush to ensure that the chimney is clear of spider webs, wasp nests, dust, etc.

- Assuming everything else is fine but you're still getting weak cooling, the ultimate step may be to install a 12 volt powered fan in the chimney, activated by a switch or a thermal sensor. The fan will help boost the air hot up and out of the refrigerator exterior compartment and can dramatically improve cooling in extreme heat.

Troubleshooting

If the refrigerator won't power on at all, start by checking the fuses. See "Fuses, circuit breakers, and Ground Fault Interrupters (GFI)" in the Electrical section of this book.

If the refrigerator comes on but then the "CHECK" light illuminates, it usually means the refrigerator tried to go into gas mode but failed. Verify that you have propane and that the gas valves on the propane tanks are open, or try plugging the Airstream into shore power and see if the refrigerator works on electricity.

If your refrigerator operates only on gas, then the problem is usually either a fuse or the electrical heating element. However, don't forget to check for loose or disconnected wires first.

The circuit board connectors can be a source of failure, especially for the older units. There are several connectors on the board that can get loose and may develop corrosion. Remove each connector separately and spray both sides with electrical contact cleaner.

If the refrigerator is operating on AC power but not on gas, check to see that you really do have gas (try lighting the stove). If there's gas, the problem may be in the igniter, thermostat, or burner. It's time for professional assessment.

If the refrigerator is not cooling in either gas or electric modes, check for an ammonia smell in the refrigerator or at the outside access door. Also check for a greenish-yellow stain of liquid or powder. Any of these symptoms indicate a leak of coolant, which means your refrigerator's cooling unit has failed. It has to be replaced. This problem particularly affects Dometic refrigerators made between 2003 and 2006.

If you have a cooling unit failure and decide to swap it out yourself (a one-day/two-person job if you are handy) be very careful about where you buy the replacement cooling unit. For some reason the RV refrigerator cooling unit industry is abundant with scam artists. Check references before you buy a cooling unit and use a credit card so you have recourse if the product isn't delivered.

If you're still stuck, it's probably time to get some help. Gas refrigerator diagnosis is a specialized task, so an RV service center that has a technician trained on gas appliances is your best bet. Don't give up on the refrigerator too easily. Often the fix is simple, like a gas flame adjustment, and even if the worst-case scenario emerges (bad cooling unit), replacement of the cooling unit can be done for less cost than an entirely new refrigerator.

Gas burner maintenance

Dometic recommends you get a qualified technician to do maintenance on the gas components of the refrigerator. The burner housing has to be removed to expose the burner jet. When running on gas, there should be a clear blue flame, centered under the flue tube.

The technician will verify the quality of the flame and make any adjustments needed, as well as clean the burner jet, clean the burner tube, inspect and/or clean the spiral flue baffle, check the electrode for location and gap, check the gas system pressure (at the test port provided on the refrigerator) and check the gas fittings for leaks.

Dometic recommends this be done "once or twice a year," but if you inspect for gas leaks, keep the area clean, and verify proper operation, you may find that's all you need. The absorption refrigerator is a pretty reliable device.

Stove/oven

The stove/oven is a generally maintenance-free appliance, except for periodic cleaning of course. The most common problem people have is lighting the oven, and they often think it's broken because they can't get it to stay lit.

Actually, the problem is almost always that they don't have the technique quite right. It's difficult to light and you have to be very patient. The full procedure is described in *The Newbies Guide To Airstreaming*.

Another common cause of this issue is air in the lines. You can easily get the air out simply by lighting the stove first. Once a burner lights, the air is out of the lines.

However, if the oven really doesn't stay lit it is possible that the oven's thermocouple has failed. This gets into a gas appliance repair and for that we recommend bringing it in to a qualified technician. Likewise, adjustment of burners, orifices, or the gas pilot are generally repairs and not routine maintenance, so instructions for those procedures are not given here.

Water heater

Airstream uses two basic types of water heaters in most late model aluminum trailers, and both are made by Atwood. Both have automatic electronic ignition, which is why all you have to do is flip a switch in the bathroom to get hot water. The only major difference between the two types is that one runs only on propane gas and the other runs on both propane and 120V AC power. (On Basecamp and recent Classic trailers hot water is provided by a combination "tankless" water heater, and this section doesn't apply to those.)

Inside the Airstream, the water heater provides little indication that it is operating, which sometimes causes confusion for new owners. When switched on to gas mode, a red light on the switch will light up for a second or two while the heater is attempting to ignite the gas. If it is successful, the light will go out and the heater will quietly go to work. If unsuccessful, the red light will stay on, indicating a fault of some type. Most commonly this is simply because there's no gas available (either the gas tanks are turned off or they are empty).

You might have heard of something called an "anode rod" or "sacrificial anode." It's designed to corrode (and be replaced periodically) instead of allowing a steel water tank to corrode. The Atwood water heaters installed in newer Airstreams do not require an anode rod because the tanks are aluminum clad. An anode rod in this case will not do anything useful.

Routine maintenance

Checking and cleaning the water heater twice a year is a good idea. You can combine these checks with your annual winterization and then check again during the summer season, since that's when spiders and insects are active.

All of the major parts of the water heater (except for the plumbing connections and AC power connections on dual-mode water heaters) are accessible from the outside. The water heater is accessed by an exterior door on the side of the Airstream. Inside you'll find the drain plug (a white nylon plug with a hexagonal head, screwed into the heater), the temperature control, the burner tube, and the pressure/temperature relief valve (P/T valve).

The P/T valve is described in detail later. For now, you need to know that it's near the top of the Atwood water heater and has a small brass lever on it. Flicking open this lever will allow water to come out, or let air in when you are draining the tank.

Routine maintenance includes draining and flushing the water heater, checking and cleaning the gas burner, and general inspections. It takes less than an hour to do the full service.

If your Airstream's water heater has been replaced with one made by Suburban, it may have an anode rod. The anode rod needs replacement periodically. It's attached to the drain plug and replacements are readily available through RV stores.

Start your water heater maintenance by first shutting off the propane at the propane tank and making sure the water heater switch is in the OFF position. If the water heater has been running recently, run a faucet until there's no more hot water coming out. Then turn off the water pump and shut off city water if it is connected.

Inspecting for leaks

Before any other maintenance, take a moment to inspect for water leaks. There are two places where water is likely to leak. The first is the drain plug, which is located at the lower left. It's a white nylon (plastic) plug with a hexagonal head. The other spot is the pressure/temperature (P/T) valve, which is located near the center top of the heater (see upper arrow on illustration). It's a brass assembly with a flip lever on it.

Both of those places should be completely dry, so any wetness is a sure sign of a leak. Also look for signs of intermittent leaks, such as a build-up of minerals or rust just below. For both the P/T valve and the drain plug, the solution to a leak is replacement. Both parts just screw in with an appropriate wrench (see instructions later in this section). Replacements should be installed with plumber's (PTFE Teflon) tape on the threads of the new part.

The illustration also marks the location of the air shutter, which we'll discuss later in this section.

Removing and reinstalling the drain plug

The drain plug is a white nylon 1/2" threaded plug at the lower left side of the water heater. It's best removed with a ratchet wrench with 15/16" socket on a short extension (or a deep socket).

Always have a new drain plug on hand. They are inexpensive and should be replaced every time you service the heater. The nylon is soft and easily damaged, and you don't want this plug to break inside the threaded hole. You can buy new ones at an RV supply or hardware store.

If the tank drains slowly, flip open the lever on the P/T valve to let air in. If it's still slow to drain, try poking in the drain with a coat hanger to dislodge any gunk, such as big chunks of minerals.

When you go to replace the plug later, be sure to wrap the threads of the plug several times with plumber's tape (Teflon or other brand). This is usually needed to prevent leaks. Be sure to inspect the tank after refilling it to verify the plug isn't dripping.

Flushing the water heater tank

Atwood recommends flushing the tank at least twice a year, and more often if you travel full-time or live in the southwest states. This is because minerals in water will leave sediment in the tank and cause corrosion which can drastically affect the life of the water heater's components.

Even after the tank has stopped draining there will still be some water in it, and potentially a lot of sediment and corrosive particles. You can get the rest out by flushing the tank with a narrow wand that fits inside the drain hole. These wands are sold in RV stores. The goal here is to stir up and flush out all sediment, so keep at it until the water from the drain runs clear.

At this point you can replace the drain plug (and anode rod, if you have a Suburban water heater).

Inspecting the electrical connections

Electronic components can often be the reason the water heater fails to operate, so we'll check those next. Since this is routine maintenance, we are assuming everything works and we're not diagnosing a problem. So the job now is to ensure that everything has solid electrical connections.

Gently wiggle each connector, one at a time, carefully removing the connectors. You're looking for clean and tight connections at every point. Reinstall each wire before going on to the next one, so you don't mix them up. Also check the green ground wire that is screwed to the sheet metal. If that screw is loose, tighten it. If the grommet is corroded, replace it.

Inspecting and adjusting the water heater burner

The burner is a long-lasting component but it will periodically need adjustment and cleaning. It's easy, so you can do this yourself. Start by looking at the flame when the water heater is running (if you've drained the tank, be sure to refill it before firing it up). The flame should be blue with a hint of yellow. If not, it's time to adjust the air/fuel mixture.

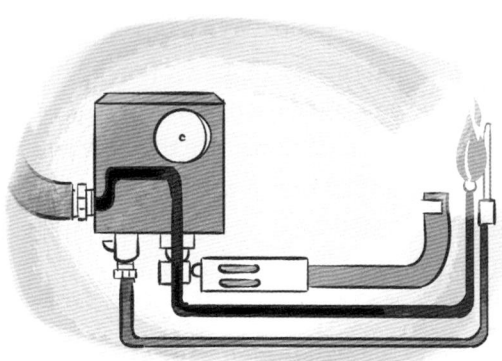

There's a single screw on the burner tube that allows the slotted air shutter to move left to right. Loosen the screw and tap the shutter with a tool such as the tip of a screwdriver toward the left to add air to the mixture, or toward the right to reduce air (enriching the mixture). You'll need to do this while the burner is running, being careful not to burn yourself on the hot tube. Tighten the screw when you're done, so the shutter stays in place.

If the flame can be adjusted to the right color, this may be all the maintenance you need to do. But periodically the flame won't be adjustable to the correct blue color, or you may notice one of these other problems:

- the flame makes a lot of noise, rather than a light hissing
- you notice ash in the flue tube (the 2.5" diameter tube where the flame enters)
- you see signs of insects (webs, nests, dead bugs)

In any of these cases, it's time to do a more in-depth maintenance cleaning and adjustment, as described below.

Disassembling and cleaning the burner tube and flue

Water heater models vary, so these instructions cover the most common Atwood water heaters used in late model Airstreams. Others will be similar.

Start by switching off the water heater at the switch inside the trailer. Then disconnect the electronic plugs to the ignitor and to the main circuit board (at top right of the water heater). This will prevent the water heater from running and allow you to remove the main burner tube.

Four screws attach the burner tube. You will need a 1/4" socket wrench or nut driver to remove these. Before you begin, mark the position of the mixture sleeve (the thing with a single screw and a series of slots for air), so you can put it back in the spot it came from. Also keep track of where each screw goes, as the threads will be different for different locations. (It may be useful to take reference photos as you work through this.) After the screws are out, the burner tube can be carefully wiggled out of the flue and off the main gas valve.

Check the interior of the burner tube for obstructions such as ash, spider webs or wasp nests, and clean it out with a brush as needed.

Inspecting the gas orifice, ignitor, and gas valve

With the burner off, you'll be able to see a brass fitting on the gas manifold. This is the gas orifice. This can be unscrewed, with some care. You will need two wrenches: one for the brass orifice, and another to hold the gas manifold in place while you are trying to break the orifice free. Keep in mind that the gas manifold is connected to a soft copper gas pipe which can easily be twisted or kinked, so don't let it move around too much.

The brass orifice is tiny, so just a little bit of dirt can affect it greatly. Clean it by soaking it in some isopropyl (rubbing) alcohol for an hour. Electrical contact cleaner can be used instead, since it doesn't leave any residue. You can also twirl a wet toothpick in the tiny orifice to remove dirt, but don't use wire or do anything that might enlarge the opening.

While you are soaking the brass orifice, use a stiff brush to clean out the flue tube. Use a flashlight to be sure you've removed any obstructions. Mud dauber wasps and spiders often clog up this tube on trailers that haven't been used regularly.

It is a good idea to spray some liquid propane leak detector or soapy water on the end of the orifice, to make sure the gas valve is closing all the way. Bubbles of leak detector fluid indicate a valve that isn't closing fully, and it should be replaced. Replacement of the valve should be left to qualified technicians.

This is also a good time to inspect the ignitor assembly. There is a sparking probe and a ground probe, which should be 1/8 inch apart. The probes should be clean and free of cracks, flaking and corrosion, and of course they should be in the path of the gas flow.

Reinstall the orifice with fresh plumber's tape on the threads. When you reinstall the main burner tube, check that the gas coming out of the orifice is going straight down the center of the burner tube. If the alignment is off, it will impede the gas flow to the spark.

Now you can switch the heater back on and run it to adjust the flame as described earlier.

This covers the basics and should be enough to keep your heater in good operation for a long time. If your water heater isn't operating normally despite good maintenance, hasn't been serviced in years, or if you find problems during this inspection, take it in for a professional look.

No hot water or very little

If the water heater appears to operate normally but delivers only a very small amount of hot water, or no hot water at all, check the winterization bypass valve. Often this valve is overlooked when de-winterizing, which means that hot water won't be delivered. Simply putting the valve in the right position will solve the problem.

The location of this valve varies by Airstream model, but it is usually located on the plumbing adjacent to the water heater (inside the Airstream, not on the face of the water heater). But in this circumstance, always double-check that the water heater drain plug has been reinstalled, or you will get a flood coming from the heater's access door.

Some Airstreams come with Atwood XT model water heaters which include a mixing valve that sometimes goes bad as a result of sediment or corrosion. Low flow or cold water is the symptom. This requires a more thorough repair, including removing the mixing valve, cleaning the screen (if equipped), and either soaking the valve in a hot white vinegar bath to remove the minerals or replacing the valve. Replacing the valve is expensive. To prevent this situation, follow the procedure above, "Flushing the water heater tank" on a regular basis.

Rotten egg odor from hot water

If your hot water smells awful, it is because bacteria have multiplied inside. This often happens during storage or when the water system has not been sanitized regularly. See "Sanitizing the water system" in the Plumbing section for instructions.

Then, treat the water heater. Remove (unscrew) the P/T relief valve following the instructions below under "Removing the P/T valve." Mix a solution of two parts white vinegar to one part water. With a funnel, carefully pour the solution into the water heater tank through the pressure/temperature coupling. Reinstall the pressure/temperature relief valve.

Turn on the water heater and allow the water to heat up fully. This may take up to 45 minutes. Let the water heater operate through three or four more heat "maintenance" cycles. Then turn it off and allow it to cool. When cool, remove the plug following the instructions earlier in the section entitled "Removing and reinstalling the Drain Plug" and drain out all the water.

Dripping P/T valve

The P/T valve is a safety device that can prevent your water heater from rupturing from high pressure or temperatures. ("P/T" refers to Pressure and Temperature.) It is located at the upper right of the Atwood water heater. This valve is set to open at 210 degrees Fahrenheit or if the system pressure exceeds 150 PSI.

In the normal operation of the water heater and the P/T valve, no water should be coming from the valve. However, if it drips a little, there are a few things to try before you replace it. Before taking any of these steps, turn off the main water supply (water pump or city water connection). Turn the water heater off and allow the water tank to cool.

1. If the P/T valve drips a small amount at a constant rate, try opening and then snapping shut the lever on the valve a couple of times. Often tank residue or mineral deposits can prevent the valve from fully seating. This procedure can be done once a year as a maintenance item.

2. The Atwood water heater is designed with an internal air gap at the top of the tank to absorb expansion of the water as it heats and reduce dripping. Eventually this gap is absorbed and needs to be restored. Open the nearest hot water faucet to the water heater. Pull the lever on the P/T valve straight out and allow water to flow until it stops. Snap the lever on the relief valve shut, shut the open water faucet, turn on the water pump (or re-connect the city water hose) and turn the water heater back on.

3. Check the temperature of the hot water coming out of the faucet. It should not be more than 150 degrees. If it is, the thermostat in the water heater may be at fault. This requires professional repair.

If none of these steps stop the dripping, the pressure/temperature valve probably needs replacement.

Replacing the P/T valve

As always, shut off the water and ensure that the water is cool before proceeding. Shut off the water pump or city water connection as well—or close the winterization valve that controls the cold water supply to the water heater.

The valve unscrews. Large pliers or a wrench will remove it. You may need to unplug some wires on the heater for easier access, so be sure to note where they go before you start.

The replacement P/T valve will be a 1/2" size (not 3/4" like home water heaters use) and can be found online, at some hardware stores and RV parts suppliers. Wrap the new valve in a rag so that it doesn't get marred by the pliers, and wind plumber's tape (Teflon tape) around the threads several times before screwing it in.

Start the water supply again, by reversing what you did to shut it off (water pump, city water, or winterization valve) and check for leaks. When the heater is full of water, turn it on and check for leaks again after it has fully heated.

Keeping Your Perspective

If you've read this book from cover to cover and are now thoroughly freaked out by the prospect of all the work you have to do, please relax.

Most of the time your Airstream will be a low-maintenance source of pleasure for you. Think about how you're going to enjoy it and forget about all the things that might go wrong. When something does need to be maintained you can flip the appropriate section of this book and refresh your memory. Most of what's discussed in here won't come up for years, if ever.

For that reason I suggest you keep this book in your Airstream when you travel, along with your basic traveling toolkit. When a job does come up you'll find it only seems hard the first time. After you've done it you'll have increased confidence because you know what to do, and you'll probably realize it really wasn't that hard after all.

If you are one of those people who isn't mechanically inclined or if you are feeling nervous about taking a wrench or screwdriver to your Airstream, let me offer a few tips:

First, it really is true that you need the right tool for the job. For example, you can remove the water heater drain plug with many different tools, but having the right socket and wrench will make it easy. An adjustable wrench wedged in there will eventually get it out, but you may have bleeding knuckles, a broken plug, and lots of pent-up adrenaline by the time you're done. Spend a little money to get good tools and a tool bag to keep them in one place.

Second, don't rush or take shortcuts. Give yourself plenty of time to study each job, understand what you are going to do, get all the tools at hand, and work methodically. An experienced person might do the job in 15 minutes that took you two hours, but that doesn't matter. Give yourself time to learn.

Taking a shortcut can turn your quick maintenance into a nightmare repair that forces you to haul the Airstream over to a professional. If you need a break, take one. If you are getting frustrated, leave the job for the next day so you can have time to unwind and maybe get some advice before proceeding.

Third, don't take on everything at once. You are holding a guide to doing all the routine maintenance on an Airstream trailer but you're not under any obligation to do things you aren't comfortable doing. Pick a few easy inspection, cleaning or lubricating tasks to get started. You won't break anything by doing those jobs. You can gradually add other maintenance items as you gain experience.

Airstreams have proven to be extraordinarily durable over the years. It's not unusual to go to a vintage Airstream rally and find dozens of trailers still on the road after four, five, even six decades of service. That's even more impressive because of the relatively low numbers that were made—the survival rate as a percentage is probably quite a bit higher than any make of car. And parts are still readily available for trailers forty years old, so there's no "planned obsolescence" with an Airstream. They are built to be maintained and kept traveling for as long as you care to use them.

With that viewpoint you can start to see how people justify the cost of an Airstream over another brand. The real return on investment comes years later, when the white box alternative is falling apart and the Airstream is just getting seasoned.

So my favorite recommendation to owners is this: use your Airstream as often as you can. You'll find that maintenance gets easier as your familiarity with the Airstream grows, and at the same time your enjoyment of life will increase. Your Airstream will appreciate it too.

The result of your awareness and care will be a travel trailer that you can enjoy for as long as you want. Your Airstream might even become an heirloom to pass on to the next generation.

I hope you'll have many happy days of travel!

Resources

Most parts and supplies mentioned in this book are readily available from general hardware stores and local RV stores. For items which are harder to find, we recommend several sources:

The **Airstream Life Store** carries specialized parts, preassembled tool kits for particular tasks, consumable supplies, and upgrades, as well as back issues of Airstream Life magazine.

We recommend only products that we use ourselves, and many of the kits come with our own instruction manuals. Visit at store.airstreamlife.com

Airstream dealers can order any Airstream specific part from the factory, and many of them also stock commonly-used parts. It's easiest if you already know the part #, but not essential. Have your trailer's serial number handy.

You can locate your nearest dealer at www.airstream.com or by calling 937-596-6111. However, if a part has to be shipped, keep in mind that you can order from any dealer you like, not just the one closest to you.

The **Airstream Inc. Store** carries some upgrade parts, supplies, apparel, replacement Owner's Manuals, and lifestyle accessories. Visit at www.airstream.com/store

Vintage Trailer Supply is the nation's leading supplier of hard-to-find vintage trailer replacement parts and supplies. Visit at www.vintagetrailersupply.com. Another source is Airstream Supply, at airstreamsupply.com.

If you are relatively new to Airstream ownership and don't already have a copy, consider purchasing *"The Newbies Guide To Airstreaming."* It's a quick-start guide to using your Airstream trailer, and available from the Airstream Life Store and Amazon.com for just $15.95.

Airstream Life magazine is the best way to stay in touch with everything related to Airstream around the world. Published quarterly in print and online, it's the favorite of thousands of Airstream owners. Learn more at airstreamlife.com.